PRAISE FOR *THE*

MW01067777

Let me make this abundantly clear: *The Next Rules of Work* is your road map to build an exponential future of work for your organization—today.

Peter H. Diamandis, MD, Founder of XPRIZE and Singularity, and *New York Times* bestselling author of *Abundance* and *BOLD*

As I've predicted for years, exponential technologies will profoundly transform our lives and our organizations. In *The Next Rules of Work*, Gary A. Bolles has shown how those same technologies can actually help to create a more human-centric future of work.

Ray Kurzweil, inventor, futurist, and author of *The Singularity Is Near*

If you're confused about what the future of work holds, *The Next Rules of Work* is the perfect companion to take on your journey, filled with practical advice and inspiring examples that will guide you through these tumultuous times.

Charlene Li, *New York Times* bestselling author of *The Disruption Mindset* and Founder and Senior Fellow of Altimeter, a Prophet Company

The future of work is in our hands but, as with any design project, we have to understand the needs and constraints. *The Next Rules of Work* brilliantly describes the canvas on which we can create meaningful work and impactful organizations, fit for the 21st century.

Tim Brown, Chair of IDEO and author of *Change by Design*

Rules change. Work changes. We adapt. Or do we? Can we? This all came together for me about page 229. Read it.

Vint Cerf, internet pioneer

I can't think of a better time to start rethinking work, or a better book to help you do it. Gary A. Bolles has produced a provocative and practical guide for reimagining how you design jobs, build teams, solve problems, and shape cultures.

Adam Grant, #1 *New York Times* bestselling author of *Think Again* and host of the TED podcast *WorkLife*

The Next Rules of Work shows how moonshot thinking can help leaders create an inclusive future of work, starting right now.

Esther Wojcicki, author of *Moonshots in Education* and *How to Raise Successful People*

The global society is facing unprecedented shifts in the way of work, amplified by the COVID-19 pandemic and an increased need for automation and digitalization. But as Gary A. Bolles points out, the most pressing question is not a potential lack of work in the future, but the need for individuals to acquire new skills and capabilities to constantly adapt in an ever-changing environment. But we can overcome any obstacles if employers, governments, and individuals work together to make the future work for everyone.

Alain Dehaze, CEO of Adecco Group

The Next Rules of Work offers a fresh and insightful view on how the world of work will look in a post-pandemic world. Gary A. Bolles does a fantastic job articulating these insights to help catalyze positive change in our organizations.

Adilson Borges, PhD, Chief Learning Officer of Carrefour

The Next Rules of Work is a must-read for anyone seeking to understand how the world is not just rapidly changing but being dramatically reshaped. Gary A. Bolles provides a playbook for leadership that prioritizes organizational purpose and deep human values as the means for what inspires people to do their best work and institutions to operate with the needs of society at the center, which in and of itself ensures institutions are built for the long term and serve the needs of all stakeholders.

Dov Seidman, Founder and Chairman of LRN and The HOW Institute for Society, and author of *How*

The Next Rules of Work is a road map to an inclusive future of work, and Gary A. Bolles is the clear-eyed guide that we all need on that journey.

Ravin Jesuthasan, recognized futurist and author of *Reinventing Jobs* and *Lead the Work*

The future of work has many challenges, but this inspiring and insightful book offers actionable steps all organizations can and must take to harness the opportunities ahead for everyone. If we follow the path laid out here, we will make a big shift from challenge to opportunity and create much more human-centric work.

John Hagel, futurist, strategist, and trusted advisor

The Next Rules of Work shines a bright light for those who have been feeling their way to a most fulfilling future of work. Gary A. Bolles writes with clarity and empathy for readers seeking to build more inclusive, productive, and dynamic workplaces.

Chris Shipley, author of *The Adaptation Advantage*

Imagine you could wave a magic wand and get a clear picture of just what you need—the mindset, skillset, and toolset to ensure success in today's rapidly changing world. Whether you're in business, or in the business of helping the next generation of children, students, or employees thrive in the 21st-century, *The Next Rules of Work* is that magic wand!

Laura A. Jana, MD, pediatrician, social entrepreneur, and author of *The Toddler Brain*

The Next Rules of Work guides leaders towards a future not of automation and substitution, but autonomy and inclusion—

providing clear strategies for transforming an organization in an accelerating world.

Vivienne Ming, Founder of Socos

An immediately practical guidebook for navigating work, career, and life in our ever-changing world—while helping create a better future of work for us all. As Gary A. Bolles says, "No human left behind."

John O'Duinn, author of *Distributed Teams*

The Next Rules of Work

*The Mindset, Skillset, and Toolset
to Lead Your Organization
through Uncertainty*

Gary A. Bolles

First published in Great Britain and the United States in 2021 by Kogan Page Limited

2nd Floor, 45 Gee Street
London
EC1V 3RS
United Kingdom

122 W 27th St, 10th Floor
New York, NY 10001
USA

4737/23 Ansari Road
Daryaganj
New Delhi 110002
India

www.koganpage.com

Kogan Page books are printed on paper from sustainable forests.

© Gary A. Bolles, 2021

The right of Gary A. Bolles to be identified as the author of this work has been asserted by him in accordance with the Copyright, Designs and Patents Act 1988.

ISBNs

Hardback   978 1 3986 0166 6
Paperback   978 1 3986 0163 5
Ebook   978 1 3986 0164 2

British Library Cataloguing-in-Publication Data

A CIP record for this book is available from the British Library.

Library of Congress Cataloging-in-Publication Data

Names: Bolles, Gary A., author.
Title: The next rules of work : the mindset, skillset, and toolset to lead
  your organization through uncertainty / Gary A. Bolles.
Description: London, United Kingdom ; New York, NY : Kogan Page, 2021. |
  Includes bibliographical references and index.
Identifiers: LCCN 2021017919 (print) | LCCN 2021017920 (ebook) | ISBN
  9781398601666 (hardback) | ISBN 9781398601635 (paperback) | ISBN
  9781398601642 (ebook)
Subjects: LCSH: Organizational change. | Leadership. | Psychology,
  Industrial. | BISAC: BUSINESS & ECONOMICS / Leadership | BUSINESS &
  ECONOMICS / Management
Classification: LCC HD58.8 .B64 2021 (print) | LCC HD58.8 (ebook) | DDC
  658.4/06–dc23
LC record available at https://lccn.loc.gov/2021017919
LC ebook record available at https://lccn.loc.gov/2021017920

Typeset by Integra Software Services, Pondicherry
Print production managed by Jellyfish
Printed and bound by CPI Group (UK) Ltd, Croydon CR0 4YY

CONTENTS

ACKNOWLEDGMENTS

If we are lucky, each of us finds a mate. If we are very lucky, we find a soulmate. And if we are very, very lucky, we find a life partner.

I am very, very lucky.

Heidi Carolyn Kleinmaus is my wife, the mother of our incredible son, the managing partner of our company, Charrette LLC, and my manager for speaking activities. She is my muse. She continually challenges me and makes me a better person. From her, I have learned constancy and courage. I hope that you either have or will find someone who can make your life as rich as it can possibly be, as Heidi continues to do for me. "You already have this book in your head," she told me. And she was right. As always.

Christian Kleinmaus Bolles is our son, and a phenomenally talented wordsmith, editor, and researcher. He is a far better writer than I am. He fights passionately for what he believes in, and is a constant source of inspiration to me. From him, I have learned about authenticity.

Shea Michael Robin Star Shawnson is my nephew. I decided from his birth that our lives would be deeply connected. From Shea, I continually learn patience and persistence.

Richard Nelson Bolles was my late father, an Episcopal minister, early member of the brainiac group Mensa, relentless manufacturer of puns, and the world's career counselor. I'll tell part of his story later in the book. Parent, mentor, and collaborator, we had a marvelously complex and caring relationship. He gave me the building blocks of creativity, perpetual curiosity, a love of words, and an early understanding of the mechanics of human work. I refer to his enduring legacy frequently. Throughout the book, I could have referred to him as Dick Bolles. Or RNB. But "my father" feels right.

Janet Lorraine Price Bolles is my mother, a perpetual caregiver and quiet saint. She gave me the building blocks of empathy and service to others.

My brother Stephen and my sister Sharon have been my great companions in childhood and adulthood. I miss our brother Mark.

And now, to my friends.

John Hagel is the former co-chairman of Deloitte's Center for the Edge, and now heads Beyond Our Edge LLC. John is a longtime friend and mentor. I depend deeply on his breakthrough insights, from "unbundling" to "big shifts."

Eric Barnett is my longtime business partner and friend, world-class software architect, and one of the best guitar players in America. Party on, Garth.

Kathe Sweeney helped me grow my global voice by inviting me years ago to create courses for LinkedIn Learning, and then by collaborating as my editor for this book. She is my cheerleader.

Charlene Li gave me the entry point for this book. "Write it all," she said. "Just keep it short." That advice allowed me to know where to start.

Megan Lubowski provided invaluable support.

Thanks to friends who have contributed to my thinking on humans and work, including Chaim Guggenheim, Leila Toplic and Cyril Glockner, Vivienne Ming, Al Perlman, Rosalee Hardin and Kevin Jones, Mark Beam, Esther Wojcicki, David Kirkpatrick, Frances Bolles Haynes, Daniel Porot, Ross Martin, Phil Cousineau, James Fallows and Deb Fallows, Dirk Spiers, Valerie Buckingham, Will Weisman, Sean Watson, David Reese, Shel Israel, David Strom, Yossi Vardi, Chinedu Ocheru, Oshoke Pamela Abalu, Nick Smoot, Matt Dunne, Erin Dobson, Susan McPherson, Megan Beck and Alex Hillinger, Nicola Corzine, John Irons, Andrew Dunckelman, Lindsey Kneuven, Vikrum Aiyer, Lorin Platto, Allegra Diggins, David Hornik, Jim Baller, Jeff Lundwall, Chris Shipley, Lisa Licht, Peter Sims, Virginia Hamilton, Dov Seidman, Pat Lencioni, Adam Grant, Markus Hunt, Tom Friedman, Flo Allen, and Ulysses. And to Laurie and Joe Rombi for the retreat time in Pacific Grove.

Referencing

Throughout the book, I use the single-person pronoun "they" a lot. My father first started doing this years ago in *Parachute*. He maintained that for centuries we have been willing to be incorrect about gender, so it's about time we shifted instead to be unspecific as to number. As so often, ahead of his time.

If I refer to someone by their first name, I know them.

As you'll see, it is deeply important to me to give credit where credit is due. If I have used any of your thinking without attribution, or through misattribution, please accept my apologies. Correct me and send me the source so I can credit your work properly.

Introduction

Humans have been worried about the future of work since the dawn of machines. But those concerns are rarely about some distant roboticized future. They're usually about today, and the nagging belief that there are cracks in the system of work that will mean that lots of humans could be left behind tomorrow.

Of course, until early 2020 many thought the seismic shift in work would be catalyzed by automation and globalization. But we know that the real impact on work comes from the pace and scale of change. Those twin forces create several possible futures of work. Yet that will be a future we will create together, by anticipating and co-creating the Next Rules of Work.

> Humans have been worried about the future of work since the dawn of machines.

It's rather ironic that I would write about rules, since I've grown up professionally in Silicon Valley, which prides itself on moving fast and breaking things like, well, rules.

And yet, when it comes to work, rules there are. (Although, in many cases, to paraphrase Paul Newman in *Butch Cassidy and the Sundance Kid*, they're often more like *guidelines* than rules.) Many of the rules are unseen, functioning not so much as strictures carved in stone, but as fluid practices intended to help optimize toward successful outcomes.

In an ideal world, we would all have been taught these practices from a young age, so we would be better prepared for constant, disruptive change as adults. But I'm guessing that didn't happen for you, either.

Instead, most of us had to figure out the Rules of Work as we went along. And then... the rules changed. Again. And again. With no roadmap. No manual.

So here's a manual. I hope it will provide you with the combination of insights and actions that can empower you, your team, and your organization.

We'll do a brief scan of the Old Rules of Work, practices that stretch back a surprisingly long time in the short history of humans. We'll see how the rules of work have always changed—but never so quickly as today. That will make it abundantly clear why we need not just New Rules, but *Next* Rules.

We'll see that there are four essential Next Rules, guidelines for the ways that a few people work today, and many will be working tomorrow.

We'll find that the three legs of the stool for tomorrow's work leverage your mindset, your skillset, and a constantly changing toolset. There are useful strategies for each of these, to help us thrive in a world of disruptive change and uncertainty.

Finally, we'll explore the ways that each of our own actions can help to create the future we all want. (I'll give you a simple preview: *no human left behind*.)

Think of this as a cookbook for ideas, not just about what's next, but for what's now. Some cookbooks give very specific recipes, exact measurements, and exacting instructions. This isn't that. It's a landscape of ideas to help catalyze. If it works, the number one deliverable will be a new mindset about work, for you, your team, and your organization. You'll also have a number of opportunities to develop a new skillset. And, you'll read about a variety of new options for your toolset. But the main deliverable is that Next Mindset.

Given the space limitations of atoms arranged on paper, my website has a lot of bits with much fewer constraints. You'll find gbolles.com a dynamic companion to the book.

The Pace and Scale of Change

In late 2019, the topic of the future of work to most people was just theory. Though many of us had been talking for some time about important strategies such as a dramatic shift to using digital technologies, and leveraging the skillsets of distributed teams, many of those who lead organizations felt little urgency to change.

Then, in early 2020, the future of work shifted nearly overnight from theory to practice. In a study on organizational change that year, the Institute for Corporate Performance (i4cp) found that two-thirds of the more than 7,000 surveyed executives said their organization had experienced disruptive change. Not much surprise there.

While many futurists have for decades projected the disruptive impact of breakthrough technology, the godfather of the vision of a tech-fueled future is Ray Kurzweil, author of books like *The Singularity Is Near*.[1] I first met Ray when he joined me for a speaking series throughout New England in the early 2000s. Spending several days driving with him from one venue to the next was a master class in innovation. In 2008, Ray became the co-founder of Singularity University (SU), and a few years later I began working with SU as the adjunct Chair for the Future of Work. Ray famously plotted the "exponential" curve of microprocessors and other breakthrough technologies, showing how dramatically they have continued to improve in function as they drop in cost, and how they have rapidly helped to disrupt a range of industries.

Many other authors have predicted never-ending waves of disruptive technologies. In *Rethinking Humanity*,[2] authors Tony Seba and James Arbib predicted a range of breakthroughs in the five "foundational sectors" of information and communications technology, energy, transportation, food, and physical materials.

These and many other futurists maintain that huge jumps forward in these industries are not a matter of if, but when. As evidence, they point to the substantial disruptions to each of these industries that are already underway. For example, renewable energy in many markets around the world is already more cost-effective than fossil fuels, disrupting those markets past the point of long-term profitability.

There is no question that new technologies are being created and widely used with increasing speed. Look at how quickly technologies like the mobile phone were adopted compared with, say, the microwave oven.

FIGURE 0.1   Technology adoption rate 1970–2016

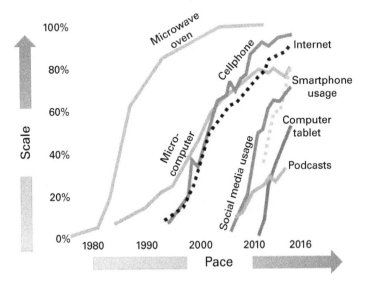

SOURCE Visual Capitalist[3]

But let's not take the Silicon Valley narrative *too* far. Technology matters. But changing customer behavior, movement in global markets, and shifts in government policy all determine if a new technology will actually trigger disruption, or if the world will simply shrug it off as "too early." The modern global pandemic catalyzed disruptive change that had little to do with technology, and everything to do with how we react to sudden shocks to the system.

Our real challenge is not simply wave after wave of technology. Certainly since the advent of the Internet era, it is the *pace* and the *scale* of change that are washing over our organizations, our industries, and our lives.

First, the *pace* of change. The influential economist Jeffrey Sachs has rightly pointed out that the inevitable conclusion is that many of our greatest challenges are coming from the pace of change, and that pace is accelerating. Of course, the pace of change is both an objective and a subjective measure. Depending on where you live and work, you might be insulated from change, or you might feel so much change that it is overwhelming your ability to manage it. But as breakthrough technologies seem to spring from the pages of science fiction books, the latter is the most common observation.

The pace of change affects the world of work in many ways. Rivers of news flood our senses, often making it difficult to sift out what is relevant to our work. Thousands of new apps are released every month, requiring us to learn new tools for our work. Perhaps most challenging, the shelf life of relevant information in many fields is shortening, requiring us to continually learn new techniques and skills.

As advertising and marketing guru Shelly Palmer, CEO of the Palmer Group, is fond of saying, "Today is the slowest day of the rest of your life."

But the *scale* of change is also a tremendous force. The sheer number of people who are affected, and the amount of change that any industry or society goes through, is increasingly larger than those who were previously affected. Today, a startup social media service can reach 1 billion users or more in a matter of months. There weren't even a billion people on the planet at the turn of the 19th century.

Of course, we were warned. In 1970, the eerily prescient *Future Shock*[4] by Alvin Toffler and Adelaide Farrell captured public imagination around the world. The wife-and-husband team talked about change—rapid, disruptive, often tech-driven change affecting societies across the planet. They warned about "the death of permanence," the rise of the knowledge economy, fragmenting families and other human relationships, the stress of adapting to change, and the cognitive load of "information overchoice." They knew that the pace and scale of change would create seismic fractures in our societies.

Happily, Toffler and Farrell offered a variety of suggestions, such as schools teaching "learning how to learn," the need to re-establish trust in relationships, and a "suitable degree of futureness"—suggesting that we anticipate enough about the future so as not to be surprised, but not so far as to fall into wishful thinking or escapist fantasy. (Hence, the Next Rules.) Unhappily, we clearly didn't listen to them. Our educational institutions don't explicitly teach us strategies for living in a constantly changing world, and other institutions, like organizations and governments, have not embraced the Next Rules to enable human-centered change.

The pace and scale of this kind of change deeply affect work markets. The difference between the skillset needed today and the skillset needed tomorrow, and the number of people who are affected, is increasing dramatically. A former coalmine worker hoping to switch to lucrative work like machine learning programming has a greater distance to go than, say, someone who once repaired mechanical car engines and now needs to learn about an electronic ignition system.

It is this impact of often tech-fueled change that has driven so much of the popular dialog about the future of work, and the ways our modern toolset contributes to the pace and scale of change.

Looking Back at the Future of Work

Since the time of the early Greeks, people have assumed that automation would displace human work. Aristotle worried that if "the shuttle would weave and the plectrum touch the lyre without a hand to guide them, chief workmen would not want servants, nor masters slaves."[5] That's a pretty good description of a robot from a guy who lived 2,300 years ago.

For exactly the opposite prediction about the impact of technology, fast forward to the early 1900s, when the influential economist John Maynard Keynes wrote about *Economic Possibilities for Our Grandchildren,*[6] which is of course talking about you and me. Keynes maintained that within 100 years, "the economic problem"[7] for mankind would have been solved:

> Thus for the first time since his creation man will be faced with his real, his permanent problem—how to use his freedom from pressing economic cares, how to occupy the leisure, which science and compound interest will have won for him, to live wise and agreeably and well.[8]

In other words, by now, you and I have so much money, we don't have to work, and we're crazy bored. Let me ask how that's working out for you.

In the decades after Keynes, many other innovators, economists, and even cartoonists weighed in, oscillating between predicting tech-fueled dystopia and utopia. MIT math professor Norbert Wiener, author of the 1949 book *Cybernetics*,[9] realized, after helping to design what we would now call robots for an auto assembly factory, that "the unemployment produced by such plans can only be disastrous."

Popular media, though, often took the utopian tack. Detroit-based artist Arthur Radebaugh in 1958 began penning the Sunday newspaper cartoon *Closer Than You Think*, predicting whizbang technologies such as electric cars, autonomous cars, hovercraft, wristwatch TVs, remote learning, electronic home libraries and computer desks, wall-sized TVs, home robots, and even electronic greeting cards (sent by microwave to the moon, of course). Soon after, the popular *Jetsons* prime-time TV cartoon treated viewers to a vision many today would have welcomed for the father's two-hour-a-week job and commute home by flying car. As a kid, this glued me to the TV screen.

Around this time, though, fears about automation began to rise again. In the early 1960s, a committee of concerned scientists warned then-President Johnson that "the cybernation revolution [would create] a separate nation of the poor, the unskilled, the jobless."[10] In speeches, Dr. Martin Luther King railed against "monstrous automation" as one of the nation's leading obstacles to African Americans achieving equal economic opportunity.[11]

Those fears were certainly borne out in various sectors of the mid-20th-century workforce. According to the Bureau of Labor Statistics, in the US in 1950, over a million people worked in clothing factories,[12] making yarn and fabric, and producing everything from footwear to knitted sweaters. Nearly 1.5 million worked in the railway system. Over half a million worked in coal mining.

But by 2020, even though the US working population had more than doubled, each of these industries employed less than a tenth the former number of workers.

There is now no question that a significant amount of technology in the modern era has inevitably shifted to the automation of human tasks. An increasing number of innovative companies coming out of Silicon Valley and beyond have trained their sights on human work in a range of industries from media to financial services. These innovators typically look at the *tasks* that humans perform and look for ways to use software and robots to replicate those tasks.

Why? It's the reason that venture capitalists (VCs) invest in those companies. VCs want a startup to find something a customer is already paying for, and "10× it." That is, the automated approach must at least be one tenth the cost, or ten times more efficient, than when the human was doing it. Only by having such a significant gain in cost reduction, efficiency, or both, is a customer likely to use a new technology.

And humans are often costly. About two-thirds of the US and European economies are driven by services. That means people. Payroll can cost from 30 to 70 percent of a business. So it's a rational (though hardly human-centered) decision by leaders to attempt to reduce those costs. Startups are all too happy to oblige, and investors are more than happy to support them. And since much of the focus is on automating tasks, they can take inspiration from people like Henry Ford, who said, "Nothing is particularly hard if you divide it into small jobs."[13]

Look at the rise of what is known as robotic process automation software, or RPA, which rapidly "learns" how a repetitive human task is performed, then repeats the task automatically. The more tasks that are automated, the more a worker is "freed up" from having to do those tasks.

Of course, in most economies there is a word for someone who is 100 percent "freed up" from their work: "Unemployed." Not exactly what Mr. Keynes had in mind.

Though automation has clearly changed work throughout the ages, all of the talk about robots and software spiked deep concerns about what is often called technological unemployment. Because we've seen this playbook before, when we read headlines about robots and software taking jobs, we immediately assume the worst impact on human work. But as Danish politician Karl Kristian Steincke wrote in 1948, "it is difficult to make predictions, especially about the future."[14]

The Three Futures of Work

While I've frequently been accused of being a futurist, I'm really more of a "now-ist." I prefer to deconstruct the trends we see today and help people to see in terms of scenarios for tomorrow. So what are those bright red threads connecting to our near future, and how should we respond? Here are three possible scenarios.

Future 1: Lots of Robots, Lots of Unemployment (Score: Robots 10, Humans 0)

Oscar Wilde wasn't the first to predict that machines would do much of the work of humans, but he was one of the most articulate. In 1891 in *The Soul of Man Under Socialism*,[15] he said that:

> all monotonous, dull labour… must be done by machinery… and just as trees grow while the country gentleman is asleep, so while Humanity will be amusing itself, or enjoying cultivated leisure which, and not labour, is the aim of man—or making beautiful things, or reading beautiful things, or simply contemplating the world with admiration and delight.

Like Keynes, though, Wilde didn't address how we would all pay the rent while the robots toiled.

In 2014, my wife and business partner Heidi Kleinmaus and I met author Martin Ford for lunch in Silicon Valley. He gave us an advance copy of his new book *Rise of the Robots*[16] and painted his own vision of technology-fueled unemployment. In the book, which he subtitled *Technology and the Threat of a Jobless Future*, Martin walked through the wide range of data points that show just how rapidly technology was changing the landscape of work. Since then, Martin's work has become frequently associated with predicting what has become the "Jobpocalypse Scenario."

Martin found many who agreed with him. The same year, Microsoft co-founder Bill Gates was quoted by *Business Insider*[17] from a talk at the American Enterprise Institute:

> Technology over time will reduce demand for jobs, particularly at the lower end of skill set. Twenty years from now, labor demand for lots of skill sets will be substantially lower. I don't think people have that in their mental model.

In "This is the most dangerous time for our planet,"[18] a column for *The Guardian* in late 2016, physicist Stephen Hawking maintained that artificial intelligence software was potentially an existential threat to human work. And a 2017 study by the Gartner research firm projected that about 30 percent of the skills listed in the average 2017 job description would not be relevant by 2021.[19]

Concern spread. In February 2016, Rice University professor Moshe Vardi was quoted in the *Financial Times*[20] as saying:

> We are approaching the time when machines will be able to outperform humans at almost any task. Society needs to confront this question before it is upon us: if machines are capable of doing almost any work humans can do, what will humans do?[21]

In a 2019 debate with Alibaba founder Jack Ma at a conference in Shanghai, China, Tesla CEO Elon Musk was quoted by Bloomberg[22] as saying that AI will make jobs irrelevant.

But much of the data fueling modern concerns about a job apocalypse came from a 2013 report, *The Future of Employment*,[23] by Carl Benedikt Frey and Michael Osborne of the Oxford Martin Programme on Technology and Employment. Their team looked at *tasks* that were considered to be "automate-able" using existing technologies, added up all those tasks, and estimated that up to 47 million jobs *could* be lost to technology by 2050.

If you want to see the Oxford study in action, go to WillRobotsTakeMyJob.com, plug in a job title, and get depressed.

Forget the theories. The tech-fueled jobpocalypse has already occurred. It's called "the media industry." Starting with the rise of the Internet in 1995, over 200,000 jobs evaporated in the US over the next 25 years. (That's why I call myself "a recovering journalist." The magazine I helped to start in 1994, *Inter@ctive Week*, which we positioned as the Internet's first newspaper, quite literally and ironically documented the demise of its own industry.)

Obviously, Future 1 is the Scarcity Scenario. The size of the work pie shrinks, because our technology makes less work available to humans.

Future 2: Lots of Employment, Assisted by Robots (Score: Robots 1, Humans 10)

The second future scenario is the exact opposite, which you might call the Abundance Scenario. In this possible tomorrow, our technologies help to create so much work that there simply aren't enough humans to do it. Or, even if a lot of work goes away, we all figure out how that won't matter, because we will have inclusive economies.

John Markoff, former *New York Times* reporter and author of *Machines of Loving Grace*,[24] wrote that he's not worried about robots taking our jobs, since our rapidly aging workforce will actually need robots to perform many of the tasks humans won't be able to do any more. And as Oscar Wilde wrote in *The Soul of Man*, "At present machinery competes with man. Under proper conditions machinery will serve man." (Hopefully, though, he didn't mean it like sci-fi writer Damon Knight's 1950 short story *To Serve Man*,[25] later a 1962 *Twilight Zone* episode.)

In his 2014 blog post, "This is probably a good time to say that I don't believe robots will eat all the jobs…,"[26] venture capitalist Marc Andreessen, whom I once interviewed when he was co-founder of the breakthrough Internet company Netscape, maintained that with widely available tools for production, things become cheaper to make instead of buy. The overall cost of a standard lifestyle drops precipitously, and though each of us makes less money, it costs less to live.

As Andreessen posited, suppose that:

> robots eat jobs in field X. What follows is that products get cheaper in field X, and the consumer standard of living increases in field X— necessarily. Based on that logic, arguing against robots eating jobs is equivalent to arguing that we punish consumers with unnecessarily higher prices. Indeed, had robots/machines not eaten many jobs in agriculture and industry already, we would have a far lower standard of living today.

A 2018 report by ZipRecruiter[27] determined that machine learning software had recently created three times as many jobs as it automated away. In early 2019, Byron Reese, CEO and publisher of technology research company Gigaom, published an article on Singularity Hub titled "AI will create millions more jobs than it will destroy. Here's how."[28] Reese maintained that innovators will begin to create technologies that will help power human skills to solve a range of new problems.

But nobody can guarantee, of course, that the jobs of the future will be *well-paid* jobs. A scan of the US Department of Labor's[29] top 12 highest-growth "jobs of the future" from 2019 to 2029 reads like a dystopian mirror image. On the high side are well-paid jobs like software developers and testers, operations managers, and medical health services managers, all of which pay a median of over $100,000 a year. But the vast majority of jobs are on the low side, jobs like home healthcare workers, fast-food workers, restaurant cooks, medical assistants, warehouse laborers, and landscape workers—none of which pays over a median $30,000 a year, or about $15 an hour. And even some of the higher-paid jobs are being "gig-ified," turned into project- or hourly-based temporary work, which are far more susceptible to descending wages.

That leads us to...

Future 3: Lots of Work, and Lots of Under- and Unemployment (Score: Robots 10, Some Humans 10, Most Humans 0 or 0.1)

In this future scenario, there is both abundance and scarcity. How does *that* happen?

In her influential and prescient 1988 book *In the Age of the Smart Machine*,[30] author Shoshana Zuboff pointed to the likelihood that

FIGURE 0.2   The Three Futures of Work

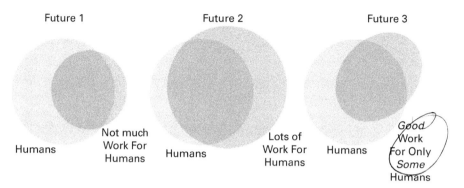

disruptive technologies would lead to both a jobs utopia *and* dystopia. Those who could navigate rapid changes in work would thrive. But those who could not adapt quickly enough would be left behind.

The publishing industry lost 200,000 jobs over 25 years, yet far more jobs were created in new media during that period. But you had to be able to make the leap.

In Future 3, many employers are still complaining that they can't hire enough of the in-demand skills like AI programming. Multiply that workforce mismatch by millions, and you have a big problem for everyone—workers, employers, societies, and economies. The executive recruiting firm Korn Ferry estimated[31] that the lack of trained workers around the world could mean that by 2030 there would be a deficit of 85 million workers and $8.5 trillion in economic activity.

We already have many examples around the world of Future Scenario 3. Rural areas with shuttered factories and relocated companies already have a work mismatch. If rural unemployed workers would simply relocate to where the jobs are, they might find work. But cities are expensive, and if the work to be done requires significant retraining, workers are far less likely to move, or to go back to school for extensive retraining.

So how does this mismatch happen in the first place?

Robots and Software Don't Take Jobs—Humans Give Them Away

We will continue to see headlines about tech-fueled workforce mismatch like this for decades, because in many cases that mismatch isn't a "bug" of the system. It's a feature. Many work economies were built on the Old Rules of Work, when far less digital technology was available, and education and hiring systems weren't as strained. But those systems weren't designed for the kind of disruptive change we're seeing in the 21st century.

As a result, you will continue to see headlines about tech-fueled work mismatches for decades. So here is how you can develop your own informed opinion about the potential impact of automation on work. When researchers try to predict these future scenarios, they are actually trying to figure out four things:

- **Will tasks be automated, or will they just be "automate-able"?** Just because, say, 40 percent of tasks in a job or field *may* be automated, doesn't mean they *will* be automated, or *when* they will be automated, using existing technologies.

- **Whether the result may be a job loss or a skills mismatch.** Those are two very different things. Someone who hires may determine that they *don't* need an older skillset, and they *do* need a lot of next skills, but will maintain they can't find enough trained workers. Yet just because they don't think they need the current skillset doesn't mean they need to make a job go away, when the worker might be retrained. (Forget the label "upskilled." Yuck.)

- **If it's a skills mismatch, what is the *net impact* of automation on work—and when?** A jobless future depends heavily on there being no easily accessed work opportunities, which may simply be due to a lack of imagination and planning on our part. In fall 2016, the World Economic Forum suggested[32] a net loss of 5 million jobs in 15 economies around the globe by 2020, and in 2017 Forrester Research projected[33] that there would be a net loss of 6 percent of US jobs by 2021. That was within the range of a mild to a major recession, but not a jobless near future. And these projections were nowhere near the actual impact on jobs in many countries from the 2020 pandemic.

- **What goes away, tasks or jobs?** Even if 40 percent of all tasks in an industry absolutely *will* be automated, that doesn't mean that 40 percent of jobs will go away.

This last point is the most crucial, because *robots and software don't take jobs. Humans give them away.* Technology simply automates tasks. It's a human's decision if a job evaporates. And we can make different decisions.

In *A World Without Work*,[34] economist David Susskind suggests that a lot of work will indeed be automated, and that we'll all simply have to figure out how to take care of those people who are affected, such as a universal basic income, or perhaps something more needs-adjusted. And perhaps all those people who work can work less, so what little work is around can be done by more people.

We'll explore some of these strategies for societies and economies in the book's Conclusion. But for now, I'll emphatically state that *job loss by automation isn't a bug of the system.* Job loss doesn't happen because we've all missed something terribly obvious. Instead, it is *a design feature* of economies and societies that have not yet shifted to a model of inclusive work. No matter how much a fan you might be of Austrian economist Joseph Schumpeter's model of creative destruction,[35] and no matter how creatively a job is destroyed, it's still a lost job if the worker can't immediately find other similar-paying work.

To illustrate this, here is a thought experiment for you. I wave a magic wand, and suddenly you are the CEO of a large corporation. (Perhaps you already are, and I've just wasted some magic.) Under pressure from your shareholders to reduce the costs of all those messy, expensive humans on your payroll, you buy technologies that allow your organization to automate 20 percent of all the tasks humans are currently performing. What are your rational choices?

- You could lay off 20 percent of your people. That's what American companies do, frequently.
- You could ask everyone in the company to take a 20 percent pay cut, temporarily, until the company rebounds. This is common in Germany and in the Nordic countries. And in some countries, it's mandated by law.

- You could offer every worker the opportunity to spend a day a week coming up with ideas for new products and features, to create new offerings for your customers, so your organization will expand its innovation portfolio. Google historically called this 20 percent time, and that's why we have services like Gmail and Google Apps, conceived of by "twenty-percenters" at the company.

- You could band together with other organizations and create software to help workers move from one company to another. That's what the country of Luxembourg did, in partnership with the consultancy PwC and the Australian software company Faethm, in an initiative called SkillsBridge.

- You could have made your organization a co-op in the first place, run by collective decision-making that would determine which inclusive strategies would be followed to avoid layoffs.

- Or, you could have been the kind of person who leads an organization that followed the Next Rules of Work, anticipated a large market shift before it happened, continually trained workers to develop new skills and to solve new problems, and never found yourself with a workforce mismatch in the first place.

Various societies have made different decisions about which of these outcomes are most preferable. The most important takeaway is that they *are* decisions that organizations, communities, and countries can make, in the face of disruptive change.

Though automation and globalization are undeniable and inexorable forces of change, it's also a false narrative to place the impact of the pace and scale of change solely on those shoulders. The International Labor Organization estimated[36] in early 2021 that nearly 9 percent of total working hours were lost in the modern pandemic, the equivalent of 225 million jobs lost worldwide. In the same period, Oxfam estimated[37] that the wealth of the 10 richest men in the world grew by over half a trillion US dollars. So many people descended or remained in poverty that year that the global economy was projected to take at least a decade to make up for the loss, with none of the net impact due to robots or trade wars.

Workforce mismatches also occur regularly in various industries. According to the Department of Labor, about 5 percent of US workers are in the construction industry. Pre-pandemic in early 2020, there was already a significant workforce mismatch, with between 223,000 and 332,000 open positions, and 85 percent of construction companies said that the availability and cost of labor was their number one concern.[38] The need for trained workers with technical skills, and the fact that most construction jobs are onsite, often requires workers to relocate where the work is—something that many modern Americans are less willing to do.

If you care about tracking the health of any work economy, though, here's one piece of advice. Don't trust government unemployment statistics, which are usually mired in the Old Rules of Work.

If your heart rate is fine, but your other major organs are failing, would you judge your health solely by your pulse? That's what many countries do with unemployment statistics. Just because a worker ticks a box that says they're working a little doesn't mean they are "functionally employed," as the Ludwig Institute for Shared Economic Prosperity (LISEP) calls it. Unemployment statistics don't include the millions who can only find part-time work but want to work full-time or are making too little to pay the bills (underemployed), and all those long-term unemployed who are discouraged from looking for work.

At the end of 2020, LISEP calculated that, rather than the published US unemployment rate of 6.7 percent, the true rate of unemployment (TRU) was actually **over 25 percent**[39]—slightly higher than the peak unemployment rate in the Great Depression.

The Fundamental Challenges Are Driven by the Pace and Scale of Change—and So Are the Opportunities

As we try to handicap the three possible futures of work, the relentless focus on a future tech-fueled jobpocalypse is a headline-fueled distraction from understanding the mechanics of work markets today. As Pulitzer Prize-winning author and commentator Thomas

Friedman wrote to me, "Who can possibly predict how many old jobs will disappear and new jobs be born by 2050?"

Late in 2017, Susan Lund and James Manyika of McKinsey Global Institute published a study[40] that rightly pointed to the real culprits for a 21st-century workforce mismatch: the pace and scale of tech-fueled change. Due to the combination of prevailing wages, economic growth or contraction, shifting demographics, and the kinds of local industries, in one region a worker might not be displaced at all. But in another region a laid-off worker might have few easy alternatives for work, becoming long-term unemployed, or becoming underemployed in a lower-paying job.

> As Thomas Friedman asked me rhetorically, "Who can possibly predict how many old jobs will disappear and new jobs be born by 2050?"

So let's stop worrying about how many jobs there may or may not be decades from now. The three futures of work aren't predictions. They're scenarios. Possibilities. Even probabilities. But one or the other will only happen due to the decisions we all make today.

Right now I think Future 3 is the most likely. But I want to convince you that we *all* need to work together to help make Future 2 a reality.

Honestly, I'm far from the perfect sherpa for this process. I admit that I'm a change junkie. I'm endlessly fascinated by a seemingly unlimited range of topics. People fascinate me. The world fascinates me. I love juggling a range of projects, an affinity that I suspect comes from an advanced case of adult attention deficit.

But there is an undeniable and significant human toll from the pace and scale of change. The tsunami of change doesn't just sweep up old technologies and jobs. Our human traditions and our values can become deeply impacted as well.

I am not suggesting that you and I conspire together to blow up the entire world of traditional work. I'm saying much of this shift is already happening, and we need to collaborate on four things:

1   We need to help every single human to thrive in a world of disruptive change. That has to begin with work, because most of us on the planet need to work to have enough money to live, and probably will for a long time.

2   We need to *throw out* the things about traditional work that are not good for many humans, like dehumanizing and unreliable work, toxic bosses, and eroding pay.

3   We need to *keep* the things about traditional work that are really good for humans, like ensuring stable income, providing meaning in our lives, reinforcing our self-worth, and generating wealth for the future.

4   We need to understand and change a work ecosystem that in many countries actually reinforces many of the things that aren't good for people, the society, and the planet. We need to co-create the changes to those financial and social systems so that an increasing number of people can benefit in a world of relentless uncertainty.

How hard can that be?

I cannot tell you that the pace and scale of change is ever going to slow down. It's hard to imagine our world shifting more rapidly than with the modern global pandemic. But I suspect we're going to look back and say that it was actually a fire drill for the coming waves of economic and societal change.

I believe that we will look back in future years to this time, and we will realize that now, today, here, is when the world of work went through a seismic shift. And the rules for success in that shift are being shaped as you read this.

PART ONE

Rules

OLD RULES   NEW RULES   NEXT RULES

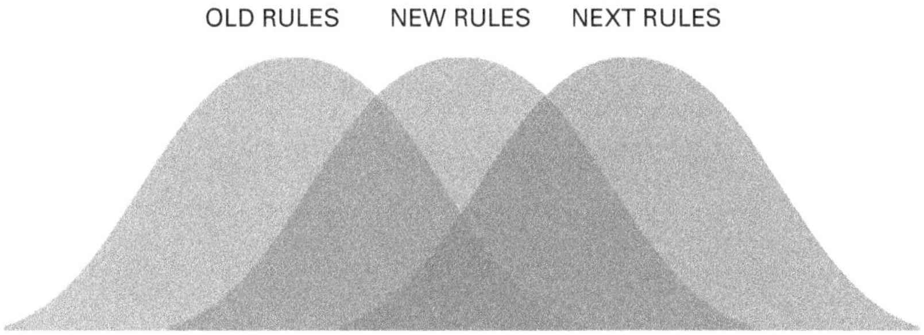

FIGURE P1 Rules of Work

SOURCE © 2021 Charrette LLC. Used by permission.

01

The Old Rules of Work

We have always worked. We just didn't think of it that way, until relatively recently.

There have always been rules for work, and those rules have changed throughout time. But many of the rules we still follow today have been with us for centuries. We have traditional definitions of work, skills, jobs, careers, teams, managers, workplaces, and organizations that still guide much of work.

And technology has always shaped human work, in a series of too-familiar patterns. By understanding the past of work, we can be better prepared to co-create a more positive future.

You Climb Into a Time Machine

Suddenly you are in a marble-walled library known as the Lyceum, in ancient Greece around 340 BC. Sitting before you is Aristotle, the philosopher who was occasionally worried about robots.

Seeing the unusual way you are dressed, he is clearly curious about you. He asks you to talk about yourself.

You begin by telling him about your work. (Forget for the moment that he actually isn't familiar with the modern-day concept of work. Or that you actually don't speak ancient Greek. You just go with it.)

You talk about your job, which is another foreign concept to him. You talk about your organization—again, a strange word, with no meaning for his time.

But he has questions for you:

- "*What* is your work? It sounds like you solve problems, with your skills. Is that correct?"
- "*Who* do you work with? Tell me about them, the kinds of people they are."
- "*Where* do you work? Describe that 'work place' for me. Where in the world is it?"
- "*When* do you work? Do you do it all day, every day? When have you done different kinds of work, throughout your time on this planet?"
- "*How* do you work? Do you use certain tools?"
- "And, perhaps most important... *Why* do you work? What motivates you to do this thing you call work?"

After you have answered each of these questions, he is still curious:

- "And this 'organization' you mention. Tell me about its What, Who, Where, When, How, and Why, as well."

You continue speaking for hours, as you help him to understand the purpose and practice of the organization in our time.

There's a very important reason that Aristotle is asking you these "Six Ws." They are the questions he uses to decide if an act is moral.

How We Learned the Old Rules of Work

Think about your first job. I don't mean what you first did to make money, like the newspaper route I took over from my older brother when I was 15. I don't mean volunteer work in your school or community. Remember your first paid job, while in school, or after you graduated. (I hope you're not embarrassed by that job. Mega-investor

Warren Buffett delivered newspapers too. Amazon founder Jeff Bezos was a fry cook at McDonald's. And Netflix CEO Reed Hastings sold vacuum cleaners door-to-door.)

Why did you work, back then? The answer was probably pretty simple. You needed the money.

For many of us, that first job was a little scary. You were being asked to do something new. You probably guessed that there were rules you should be following. But there wasn't any rule book you could use as a reference.

So how did you learn those rules?

Maybe your parents taught you a few things to prepare you. Hopefully you had a mentor who showed you the basics. Show up on time. Work hard. Follow instructions. Finish what you start.

But there were also many other unwritten rules, about work in general. Rules like, work often happens in an office, or in a restaurant, or at a construction project. That workplace operates onsite from 8 or 9 am to 5 or 6 or 7 pm. People are at the workplace five days a week. Many people also work from home on weekends, to catch up or to keep from falling behind. A job has a job description that outlines the tasks you regularly perform. Your organization has a hierarchy. Most workers have a boss, and that boss has a boss. You get a paycheck every few weeks.

But *why*? Why were these the rules of your work? It's likely that nobody explained.

Some work rules are clear and explicit, while others can be opaque or unclear. Some rules make some sense, and many rules seem to make no sense at all. In fact, a lot of the rules you were encouraged to follow felt like holdovers from a time long ago. To a young worker, some rules sound like they were simply made up by older people to ensure that work would be more challenging for the inexperienced, so they could "pay their dues," whatever that means. (What it often means is "payback time.")

Eventually, though, you learned the rules. And then, when someone new came to work, you did the same thing your mentors did, helping the new person to understand the rules of their work role and of the organization's culture.

Now, maybe the word "rules" sounds a little too prescribed for your tastes. Perhaps you prefer "guidelines" or "practices" to "rules." How strict the rules are in, say, a branch of the military is a very different situation from the rules of a creative agency. Yet no matter how much you may feel that you are an innovator who continually challenges norms, our actions at work are continually structured by sets of rules.

In every era, there have been rules defining what, when, where, why, how, and with whom we work. And those rules have gone through a series of evolutionary changes. Think of that constantly shifting set of practices as Old Rules of yesterday that are always phasing out, to be replaced by the New Rules that are being adopted today.

But what about what happens *next*? In a modern world where tomorrow is coming at us with blinding speed, how can we possibly prepare? Artificial intelligence software, adaptive robots, and self-driving cars are already among us. A global pandemic already transformed work for half the people on the planet. How can we anticipate how work will be changing in the coming years and get ourselves ahead of that exponential curve?

In a world of seismic change, the rules of work can change so quickly, it unfortunately isn't sufficient to focus on learning the new

FIGURE 1.1 Rule Waves

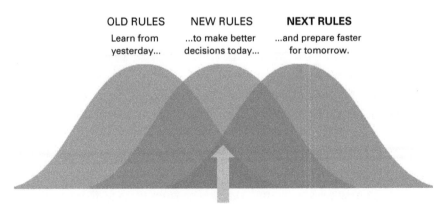

OLD RULES	NEW RULES	**NEXT RULES**
Learn from yesterday...	...to make better decisions today...	...and prepare faster for tomorrow.

You Are Here

rules of today. The events of the early 21st century made it abundantly clear that change can happen overnight. We need to be prepared today for the ways that work will work in a rapidly approaching tomorrow.

These are the Next Rules. This is how we learn from yesterday, so we can make better decisions today, and prepare for tomorrow—faster and more effectively.

Through all of these changing sets of work rules throughout history, three things have always been true about work:

- There has always been a prevailing *mindset* in the way we approach our work. Your mindset is defined by your mental model of the world of work, and by your motivation, the incentives that encourage you and the disincentives that dissuade you. Your mindset is a product of your *cognition*, the marvelous mechanics of your mind.

- There has always been a *skillset* needed to perform the work of the day. You and every other human on the planet have a unique mix of skills and abilities and experiences and interests and motivations. These all add up to a skillset for which you'll find someone who is (hopefully) willing to compensate you, in your job, or in some other kind of work role.

- And there has always been a *toolset* used to enable work. Sometimes that toolset is created to support work. In other cases, the toolset creates completely new kinds of work. And in yet other cases, the toolset can completely replace human work. Some of these tools are techniques and practices, and others are technologies and services.

By learning the mindset, skillset, and toolset of the Next Rules of Work, workers and those who lead in organizations will all be far better prepared to thrive in a world of disruptive change and perpetual uncertainty. And if there is anything we have learned in recent decades, it is that disruption and uncertainty are the new death and taxes.

Yet even though we think of ourselves as 21st-century problem-solvers enabled by technologies born out of science fiction, a surprising number of the work rules we follow today remain deeply rooted in practices stretching back through the 20th century into the distant past history of work.

> If there is anything we have learned in recent decades, it is that disruption and uncertainty are the new death and taxes.

You may think that you are a completely modern worker, and that none of the Old Rules apply to what you do in the new millennium. But many of the invisible guardrails of the Old Rules of work continue to guide and shape a surprising amount of our actions today. If we want to free ourselves of the Old Rules that keep us from being effective today and tomorrow, we first need to understand where they came from, and why they are still so influential today, so we can unlearn them for tomorrow.

A Brief History of Human Work

Throughout the early millennia of the Western world, we worked, but we didn't think of it in the same way that we think of today's jobs. Our mindset was to do the tasks that were needed, and not much more. And we certainly didn't think of performing those tasks as some noble pursuit. In his 1930 book *Work: What it has meant to men through the ages*,[1] author Adriano Tilgher wrote, "the Greek philosophers maintained that manual labor and even most forms of mental work 'brutalized the mind till it was unfit for thinking of truth.'" Vicki Smith says in her 2013 anthology *Sociology of Work: An encyclopedia*[2] that both the Greeks and the Hebrews actually thought of work literally as a curse by the deities or deity.

In fact, Tilgher pointed out that the Greek word for work was *ponos*, from the Latin word *poena*, which means pain, or punishment, or sorrow. Like me, that's probably how you felt about that first job out of school. And it's why Aristotle was so curious about your "job," since he wasn't quite sure why you were looked on so unfavorably by the gods as to be cursed with work.

All the way up to the Middle Ages, disdain for work continued to permeate Western culture. As the Greek and Roman gods were left behind for one Christian god, the mindset toward work went from a pantheistic curse to a punishment by God for original sin. Work was only acceptable if it could make you money, and if that money could make you independent from others. But going from a curse to a punishment wasn't exactly an upgrade.

Then suddenly, about 500 years ago, the Western view toward work took a dramatic turn, laying the groundwork for a mindset that persists in many cultures and families today. As Vicki Smith describes it, "A new perspective on work came with the Reformation. Martin Luther believed that people could serve God through their work, and that people should work diligently in their own occupation." And as author Roger Hill writes in *Historical Context of the Work Ethic*,[3] Luther also disdained what we would call today career pivots, maintaining that since you were born into a certain kind of work, God wanted you to stay in the profession for which you were trained.

The contemporary reformist John Calvin one-upped Luther on the purpose of work. Calvin believed it was actually the will of God that we should *all* work. The Calvinistic mindset was that industrious people were far more likely to get into Heaven, while lazy people might never be admitted.

Today we call that doctrine the Protestant work ethic.

Have you ever praised someone for being a hard worker? Have you ever admonished a relaxed teen for being lazy? From that mindset today, you can draw a straight line back 500 years to one of the Old Rules of Work.

The Protestant work ethic eventually incorporated a key tweak that laid the groundwork for future economies. Many came to believe that God not only wanted you to work hard, but also to acquire wealth. It was through this mindset that the seeds of modern capitalism were sown. And what helped to build that foundation was the toolset we call technology.

Work, Meet Technology

From fire and the wheel through the scythe and the plow to the personal computer and the mobile phone, our technology toolset has always transformed work. But technologies that could actually perform tasks similar to humans, and do that work independently and at scale, are a relatively recent innovation in our history.

Gutenberg's printing press in the mid-1400s quickly impacted the hand-duplication profession for books, and by the early 1500s there were hundreds of printing presses in dozens of cities in Europe and beyond. The technology of scaled production slowly began to transform work in a range of other industries. In 1589, William Lee, a minister and amateur inventor living in Calverton, England, used his mechanical mind to invent a device that could knit stockings much more rapidly than by hand. He built what became known as a framework knitter, a rack with several needles stitching several rows simultaneously.

But Queen Elizabeth I, whose patronage was needed for its adoption, would have none of it. "I have too much love for my poor people who obtain their bread by the employment of knitting," she said, "to give my money to forward an invention that will tend to their ruin by depriving them of employment, and thus making them beggars."[4]

Imagine those words coming from a modern-day venture capitalist.

Lee's knitting technology became widely adopted in the 1600s, but by the early 1700s the machines had become so expensive that only the rich could afford them, and they would employ knitters to run them, often with low wages. The knitters who rebelled against this arrangement called themselves Luddites, burning frameworks across the country. Yet despite our use of the word Luddite today to describe a techno-skeptic, it wasn't really the technology that they fought against. It was the drop in income engineered by the framework owners, meaning that people doing the real work made much less than those who owned the technology.

If you immediately thought of modern calls for taxes on the owners of robots displacing human workers, you're not alone.

Also in the early 1700s, an English farmer's son by the name of Jethro Tull,[5] whose poor health kept him from completing college, returned to the family farm and began noticing how inefficient the family's field workers were at planting seeds. Tull designed and eventually perfected a seed drill, the first agricultural machine with moving parts, which could place seeds at exactly the right depth. Soon an entire field could be seeded by a single worker and a horse-drawn drill.

Tull's invention helped in part to catalyze the Second Agricultural Revolution, dramatically increasing the food-growing capacity of farms across the country, and eventually around the world. But that revolution was also a textbook study for how changes in our technology toolset change the power dynamics of work. The British passed laws called "Enclosure Acts"[6] allowing the wealthy to buy what used to be common areas between farms, spawning an era of large businesses and displacing countless small farmers. No antitrust laws to slow things down.

Stripped of the chance to use their skillsets on farms, those displaced workers left their rural areas for cities like London and Dublin, itinerant workers ready to become the nascent workforce to populate factories. But the machines of the time were still powered by inefficient human hands, so having a large unemployed workforce by itself didn't spark a production revolution. Some kind of new technology that could transform human work would be needed.

Technology, Rising

The Second Agricultural Revolution meant more food. More food meant more people. More people meant more customers for goods from factories. More goods meant a dramatically increased need for raw materials like iron, copper, and coal. More demand meant digging deeper and wider for more raw materials. But deeper mines meant lots of subterranean flooding. So in the early 1700s, British steelworker Thomas Newcomen invented a steam-powered cylinder pump, a machine that could work tirelessly, made from the iron and copper it was helping to excavate, and feeding itself on the coal and water it helped to extract.

Newcomen's pump morphed into the steam engine, and suddenly machines were no longer limited by the power of a human or a horse or a stream. Now the First Industrial Revolution could begin. And with it, yet another new mindset toward human work.

Up to the 18th century, most craftwork was artisanal. A wood-worker usually built an entire cabinet. A shoemaker cut and assembled all of the parts of a shoe. Apprentices might do many of the most mind-numbing tasks, such as preparing the wood or leather. But once the work was mastered, a craftsperson knew and performed every step of the process.

As the First Industrial Revolution began to sweep the Western world, production increasingly shifted from human hands to big machines in factories. Adam Smith, the influential 18th-century econ-omist, was one of the first to point out that the craftsperson model was actually pretty inefficient. By having people specializing in doing just one or two things in a production process, early factories could dramatically increase production output. That approach required a fundamentally new mindset by the worker. You weren't the craftsper-son building the entire product. You performed just part of the process, or you tended the machine.

That mind-numbing repetition made for much less interesting work. And those early factories weren't exactly iconic examples of inclusive management. Often run like a fiefdom, the manager of the factory would peremptorily issue autocratic orders. Working conditions in factories were often brutal, with work weeks of 80 to 100 hours not uncommon. This was work as *toil*, with little regard for—or even search for—satisfaction in work. People worked mostly for food, which could cost up to half their wages.[7] Shelter was, by comparison, pretty cheap—only about a tenth of their income. (For laborers in cities today, those percentages are usually flipped.) Yet many city workers could still make more than on the farms they had left, and the wages of most workers in the first half of the 19th century eventually doubled.

After a brief lull in global innovation, the late 19th century saw the rise of the Second Industrial Revolution. Standardization of machines and production practices gave the last big shove, and by the end of the 19th century human work had completed the shift from farm to factory.

The Century-Old Rules of Work

With so many people now working in factories, starting in the early 20th century a series of engineers and economists began offering a variety of scientific and mechanistic principles defining the roles of the manager and the worker. First came Frederick Winslow Taylor, the American mechanical engineer who is considered the father of industrial engineering, which is the scientific management of an organization. Like Adam Smith, Taylor pushed for division of labor, so that people would do the same tasks over and over again. But Taylor decided that it was a factory leader's responsibility to tell workers what to do and how to do it, to ensure greater consistency in the performance of tasks, to increase the quality of output.

With Taylor's 1909 publication of his *Principles of Scientific Management*,[8] modern management theory was born. If you were to dig into the machine learning algorithms that help to automate human work in today's enterprise resource planning software, you would see much of it infused by Taylorism's mentality around the data-driven science of work.

In the coming decades, a series of other theorists offered their own sets of management principles. One of the most influential was Henri Fayol, a French mining executive, who in 1916 suggested his own precepts of people management. They included:

- **division of work**, breaking work into tasks that each person performs based on their skills;

- **authority and responsibility**, giving bosses control over subordinates, in a "scalar chain" (hierarchy);

- **discipline** (by which Fayol meant "obedience");

- **unity of command and direction**, with just one boss telling any given worker what to do;
- **order**, which meant a place for everything, and everything in its place, like machines, materials, and humans;
- **subordination of individual interest**, meaning that the collective mattered the most.

If many of these 100-year-old practices sound to you like today's classic command-and-control organization, it's not an accident. Fayol laid the groundwork for much of today's mindset about "optimized human work." But often forgotten are Fayol's counterbalancing principles, laying the precepts for more human-centered work. Fayol's principles included:

- **Fair wages, with equal pay for equal work**—How is your company doing on gender pay balance, and the ratio between line worker and executive pay?
- **Equal respect for all workers, including justice and kindness**— Does *your* HR department help enforce kindness?
- **Initiative, encouraging workers to solve problems, paired with "balanced decision-making," allowing for decentralized initiative**— How "bossed" are you?
- **Esprit de corps, encouraging a culture of community in the organization**—What is your organization's employee engagement score?

After Fayol, many other influential waves of management theory washed over the early modern organization, especially starting in the late 1940s with the Third Industrial Revolution, which ushered into the organization a range of new technologies that helped fuel the rise of office-based work.

At the same time as the appearance of that new toolset, international lawyer and economist Peter Drucker wrote his landmark book, *Concept of the Corporation*,[9] laying the groundwork for the mindset and skillset of the worker and the manager in the modern organization—and for many of the definitions of work and management that we still hold today.

So Now... What's Work?

As James Suzman says in his excellent book *Work: A deep history, from the stone age to the age of robots*,[10] "The work we do... defines who we are; determines our future prospects; dictates where and with whom we spend most of our time; mediates our sense of self-worth; molds many of our values; and orients our political loyalties."

We often use the word "work" without much thought. But *mechanically*, human work is just three things:

1 It's a **problem** to be solved. It doesn't matter if the problem is a dirty floor, or a complex market entry strategy, or a thorny social challenge.

2 How do we solve problems? We perform **tasks**. If it's a dirty floor, we go to the closet, get the broom, sweep, and so on.

3 How do we perform tasks? We use our human **skills**.

Skills > Tasks > Problems

That's it. Our human *skills*, to perform *tasks*, to solve *problems*. That's why people pay us, and why we pay other people: to solve problems. (Of course, in any organization, there are one or two people who think it's their job to *create* problems. And you know who those are in your organization. But for the most part, we are problem-*solvers*.) And tasks are frequently enabled by tools, from lowly pencils to powerful computers.

Every organization has a range of problems. The problems that organizations most frequently focus on solving are those of its customers. For example:

· A fast-food company has *problems* like customers who want to get food into their hands quickly. Behind the Formica counter, a worker in a colorful uniform performs *tasks* such as taking orders and making change, using *skills* like listening, pressing buttons on a keyboard, making change, and so on. These are mostly repetitive problems to solve, except when the occasional high-maintenance customer wants something unusual, like a well-cooked hamburger.

- A consulting company has *problems* like clients who need sophisticated market-entry strategies. A team member in a suit performs *tasks* such as walking a client through a design process, using *skills* like interviewing, analyzing, synthesizing, and writing.
- A non-profit or NGO servicing a homeless population has *problems* like needing temporary housing for the displaced. A volunteer or staff member performs *tasks* such as making phone calls, doing site visits, and stopping by homeless shelters, using *skills* like researching, communicating, and empathizing.

In many organizations, tasks are grouped into processes, sequences of activities intended to be performed the same way again and again. Then as workers we often fall in love with our processes, losing sight of the problems we were originally trying to solve.

When a (typically young) worker comes along to challenge those processes by suggesting a new approach, it's not uncommon to find that person pulled aside after a meeting to receive the admonishment, "That's not how we do it here." That's a behavior buzzer signaling that someone has violated an unwritten Old Rule of Work in that organization.

In many organizations, there is tremendous pressure to continually hone tasks and processes to make them as efficient and productive as possible. As a result, a huge amount of work today remains task- and process-centric.

What's a Skill?

If work is our human skills performing tasks to solve problems, then what's a skill? There are few words that have as many definitions in many languages, yet are so generally misunderstood, as "skill."

The good news is that there is extremely valuable research going back to World War II that helps us gain a clear understanding of the different kinds of human skills. Unfortunately, not only have we not taught workers about the different kinds of skills they have, most of us don't even understand our own skills in the first place.

THE MODERN HISTORY OF SKILLS

In the late 1940s, as America was shifting from a war footing to what became a more consumer-driven economy, the US Department of Labor had the unenviable task of trying to get its arms around the kinds of work that would be needed, and the jobs that would be required.

Dr. Sidney Fine had earned a PhD in Industrial and Counseling Psychology from George Washington University. At the time, the general arena of understanding jobs fell to the field of industrial psychology, which was as reliant on an industrial-era perspective as its name implies. Researchers would develop straitjacket job classification hierarchies, locking workers into metaphorical boxes that severely limited their career mobility. The corporations, government agencies, and military organizations of the time used these classifications to structure job responsibilities and pay, as if humans were as easily sorted as the products they produced in factories.

Dr. Fine had a different approach. For nearly 10 years, he guided research that looked differently at the patterns of work and jobs. Rather than continuing to pigeonhole people based on tasks, he focused on understanding the kinds of skills that people were using. Imagine sifting through tens of thousands of job descriptions, and looking for the common threads, without any of the flexible technologies that we have today.

I first met Sid in my late teens. As my father was doing the research that led to the writing of *What Color Is Your Parachute?*, he interviewed Sid, and later invited him to join him as a staff member of our two-week workshops in Overland Park, Kansas. Sid was a mensch, a warm and caring human being who saw his work as helping enable the careers of millions of people across the country.

As the post-War US Department of Labor analyzed the data about human activity in work, they saw a number of patterns emerging. One of the most fundamental is that they realized humans have three very different kinds of skills: *know* skills, *flex* skills, and *self* skills. (These are my labels; the DOL team had several for each category.)

- **Know skills** (also called special knowledges, rooted skills and work content skills) are what were classically thought of at the time as skills. Because knowledges are bodies of information anchored in a field or arena, these skills could often be tested (what we unfortunately call "assessments"), and a level of understanding or proficiency assigned. Know skills are not easily transferable between different work activities without adaptation. For example, your knowledge of a programming language probably won't help you cook an omelet, or vice versa.

- **Flex skills** (transferable, functional, or reusable skills) are those abilities that are usable in a range of situations. These skills aren't anchored in a particular field or arena. The same fine motor skills you learned while taking apart a vacuum cleaner give you a skill you can flexibly use to assemble the ingredients for a recipe. Important flex skills include critical thinking, creative problem-solving, basic interpersonal skills, and collaboration. Flex skills have an *object*. Sid Fine and his team grouped these objects into three categories: people, things, and data or information. So, if you're good at analyzing, we need to be a little more specific: You could analyze people, or machines, or the information in a spreadsheet. In each of those cases, analyzing could be paired with a know skill, such as psychology with people, engineering with machines, and data science with information.

- **Self skills** (self-management skills, often called traits) are skills focused on ourselves. Arriving on time, completing tasks, and managing anger are all traits we use in our daily lives so we can perform tasks and solve problems. Each of us starts with a basic toolkit of self skills, some from nature that we are born with, and some from nurture that we are taught to develop. These are foundational skills that provide us with the basic building blocks of doing work and solving problems, skills we hone throughout our lives.

As you've guessed, today many often call know skills "hard skills," and we group flex and self skills together and call them "soft skills." But there is nothing soft about flex or self skills. They are the kinds of skills that will allow us to solve problems in a range of situations. They are the skills that allow us to manage our interactions with other human

FIGURE 1.2 The Three Categories of Skills

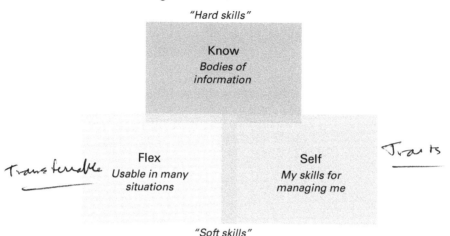

"Hard skills"

Know
*Bodies of
information*

Transferable

Flex
*Usable in many
situations*

Self
*My skills for
managing me*

Traits

"Soft skills"

beings, and to manage our own time and energies. And they form the foundation for virtually every list of critical 21st-century skills.

Where Do You Begin to Learn Skills?

The industrial-era model of learning that we call school provided a structured production process taken directly from the factories whose workers the schools were intended to prepare. The teacher was "the sage on the stage," as Esther Wojcicki says in her iconic book, *Moonshots in Education,*[11] "the one with all the answers." Mass production teaching delivered mass production learning.

In the Old Rules, you made a significant investment in learning early in your life. When you shifted into the work arena, you were able to amortize that learning investment over your career. After spending all that time learning to be an electrician or a doctor or a lawyer, you could be reasonably assured of never having to immerse yourself in a deep learning experience again. Sure, you might have to do some professional development now and then. But the pace of change in many fields wasn't very fast. Besides, maybe you didn't even like school all that much. Why would you subject yourself to it again? Just graduate, go to work, and don't look back.

As a result, traditional school systems often focused on the rote acquisition of know skills, and rarely explicitly taught flex and self skills. It's possible that some students would learn those skills in college, and certainly the lucky student who found teachers dedicated to critical thinking and team collaboration would be better prepared for work. But the traditional college system wasn't designed to ensure that outcome, either.

What's a Job?

See how many of these Old Rules of Work apply to a current or past job of yours:

- If you have a job, you are an employee, and the organization is your employer.
- A job has a title. But it may not be very descriptive. Someone with the exact same title as yours might have a completely different set of responsibilities. (My father used to call a job title "a poetic metaphor.")
- A job has a salary, and may have benefits.
- A job has a workplace, and that workplace is located somewhere geographically.
- A job may have a set number of hours during which you must work, either on a given day, or in a given week. Or it may have a set number of shifts to be worked.
- A job has a set of functions, responsibilities, and tasks. Sometimes these are loosely prescribed, and sometimes they are very specific and exacting.
- A job almost always has a supervisor, or a manager, or a boss.
- A job may also have team members and co-workers. Your job might also have other workers reporting to it.

Not all jobs have these characteristics. But we call work that has many of these characteristics "a job."

WHAT COLOR IS YOUR PARACHUTE?

In the mid-1960s, Richard Nelson Bolles was an Episcopal minister in San Francisco, at Grace Cathedral on Nob Hill. He had been a small-town priest just east of New York City in the 1960s and had coordinated the merging of a black and a white congregation in Passaic, New Jersey. His local bishop recommended him for an opening at Grace. The charismatic bishop at the time, Jim Pike, recruited my father to become Canon Pastor at the cathedral, and our family drove westward in early 1966 in the family station wagon, when I was nine years old.

Yet after a few years, Pike stepped down, and in the ensuing budget and political turmoil at the cathedral, my father's job was eliminated. Suddenly, in his early 40s, he found himself unemployed, with a wife and four kids, and no nearby parishes where he could work. After a gut-wrenching job search, he eventually found work helping other ministers on college campuses in the western US, funded by a consortium of Protestant churches originally known as United Ministries in Higher Education.

The first challenges those ministers were faced with in the late 1960s were recreational drugs, so my father wrote a pamphlet to help them help students deal with addiction. The second problem the ministers had to deal with was being laid off themselves, as the churches supporting them cut back their budgets.

My father ended up getting a grant from the Eli Lilly Foundation, so he could travel around the country and find the best techniques for job-hunting and career change, of which there were very few. Sidney Fine, known as the Father of the Dictionary of Occupational Titles, was the leading expert on human skills. John Holland, a former federal job counselor, had developed what is still considered the leading model for people environments. And John Crystal, a former World War II spy, developed the research techniques we now call information interviewing.

Though my father originally intended to knock out a job-hunting pamphlet, he ended up writing a book, which he self-published. He typed it on an IBM Selectric typewriter, the illustrations were block-cut pictures from open-source books, and my brother Stephen did the calligraphy for the chapter titles. The book talked about vocation and mission, giving ministers insights and techniques to find work outside the Church.

As a teenager I would visit my father at his small apartment below Nob Hill after my parents had split up, helping mail books to his readers. (It cost $5 to print and mail, and he sold them for $5. Minister, not business guy.) I would ask him, why are some of these going to corporate executives, teachers, and even the Department of Labor? He would write to them, and they responded: It's the best compendium of job-hunting techniques we can find.

Sensing a market opportunity, my father was introduced to a local publisher, Phil Wood of Ten Speed Press, who at that point had only released a single book. That's how *What Color Is Your Parachute?*[12] came to become the world's career manual. Over 10 million copies in print, in 17 languages. The reason it retained its relevance through the decades is that my father updated the book nearly every year. In fact, one of his favorite jokes was that he had written 42 books, they just all had the same title. He passed away in 2017, soon after his 90th birthday. And he left behind an amazing legacy.

What's a Career?

When you were born, nobody told you that there would be three phases to the arc of your life. You'd start with a **learning** phase. Once you had learned for a dozen to a dozen and a half years, you would suddenly hop into the **work** phase. Then, after you had worked for decades, at some point you would no longer need to work, and you could just **live**.

In the Old Rules, that third phase is what I call "The Period Formerly Known As Retirement."

In *The 100 Year Life*,[13] Lynda Gratton and Andrew Scott call this the "three-stage life." My father called them *The Three Boxes of Life*[14] in his 1976 book by that name. During the Western transition to industrial economies, this approach was a huge leap. By subsidizing schools, many governments ensured that everyone—not just the elite—could get a basic education. But in many countries, this helped to bake into the culture and the economy a three-stage model, and encouraged the creation of the mass-production education system that many countries have today.

After you were born, you needed to learn quite a bit before you could become a functioning adult. So you became immersed in the process of learning. You would eventually reach the age where you

FIGURE 1.3 The Old Rules of Careers

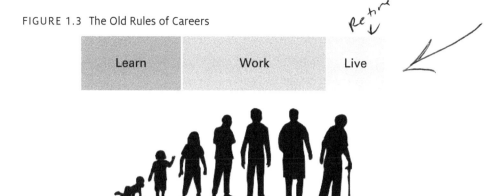

SOURCE © 2021 Charrette LLC. Used by permission.

might learn a trade or get a degree, hopefully teaching you the *know* skills you would need for your future work.

With little or no preparation, you would then shift into the *work* phase of your life. In a traditional career you would likely be doing the same kind of work for a long time. You'd be a lawyer, or a doctor, or a mechanic, or an assembly-line worker. That meant that getting the right kind of educational preparation for the work stage made a lot of sense, because more education often meant better pay and better opportunities. So once you (or your parents) spent a lot of money for you to go to college, so long as you worked in the field for which you studied, you could literally work off that investment over decades, as your student loans were repaid.

Then, when your relationship to work was mostly over, you would enter the *live* stage, in "The Period Formerly Known As Retirement." Now you could finally rest, you could finally travel, you could spend time with the grandkids—that is, if you have the health, the savings, and the energy for it.

What's a Team?

Throughout your career, you would typically work as part of one or more teams.

In the Old Rules of Work, a team is a group of workers focused on a set of connected tasks. Members of a team might be responsible for tasks like creating plans, thinking of solutions, and making decisions. A team is assumed to know how to understand the strengths that each team member brings, collaborate efficiently, communicate effectively, and achieve a common goal.

If that defines teams you've worked with before, congratulations. Yet in many organizations, though these are all an ideal skillset for a team, few teams would say they do all of these things well. Instead, the culture of traditional organizations often rewards members of the team for following a set of prescribed tasks, which are grouped into processes. And, again going back to Taylorism, since many managers define their roles as simply telling team members what to do, those workers might have had little freedom to experiment and innovate.

What's a Manager?

I don't know if anyone has actually counted all of the management books that have been written in the past 100 years since Taylor advanced his scientific theories. A stack of those books might not actually reach the moon. But I'm guessing it would at least be stratospheric.

Why so many attempts to teach the work of managing? As we've seen going back to the days of Taylorism, helping to coordinate the work of other people can be hard stuff. Helping a team of humans to effectively solve problems for the organization's stakeholders can require a breathtaking range of skills. Yet despite a never-ending river of books on management, over and over again traditional organizations default to teaching and reinforcing manager practices from the Old Rules of Work. Why?

The simple answer: It's a self-perpetuating system.

Stephen Denning, author of books like *The Leader's Guide to Radical Management*,[15] criticizes the traditional management approach that simply guarantees those traditional practices will be perpetually reinforced. Corporate cultures encourage conformity. Compensation structures include rewards for keeping things the same. Organization leaders often don't want to actually have to change their own behavior, so others follow their lead and don't change, either. And the new generation that should be the change agents are simply taught the same techniques in business schools. The result is that many organizations fell into the trap of encouraging managers to follow the Old Rules of Work, with the manager expected to have all the answers.

The Old Rules encouraged what I call "management-by-surveillance." If a manager didn't see a worker on a given day, how could the manager know if the worker was doing their work? Look at how few organizations trusted their workers enough to have consistent work-from-home practices before the modern global pandemic. That lack of trust was a clear sign of a transactional mindset between managers and workers. And if a manager trusted one or two workers enough to let them work offsite, those were often "remote" workers, second-class team members dissociated from the core team.

What's a Workplace?

As managers increasingly practiced management-by-surveillance, the model of the industrial office-as-production-environment took hold. That high-density approach to physical workgroup space met its defining technology with the invention of the cubicle. Robert Probst, research director for the Herman Miller furniture company, originally envisioned "the Action Office"[16] in 1968 as a flexible, creative work-space. Slow at first to catch on, the combination of tax depreciation laws for office equipment and the subsequent drive toward corporate productivity drove the creation of "cubicle farms" of ever-increasing size to pack people into vast worker warehouses. And the high-density urban work environment also meant more time spent in cars getting to that workplace. By 2016, the average American spent about nine full work days a year just commuting to and from work.[17]

You might think that technology companies invariably hire digital natives who could conceivably work anywhere and still coordinate their efforts. But companies like IBM and Yahoo, which at one point had widespread work-from-home standards, in the late 2010s revoked those policies. In fact, pre-pandemic, many tech companies embraced the trend toward human density. For example, Apple's "spaceship" headquarters, opened in early 2017, can hold over 12,000 workers in one 2.8 million-square-foot building. That's about three-quarters the size of the Pentagon in Washington, DC, which is the largest office building in the world.

What's an Organization?

Under the Old Rules of Work, the model of the traditional organization was what I call The Box. There is abundance outside The Box, with many people who would like jobs. There is scarcity inside The Box, with only so many available jobs. How have organizations traditionally managed that scarcity? With a hierarchy. Workers have bosses, and bosses have bosses. It's bosses, all the way down.

Box models led to the solidification of a wide range of management practices. One of the most widespread is what I call Binary Set Thinking. Workers would typically fit into one of two categories: You were either an employee, or you were not. (Mathematicians call this traditional set theory, or crisp theory.) The answer to the question, "Is this person an employee?" was either true or false.

If you were in The Box, you were an employee. The Old Rules positioned employees as either personnel, or human resources. But they were actually thought of more as human *assets*. Because the organization's core stakeholder was a shareholder, the organization was judged by its ability to maximize the productivity of those human assets.

Of course, I'm oversimplifying for dramatic effect. But think about some of the organizations in which you have worked. Is this really an exaggeration? Aren't many organizations actually run as if they are boxes?

How Have Organizations Managed Change?

Many of those who lead organizations have traditionally tried to catalyze organization-wide change through change management initiatives.

Change management is simple. A group of those who lead the organization—typically a decision-making black hole called "the leadership team"—goes to a weekend retreat. They look at what the organization is doing today (A), develop a five-year plan (B), subtract what is being done today, and voila: change management plan.

It's not clear if this was a consistently effective methodology. But in a time when the pace of change was slower, and the scale of change was smaller, it may have been more possible to envision that future static state to the point where meaningful change could be catalyzed.

FIGURE 1.4 The Old Rules of Change Management

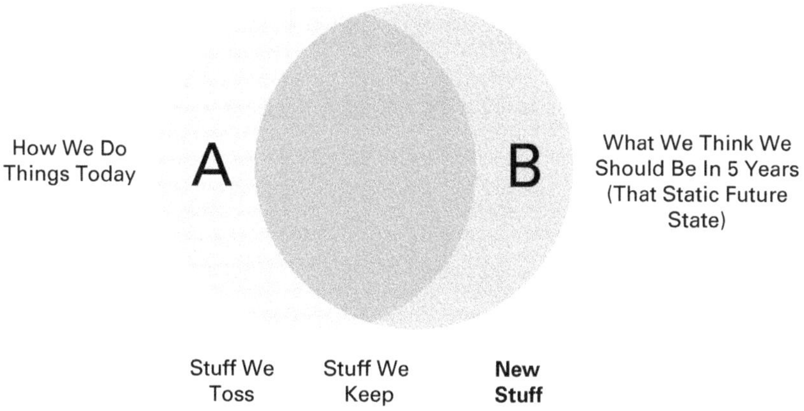

How We Do Things Today **A**   **B** What We Think We Should Be In 5 Years (That Static Future State)

Stuff We Toss   Stuff We Keep   **New Stuff**

SOURCE © 2021 Charrette LLC. Used by permission.

What Is the *Purpose* of an Organization?

Most people don't question why we have organizations. If they give it any thought at all, they may think that it's so people can have jobs and be productive members of society. Others may think that the purpose of for-profit organizations is to make happy customers.

But the organization as we know it is a pretty recent invention. Early organizations in Europe and America were often incorporated solely for public projects like waterways and dams. But changes in post-Depression investment and taxation laws started to guide Western money into stock markets. Around the same time, a British economist named Ronald Coase offered a set of arguments that only economists could find exciting. (It's not called "the dismal science" for nothing.) Coase speculated that there were market and social costs that all had to be managed for the benefit of economies and societies, and a company was the best-designed vehicle for balancing those costs.

Then along came a guy named Milton Friedman.

In the 1960s and 1970s, Friedman and fellow economists from the University of Chicago offered the persuasive argument that making lots of money was a counterbalance to socialism, which carried a lot of political gravitas during the Cold War. Friedman won the Nobel Prize in Economics in 1976 and became an influential adviser to US President Ronald Reagan and UK Prime Minister Margaret Thatcher.

Remember that the seeds of capitalism were sown going all the way back to the Protestant work ethic, encouraging not just work, but amassing wealth. In the latter half of the 20th century, amassing wealth often became synonymous with investing in the stock market, providing working capital to organizations large and small as they jockeyed for market dominance. Happily for that stock market, Friedman maintained that the number one responsibility of a corporation was to satisfy the needs of its shareholders.

Sure, there are other *stakeholders* of the organization, such as customers, partners, suppliers, the communities in which the organization operates, and even the planet. Yet just as in George Orwell's *Animal Farm*,[18] all of an organization's stakeholders are equal—but some are more equal than others. And in the peculiar form of capitalism we practice here in the US, shareholders became *far* more equal than others.

You might think that all this discussion about economics has nothing to do with the Rules of Work. But these dynamics actually define *everything* about work in corporations, even in private rapid-growth hi-tech companies. For example, if one worker in an organization is a "high performer," and another is a less productive "low performer," it doesn't take a complex calculation to see that shareholders win if the company simply fires the "low performer," making room to hire more high performers. Why would you pay to train or coach the low performer? Toss the worker and move on.

The same rationale goes for high executive pay. The more you pay "top" executives in the organization, the more you have to compensate them to remain "competitive" in the "job market." That's why upper executive pay—which often is through stock—has skyrocketed. According to the Economic Policy Institute, from 1978 to 2020 the average non-executive worker pay in public companies in the US increased 12 percent, adjusted for inflation. But in the same period, executive pay increased 940 percent.[19]

Check my math here, but I don't think the value of an executive today has increased 78 times faster than that of workers.

As we'll see, the Next Rules are nearly impossible to follow unless you and I can co-create a vision for a new purpose for the organization. And for bonus points, we'll dive into revamping business and capitalism in the book's Conclusion.

This Is Why We Need the Next Rules

I've obviously oversimplified many of the Old Rules. But not much.

There is nothing that is inherently wrong about the Old Rules. In fact, back at the dawn of the Third Industrial Era, they *were* the Next Rules.

Today, though, many of the Old Rules of Work are increasingly a tax on nimbleness and innovation. The more that organizations and leaders follow those Old Rules, the slower they will react, and the less likely they will be able to adapt.

Even though our world has recently gone through a series of seismic changes, from the rapid introduction of disruptive technologies to the Great Reset of the modern pandemic, the Old Rules of Work still guide far too many of the ways that organizations function today.

That's why we need to understand the Next Rules for the 21st century.

02

The Next Rules of Work

The Next Rules illustrate how rapidly work is changing, and what it is becoming. In the Next Rules...

- Work becomes a process of creating value for customers and other stakeholders.
- A worker becomes a problem-solver who is adaptive and creative, with empathy.
- A career becomes a portfolio of work.
- A job becomes just one of many use cases for work.
- An employee becomes a worker, and the employer becomes a hirer.
- A manager becomes a team guide.
- A team becomes a distributed band of problem-solvers.
- A workforce becomes a worknet.
- The workplace becomes a co-working collaboratory.
- Change management becomes managing change.
- The purpose of the organization is as a platform for channeling human energy.

Time Machine Time

You and I set our time machine for 20 years in the future. We step out into the main office of a typical organization, and suddenly it is apparent to us that people are working very differently than before.

The entity we once thought of as an organization has changed dramatically. There are no perceptible boundaries. People flow in and out of the organization in a frictionless process of identifying problems, creating value, and moving to the next problem. That "worknet" is at once local, regional, and worldwide. People collaborate remotely, frequently, and effortlessly.

Workgroups here seem to function without traditional managers. Every worker is empowered with the agency to solve problems. The team's work is continuously synchronized like a co-created, global dance.

The traditional workplace as we know it is gone. In its place is a flexible work environment that is continuously adapted to the needs of those onsite. And those who are working in distant locations are seamlessly interconnected.

And then... we realize that the time machine didn't actually take us *anywhen*. The time is now. What we are witnessing together is how an increasing number of people are working, today. But no single organization follows all of these practices. They are being continually adapted and improved in a range of organizations, in a variety of different ways, as groups of workers continuously coalesce toward what works.

As the science fiction author William Gibson has often been quoted as saying, "The future is already here—it's just not very evenly distributed."[1]

The Four Core Next Rules

Disruptive technologies, increased competition, and global trends will all continue to place increasing pressure on organizations and their leaders. Customers will demand new value more rapidly. Older human skillsets will become less needed, and new skillsets will continually be in demand.

As a result, workers and those who lead in organizations must become more nimble and adaptive. They will need to follow a brand new set of rules that can define the ways they will continue to deliver value.

I want to encourage you to embrace a completely different language and perspective, not just about work, but also about jobs, careers, teams, managers, leaders, and the organization. That's a lot to digest, I know. But I urge you to open the aperture, take a deep breath, let it out, and come along for the ride.

Despite the mind-numbing complexity of the world of work, the Next Rules provide a simple framework for those who lead in organizations to develop the mindset, skillset, and toolset for the work of today and tomorrow. There are only four core rules:

- Empower Effectiveness.
- Enable Growth.
- Ensure Involvement.
- Encourage Alignment.

(EGIA. I know. Not exactly a catchy mnemonic.)

FIGURE 2.1   The Next Rules of Work

Each rule is the container of some rather large problems to be solved.

Empower Effectiveness

How can workers continually do their best work? How can they solve problems the most effectively?

How can people continually innovate to solve problems and create value for customers and other key stakeholders?

What rewards will appropriately encourage and compensate those workers for their contributions?

Enable Growth

How can people understand their own skills, develop a growth mindset, rapidly learn new skills, and become lifelong learners?

How can every worker continuously maximize their human potential?

How can each human continually thrive as a whole person?

How can human growth become a team sport?

Ensure Involvement

How can the organization hire, develop, and promote inclusively, ensuring human diversity and equity are supported in all their forms?

How can the organization encourage individual- and team-driven growth, effectiveness, and alignment across its entire work ecosystem?

How can involvement remain anchored in the needs of key stakeholders, especially communities and societies?

Encourage Alignment

How can workers understand the problems that need to be solved for key stakeholders, and the value that needs to be created for them—and continually and perpetually align their work with that strategic value?

How can teams of workers coordinate their efforts most effectively?

How can many independently innovating and widely distributed humans continually stay aligned with each other's work, and with the strategic goals of the organization?

How can those workers ensure that their own sense of meaning and purpose, and the purpose of the organization, are in alignment?

Focusing on the Next Rules isn't about surfing the fad-waves, nor is it about trying to emulate the latest *strategy du jour* out of Silicon Valley. The Next Rules point the way to a new mindset, skillset, and toolset to solve the problems and create value for stakeholders, today and tomorrow.

These Are the Transformed Rules of Work

We'll explore the various facets of the diamond for the four core Next Rules throughout the book. Let's start by revisiting the Old Rules of Work to see how they are being transformed, today.

Work Becomes a Chain of Activity to Create Value for Stakeholders

I said earlier that work is essentially three things: our human *skills*, applied to *tasks*, to solve *problems*. But there is a fourth element: the *value* that is created for stakeholders by this chain. That value can be a solution, a product, a service, or a result. Here's what that full chain looks like.

The Next Rules Value Chain

Skills > Tasks > Problems > **Value for Stakeholders**

This simple model has several important ramifications for the work of your organization.

STAKEHOLDERS

Every organization has one or more core stakeholders. Whether you work in a for-profit company, a non-profit/non-governmental organization (NGO), or a government agency, the primary stakeholder is usually a customer, a citizen, or a constituent, such as an impacted population. But in addition to that primary stakeholder, there are other core stakeholders such as workers, contractors, partners, suppliers, the communities in which you operate and live, the planet—and, for some, shareholders.

VALUE

Value is created for a stakeholder. For example, the value for the customer often comes from *the result* of the product or service you offer. The value for a rideshare user isn't usually the ride: It's to arrive at point B, after having been at point A. The ride is simply how their problem is solved, unless it's also a great experience, in which case that's an additional value created for that stakeholder.

Your organization may have only a single kind of stakeholder, such as a customer with consistent needs for the value to be created. Or, you may have lots of stakeholders, with varying and changing needs. The value for a partner might be getting consistent business from you, and the value for a community might be having income for some of its citizens.

PROBLEMS

A stakeholder's problem can be well defined, such as hunger or boredom. Or the problem can be poorly defined, such as when a customer simply stops using an app, and a product designer has no data about why.

Problems can also be repetitive, such as needing to sweep the same floor every day. Or they can be unique, one that a worker has never encountered before, like the failure of a car engine's computer chip faced by a mechanic who has only repaired mechanical engines before.

Problems need to be viewed from the perspective of one or more stakeholders, because a problem to one stakeholder may not be a problem to another. Also, some stakeholders such as customers and citizens are external to the organization, and others are internal, like co-workers in other divisions, or your boss.

TASKS

Tasks outline the steps we follow to solve a problem. But continually honing, improving, and even discarding tasks is an important part of the process in defining how best to solve problems.

Some problems require just one or two tasks to solve, like bagging a few groceries. Others are devilishly complicated. A single car can have 30,000 parts, each of which must be produced to exacting specifications. Picture every one of those thousands of parts as a series of tasks to be performed by potentially hundreds of supplier organizations. Now picture a global supply web so that all of those parts eventually coalesce together into one geographical location so that a car can be assembled. That's a lot of tasks.

Tasks are most effectively performed with the right *toolset*, which is often a combination of techniques and technologies. Rather than becoming mired in tasks that are simply bundled into processes, Next Organizations need to focus on flexible techniques and technologies that can be rapidly adapted or exchanged to ensure that stakeholders are continually receiving the intended value.

SKILLS

We've already deconstructed a three-part model of human abilities: know, flex, and self skills. Every human skill can be thought of as having a *level*, from neophyte to mastery. Skills can be grouped into *families*, and multiple families grouped together into a *skillset*. The aggregate total of skills that any single person has, or that are in an organization, I think of as *a portfolio of skills*.

Note that we are talking specifically about *human* skills. You might not think I need to make that distinction. But since technologists increasingly refer to the tasks performed by software and robots as skills, such as Amazon's "Alexa Skills," I need to repeatedly reinforce that the Next Rules are specifically about human-centered work. The robots and software will be just fine. Let's make sure we're designing human-centric systems so people can continue to use their skills.

So now we have the entire value chain for work, in the context of the organization: our human skills, applied to tasks, to solve problems and create value for one or more stakeholders.

> The robots and software will be just fine. Let's make sure we're designing human-centric systems so people can use their skills.

Whether the value to be created is a potentially simple need like solving a customer's support query, or the manufacture of a complex product like a car, think of the entire integrated set of functions for stakeholders—skills, tasks, problems, and value—not just as a linear chain, but as *a value web*, an ecosystem of value creation optimized for a group of stakeholders.

Visualizing the value web of your organization is essential not just so you can better understand the current ecosystem, but so you can anticipate future demand as well. As enterprise analyst, consultant, catalyst, and CxO coach Charlene Li outlines in her book *The Disruption Mindset*,[2] organizations that want to be nimble innovators must have part of their value creation portfolio focused on their *next* customers. To use this approach in envisioning future products and services, simply plug in the future customer as the stakeholder, and use a design process to envision the problems you will solve for them, and the value that will create.

A Job Becomes Just One of Many Use Cases for Work

Remember that in the Old Rules of Work, a job is often a set of tasks. In the Next Rules, a job is *just one kind of work role*. You may have a day job. Or you might work part-time, in an apprenticeship, as a volunteer, on a project basis, as a contractor, as a gig worker, as a worker through a temporary agency, as an unpaid team member of a startup—or all the above, simultaneously. Each of these is a different *use case* for work, a different context for how you might work.

"The End of the Job" has been predicted for decades. *Fortune* magazine published a cover story[3] in 1994 by that title. Authored by William Bridges, a historian turned expert on life transitions, the article's subtitle read, "As a way of organizing work, [the job] is a social artifact that has outlived its usefulness. Its demise confronts everyone with unfamiliar risks—and rich opportunities." A longtime friend of my father's, Bill was a warm and brilliant thinker who was as comfortable helping someone to explore their spiritual development as he was coaching CEOs on life transitions. In his subsequent book *Jobshift: How to prosper in a workplace without jobs*,[4] he wrote:

> We all will have to learn new ways to work… While in some cases, the new ways of working will require new technological skills, in many more cases, they will require something more fundamental: the "skill" of finding and doing work in a world without clear-cut and stable jobs… Today's workers need to forget jobs completely and look instead for work that needs doing, and then set themselves up as the best way to get that work done.

That's as clear a rationale for the Next Rules as I've ever heard.

The Employee and the Employer Become the Worker and the Hirer

The trusted relationship from the Old Rules between the organization and those who worked for it has eroded. With the range of new use cases for work, "employee" and "employer" no longer accurately label the modern context. No matter whether you have a full-time job or a gig project, you are a worker. And no matter whether you need someone to solve problems for you temporarily or for a long time, you are a hirer. I know that "worker" sounds rather industrial, and "hirer" sounds rather transactional. But I think these more accurately describe the true state of play today.

Work Becomes Problem- and Project-Centric

Think of the kinds of problems you most love to solve. Perhaps you enjoy taking apart something that isn't working and putting it back together again. Maybe you like figuring out how to help people navigate complex social issues. Or you could have fun trying to digest large amounts of data or wrestling with complex ideas.

Now think of the kinds of *skills* you most enjoy using. They usually match up to the kinds of problems that you like to solve. That's because, as we discover throughout our lives the kinds of problems we are good at solving, we hone our skills so that we can continually improve our ability to solve those kinds of problems. In the Next Rules, work will increasingly become more problem-centric, and the context for solving problems will become increasingly project-centric, with problem-solving that has a beginning, middle, and end. Those projects will often overlap, creating a potentially never-ending stream of work.

Think of problem-solving as a mindset *and* a skillset, enabled by a constantly changing toolset.

I sometimes get pushback when I tell people that work is fundamentally about solving problems, usually because of cultural issues in different countries. For example, when I hosted a group from Germany's labor and unemployment agencies, they told me, "We don't talk about problems. We focus on solutions." So, if "solution-solvers" is better language for your culture, by all means, do a mental global search-and-replace from "problem-centric" to "solution-centric."

As we will explore in subsequent chapters, anchoring work in problems and projects is a critical mindset, skillset, and toolset for Next Organizations.

With the shift toward more problem- and project-centric work, those who lead in organizations must be far more intentional about the actual amount of work that someone does in a given week. The Silicon Valley and Wall Street narratives of obsessive work and unlimited work hours can lead to a raft of burnout-related challenges. Project-centricity must be counterbalanced with quality-of-life metrics and guardrails around the amount of work that humans are consistently encouraged to do.

A Career Becomes a Portfolio of Work

Remember that in the Old Rules of Work, a career was in three stages: education, work, and retirement. Many workers around the world will continue to follow that three-stage approach.

But a new model is emerging.

Imagine a young person coming out of high school, or college, or trade school. They might get a day job. But they could still be taking courses online. Then they might take a gap month and travel with their friends. Then they might get a day job, but drive for a gig company at night, and on weekends work on a startup company with their friends.

Think of this as *a portfolio of work*, a constantly changing landscape of work, learning, hobbies, fun, and life activities. It's the same mindset that your investment adviser suggests you should think about risk with your financial investments. A good part of your portfolio should be reasonably safe (your day job), some amount can take a little more risk to make more money (driving for a gig company), and a small part can take a lot more risk (the startup).

Parents around the world ask me all the time, "Why won't my adult kid get a real job?" This is why. A portfolio of work is a hedge strategy against a world of exponential change. As the traditional contract between employers and employees erodes, young workers are increasingly expanding their work options to lay the groundwork for an uncertain tomorrow. They don't know what option will bear

FIGURE 2.2   Portfolio of Work

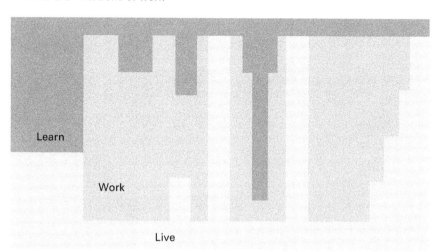

SOURCE © 2021 Charrette LLC. Used by permission.

fruit, so they continually sow new seeds that might lead to future opportunity, and help to mitigate future risk.

> A portfolio of work is a hedge strategy against a world of exponential change.

Smart people have talked about this "atomizing" of traditional work for decades. In 1979, Jay Conrad Levinson was a Madison Avenue executive who helped to create iconic marketing campaigns including the Pillsbury Doughboy, Tony the Tiger, and the Jolly Green Giant. Believing that the project-centered approach of the advertising industry would spread to other industries, he wrote *Earning Money Without a Job,*[5] offering strategies for juggling multiple projects without a formal work role. Jay's focus on projects—a model he'd learned from the ad industry—was an early glimmer of the project-centric model frequently practiced in Silicon Valley and beyond.

For many young people today, the Old Rules categories of learning, work, and life can blur. Workers who are motivated by change and variety, and who have a lot of agency and access, will thrive in this model. But those who are less advantaged are more likely to be challenged, and will therefore need new ways to empower them in their efforts to find or create meaningful, well-paid, steady work.

You Also Have a Portfolio of Lifelong Learning

In a world of uncertainty, where the shelf-life of information is rapidly evaporating, the Old Rules model of front-loaded learning is no longer sufficient. You will need to be a lifelong learner who maintains a portfolio of learning, a range of experiences, from mild interests and hobbies to long-term learning leading to mastery. That learning will follow two parallel and intertwined tracks: developing your know skills, as you continually gather bodies of knowledge, and a separate thread of your flex and self skills.

That portfolio of learning and skills is sometimes called "T-skills." Specialization requires you to be deep on a particular subject or in a profession. But a world of constant change requires you to have a range of skills that can span traditional industries. So, you still need the *depth* of learning a trade or field (the upright bar of a T), but also the *breadth* of flex and self skills (the crossbar of the T). One of the first public references to "T-shaped" skills is from a 1978 issue[6] of *IEEE Engineering Management Review*. In the 1980s, the management consulting company McKinsey began using this approach for training its professionals. Tim Brown, chairman of the iconic design firm IDEO, has long championed the breadth and depth of T-skills, and IBM is most frequently associated with the mindset and skillset of T-skills. For more, read *T-Shaped Professionals*,[7] co-authored by IBM's director of cognitive open technology, Jim Spohrer.

Learning Skills Often Becomes Just-in-Time and Just-in-Context

The Old Rules approach to investment in education years in advance of its use may have made sense in the industrial era. But the decaying shelf-life of information, paired with our increasing understanding of human learning, make it quite clear that we learn best when we can learn *when we need it*, and *when we can apply it*. I call this *just-in-time* and *just-in-context* learning. Just-in-time, because you need it now, to solve the problem in front of you. And just-in-context, because you are learning as you solve a specific problem.

This doesn't mean, of course, that I want my brain surgeon to watch a YouTube video, then walk into the operating theater. A substantial amount of learning is a wine that should not be sold before its time. But not everybody requires Malcolm Gladwell's much-publicized and often-questionable 10,000 hours of training. (See in Chapter 8 how rapidly the Next Organization Catalyte can train a programmer.) A huge amount of human learning can be atomized into smaller chunks and infused into learning situations where it can be immediately applied, so you can continuously develop your portfolio of learning and skills.

Your Portfolio of Learning and Skills Becomes a Set of Intersections

A portfolio of work and learning enables multidimensional problem-solving. Suppose you're the founder of a startup company, and the problem you focus on is that some neuro-diverse people learn more slowly than they would like. Your thesis is that music customized for each learner might help them learn faster. To develop software, you might try to hire a cognitive psychologist, a programmer of machine learning and artificial intelligence software, and a specialist in music theory, in the hope that the three of them might collaborate effectively to actually come up with a viable product.

Or, you might hire one person who has a portfolio of skills at the intersection of those three fields.

In Chapter 6, we'll cover some other examples of intersection skills. But even though it is now 45 years since I was trained to do career counseling, I am still continually astonished at how many people are doing fascinating work at intersections of interests that I could never have imagined.

CASE STUDY

An Overlapping Portfolio of Skills

John Venn was a Victorian-era minister born in Yorkshire, England, in 1834. He came from a line of evangelical ministers and practitioners, so perhaps it was inevitable that he would become a man of the cloth himself. But he had many interests beyond the church.

Venn was a trained mathematician, whose book, *The Logic of Chance*, advanced probability theory as a way to leave behind guesswork and assign numeric risks to possible outcomes. He became president of the college where he worked. He was also an amateur inventor, delighting in designing and building machines that could perform human functions, and he was an avid cricket aficionado. The intersection of those two passions resulted in his invention of a cricket pitching machine that actually beat a local cricket team. (As an American, I have absolutely no idea what that means.)

One recurring problem for mathematicians of the time was the difficulty of envisioning the interactions between sets of numbers. Looking at the data in Set A

FIGURE 2.3   John Venn's Overlapping Portfolio of Skills

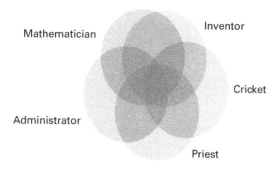

and the data in Set B, there might be some overlap in them. That was easy enough to describe in math. But how could it be visualized?

It turns out that Venn's flex skills from inventing, such as analysis, problem definition, and ideation, were also extremely useful in visualizing math problems. He realized that these overlaps in sets could be illustrated with a simple set of images. Each data set would be represented as a circle, and the overlaps between them would show in alternate shades or colors. Multiple data sets could show the additive properties of multiple overlapping circles.

Today we call these Venn diagrams. I use them throughout the book to boil down complex concepts related to work and learning, so we can better understand the inevitable and fascinating overlaps of domains and ideas.

Have you ever heard of the work roles of neuro-economist, astro-chemist, or astrobotanist? They sound straight out of science fiction. But they all exist, at the intersection of multiple disciplines.

A Team Becomes a Distributed Band of Problem-Solvers

Remember that in the Old Rules, a team was a group often focused on performing complementary tasks. But in the Next Rules, teams must become problem- and project-centric, just as individual workers do.

A team has to be adept at *dynamically binding around those problems*: first, by collaborating to understand the problems they're solving, then collaborating on solutions, agreeing on responsibilities and accountability, knocking problems down individually and collectively, and continually aligning their efforts. They need to understand each other's *superpowers*, so they can break up the work to be done and use their complementary skillsets to achieve the best outcomes.

Since many teams learned during pandemic times that they could actually trust each other, many are remaining distributed. As we'll see from companies like Procter & Gamble, team members are intentionally coordinating their work to determine when each needs to be onsite, and when they can work outside the traditional office. Next Organizations will increasingly hire talented people wherever they are found, and leave them in place.

Your Workforce Becomes Your Worknet

Remember that in the Old Rules, the organization was a box. There was abundance outside The Box (lots of job-hunters) and scarcity inside The Box (few jobs). You managed that scarcity with a corporate hierarchy. And the organization's workforce was a binary set, either employees or not-employees.

Remember also that a traditional job is a use case for work. Yet look at all the other use cases for work. Who else helps to create value for your organization? Part-time workers, distributed workers, temporary workers, contractors, subcontractors, gig workers, apprentices, mentees, consultants, partners, and suppliers. Your customers can help create value *for themselves*, by participating in design thinking sessions, and through crowdsourcing and crowdfunding. Even your former employees can help create value, by continuing to promote the brand of the company, and by helping to channel new talent to the organization.

The old Box model is no longer sufficient to manage this human ecosystem of sophistication and complexity. We need a Next Mindset that allows us to encompass all of these different use cases. As a result, your workforce is now a *worknet*, a network of humans who can help create value for the organization's stakeholders. Your organization suddenly has *soft walls*, functioning as an interconnected part of a

FIGURE 2.4   Your Worknet

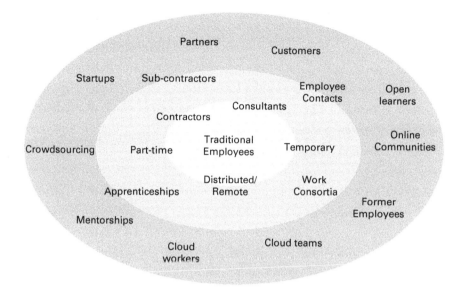

SOURCE © 2021 Charrette LLC. Used by permission.

larger ecosystem of talent and organizations, all of whom comprise a shared value web. By thinking of all these different humans as part of your worknet, you will become far more adept at finding and involving talented workers, and helping them to align their skills to solve problems and create value for stakeholders.

The Manager Becomes the Team Guide

In the Old Rules, the manager was the one in charge, hoping to have all of the answers. In the Next Rules, the manager is the team guide, the one who works hard to offer the best questions.

The inspiration for the label of "guide management" comes from *Moonshots in Education*[8] author Esther Wojcicki's insight that a teacher needs to shift from being "the sage on the stage" to "the guide on the side." The same needs to be true for the "person who used to be known as the manager."

Guide management is the Next Mindset toward empowering the work of others. The team guide isn't a career or life coach, nor a mentor, though they should have some of those skillsets. Instead, the team guide is deeply invested in understanding the capabilities of each team member, helping team members understand and agree on the problems to be solved, and—*only when necessary*—guiding the team individually and collectively to solve those problems. The team guide is a clear and direct communicator, asking questions to help each team member draw insights and solve problems on their own. The team guide is dedicated to helping each team member to work toward realizing their human potential. The guide is committed to each worker's effectiveness and success, which includes serving as an agent of accountability. And in many cases the guide is also an individual contributor, something like the "player-coach," who demonstrates their own skills as a problem-solver for work that supports the goals of the team.

I personally hope the traditional "manager" label will go the way of the dodo. It's not that Peter Drucker's original vision was wrong, seeing the manager as both "composer and conductor" of the activities of the business, and managing as a "creative task." But the traditional approach to the manager role is no longer sufficient for a world of disruptive change.

We will explore the positive mindset of guide management in Chapter 4, the most effective skillset in Chapter 7, and the enabling toolset in Chapter 8. We will also look at the practices of "leaderless" organizations, so we can take away some of their best insights for what can happen when the manager completely disappears.

The Workplace Becomes a Flexible, Co-Working Collaboratory

In the pandemic economy, many organizations learned that their teams and workers were able to function quite well working outside of the office for at least part of the week. Many workers also discovered the joys of avoiding the daily rush-hour commute and foregoing the faceless work environment of the cubicle jungle. As teams become increasingly distributed, the workplace is increasingly being seen as the space where team members come together for intentional collaboration.

Cubicle jungles won't completely disappear, and many workplaces will remain static environments. But for many organizations, the workplace will become more flexible and fluid, continually adapted to meet the constantly changing needs of a constantly changing mix of workers. The decision as to whether a worker will function onsite in a workplace will include the Venn diagram overlap of the worker's overall work role, the kinds of projects they're working on, the phases of each of those projects, their health, the health of their co-workers, the geographical proximity of their co-workers, the usage level of the facility, and what is happening in the worker's personal life at that moment.

If you're a project lead, you're working on a project that requires close collaboration, you're at the front end of the project when collaborative design is needed, you're healthy, your team members are healthy, you're not traveling, you live close enough to the office to come in that day, and the workplace can accommodate you and your team that day—well, then you'll probably go into the office.

But if you're a software user interface designer working on a new website, you're in the execution phase of the project, you're not feeling well, neither is one of your teammates, you live in a rural town several hours from the office, and you see online that the office is at capacity—you're probably *not* going into the office today. That may not have been a regular choice pre-pandemic. And there are certainly many work roles that don't allow that kind of flexibility. But many teams will find themselves doing this kind of day-by-day calculus to determine whether any particular worker needs to be onsite or distributed.

In a mid-2020 report,[9] the commercial real estate services company JLL predicted that 30 percent of *all* office space will be "consumed flexibly" by 2030. That level of dynamic use will require a new mindset by everyone involved, a new skillset (especially for the team guide, and for the organization's operations coordinators), and a new toolset of software that helps to manage all of these "fuzzy sets." From the organization's perspective, its physical assets will become a "portfolio of space" including offices, distributed work hubs, memberships in co-working facilities, partners' facilities, the local coffee shop, and even workers' home spaces.

Change Management Is Dead; All That's Left Is Managing Change

Remember that change management in the Old Rules was a common methodology for envisioning a future static state years in the future, then developing a plan to catalyze the changes needed to create that hoped-for future.

But in a world of constant disruption, change management is dead. All that remains is managing change. Organizational transformation is a journey, not a single reachable goal. Those who lead organizations must continually reward innovative approaches that encourage new mindsets and behaviors. It's a morphing process through a series of "phase changes."

In computer animation or through Photoshop wizardry, *morphing* is the process of seamlessly transitioning through a series of states. The later image in a series may look nothing like earlier images, but the changes were so incremental that there's no point when there was a huge, jolting difference. A significant amount of transformation rarely

FIGURE 2.5   Next Rules: Managing Change

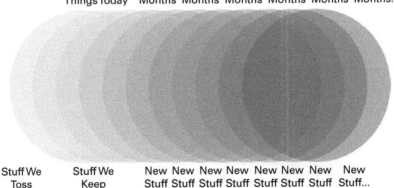

| How We Do Things Today | In 3–6 Months | In 3–6 Months | In 3–6 Months | In 3–6 Months | In 3–6 Months | In 3–6 Months... |

| Stuff We Toss | Stuff We Keep | New Stuff | New Stuff | New Stuff | New Stuff | New Stuff | New Stuff | New Stuff | New Stuff... |

SOURCE © 2021 Charrette LLC. Used by permission.

happens in big leaps: It's usually a series of incremental steps in changing mindsets and skillsets.

The Next Organization Is a Platform for Channeling Human Energy

The Old Rules of the organization focused on maximizing value for shareholders. Sure, many Old Rules leaders cared about customers as well. But if shareholders were happy, leaders got big paychecks. So shareholders came first.

But every organization has a much broader set of stakeholders, including customers, workers, business partners, the communities in which it operates, and the planet. The Old Rules Organization often didn't treat them as *core* stakeholders. The Next Organization must.

I have said that, mechanically, work is our human skills applied to tasks to solve problems and create value for customers and other stakeholders. Spiritually, though, work is *channeling human energy*. When we use our skills, we expend energy. Whether we are simply using our cognitive powers to envision a solution, or we are using physical skills to perform a task, we are channeling our human energy. The Next Organization, then, is *a platform for channeling human energy to create value for its customers and other stakeholders.*

How exactly can you help to make that happen? That's what the Next Rules are for.

Mini-Workbook: An *Aristotle Canvas* for Individuals and One for Organizations

Those are the main takeaways for the effects of the Next Rules on work. Throughout the rest of the book, we'll explore the ramifications of these shifts through the lens of mindset, skillset, and toolset. But first, a brief exercise or two.

The Next Rules aren't simply theoretical. They are only useful if it's clear *why* they are relevant to your work and your organization. That's why I'm going to ask you now to do a few quick exercises to limber up your mental muscles.

Remember that when you sat down with Aristotle after your time machine trip in the first chapter, he asked you a half dozen important questions, the six Ws: Why, What, Who, Where, When, and hoW. I've put them into a *canvas*, a single-page overview that contains the most important elements to consider for a strategy. In the canon of author Dan Kahneman's *Thinking, Fast and Slow*,[10] this is fast thinking.

I've included two versions of the Aristotle Canvas (see Figures 2.6 and 2.7), one for your work as an individual, and one for your organization. These are to help you flex your mental muscles around the meaning for your work and the purpose of the organization.

The Canvas for Individuals (Figure 2.6) covers the six Ws in the context of your current work role, if you are working in one role full- or part-time. If you have a portfolio of work, or you aren't currently working, you can complete it for your most recent work role, or for an ideal work role that you'd like to have.

You can complete the Aristotle Canvas for Organizations (Figure 2.7) no matter what your work role in the organization might be. If you're not currently working with any organization, you can complete that canvas for the most recent place you worked. Or, you could do it for the organization you'd ideally like to work for, or for one that you'd like to start yourself.

Note that the Aristotle Canvas for Organizations is related to *the human work* of the organization, not its industry differentiators or go-to-market strategy. For those, you can refer to any of the many business canvas options you can easily find with an online search. The most popular in Silicon Valley is the Lean Canvas, promoted by Eric Ries, author of *The Lean Startup: How today's entrepreneurs use continuous innovation to create radically successful businesses*.[11] Ries has created the gold standard for effective business decision-making with limited time, money, and information.

These are "fast-thinking" exercises. Just jot down brief thoughts.

I know what can happen as you're reading through a book, and the author suggests doing an exercise. You might want to skip past it and tell yourself you'll come back later. But I want to urge you to take even 15 minutes now and jot down brief answers to each of the questions, at least for yourself. The goal is to get ideas down on paper quickly, which you can always modify later. These insights will be very useful in subsequent chapters. (You can of course take as much time as you want. But don't let "perfect" be the enemy of "done.")

Personal Inventory Exercise: The Aristotle Canvas for You

You are unique. You have a set of skills, interests, motivations, and experiences that is unlike any other person on the planet. And no matter whether you are a sole contributor, or you lead a small team, or you help guide a large organization, each of those with whom you work also are unique. But there are so many potential elements of your work and your life to try to inventory, it can be a little daunting. The Aristotle Canvas for Individuals is intended to help quickly capture a variety of elements of your work, so you can reflect as we delve into each of the Next Rules throughout the rest of the book.

WHY

Meaning: Why do you work? What is the meaning or purpose of your work?

Rewards: How do you want to be compensated for your work? What income, benefits, and vacation time do you need? What kind of chances for advancement? (Include psychic benefits if you like, such as job satisfaction.)

WHAT

Problems: What kinds of problems do you most love to solve? Or, if your core motivation is a *process*, like using creativity, with what kinds of activities do you most enjoy using your creativity?

Skills: What skills (know, flex, and self) do you most love using?

WHO

People: Who are the kinds of people you most enjoy working with? How would you describe them?

FIGURE 2.6 The Aristotle Canvas for Individuals

WHY	MEANING *Why do you work? What gives your work purpose?*	REWARDS *How do you want to be compensated for your work? Income, benefits, advancement, etc.?*	PEOPLE *Who are the kinds of people you most enjoy working with?*	MINDSET *What kind of organizational culture is the best fit for you?*	WHO
WHAT	PROBLEMS *What problems do you most love to solve?*	SKILLSET *What skills do you most love using to solve those problems?*	VALUES *What beliefs drive your work? What values must be reflected in your work?*	TOOLSET *What strategic and technical tools do you most like to use in your work?*	HOW
WHERE	GEOGRAPHY *Where in the world do you want to do your work?*	ENVIRONMENT *What kind of working environment helps you do your best work?*	PORTFOLIO *What is the ideal mix of work for you today? How will you manage that portfolio of work?*	PATH *When would you like to do certain kinds of work in the future? What future scenarios most excite you?*	WHEN

SOURCE © 2021 Charrette LLC. Used by permission. A blank version of this canvas is available at gbolles.com/canvas.

Mindset: What kind of organizational culture is the best fit for you? What values and behaviors do you want those around you to follow?

WHERE

Geography: Where in the world would you love to do your work? (A love for a particular place is known as *topophilia*. For where in the world are you a "topophiliac"?)

Environment: What kind of workplace helps you to do your best work? What percentage of your time would you like to be at a work location, working from home, and any other options?

WHEN

Portfolio: What is the ideal mix of work for you today? Is that a single job, or a variety of projects?

Path: When would you like to do certain kinds of work in the future? What future scenarios for your work most excite you?

HOW

Values: What are the two or three core beliefs that drive your work? What two or three top values *must* be reflected in your work?

Toolset: What two or three techniques and technologies do you most like to use in your work?

The core questions of the canvas are supported by a variety of recent studies of human well-being. For example, research at the University of Wisconsin-Madison identified key aspects of well-being: awareness (using your cognition to deeply sense your lived experience), connection (caring about others in your life), insight (a growth mindset fueled by understanding you), and purpose (understanding your own beliefs, values, and goals). Awareness is your how, connection is who, and purpose is your why.

> **Try This #1: For you, personally.** Print out the Aristotle Canvas for Individuals (Figure 2.6). You'll find a PDF version at gbolles.com/canvas. Write down your answers to the questions above. Don't spend

a lot of time on it, initially. Just jot down bullet points for each, to get your thoughts quickly on paper.

If you already know your own motivations for your work, that's excellent. The canvas will go very quickly. If there are one or two open questions in your mind, this exercise can help fill in those blanks.

Try This #2: Treat the canvas as a team sport. Ask members of your team to fill out the canvas for themselves as well. Then conduct a brainstorming exercise to see where you each have complementary skillsets and aligned values, and where you disagree, to see if you can synthesize your perspectives.

If you want to delve more into any of the canvas elements, such as inventorying your skills or clarifying your values, each of these elements is covered in much more depth in a variety of self-inventory tools, ranging from books to online services to coaching and training. You can find a variety of references at gbolles.com/canvas.

Organizational Inventory Exercise: The Aristotle Canvas for Your Organization

Now let's apply the six Ws to the Next Rules characteristics of your organization.

WHY

Vision is a statement of the purpose of the organization. It usually begins something like, "A world where…" It's the organization's image of the future it wants to help shape. The organization's vision should be so big, it's not likely to be achievable in our lifetimes. The organization's vision doesn't usually change over time. It remains the North Star or Southern Cross of the organization, its navigational direction. (If you can't find your organization's vision statement, that's a future problem to solve. For now, just write what you *think* it should be.)

Mission is the long-term thesis for how the company will work to further its vision, and who will benefit. It should list the key

FIGURE 2.7 The Aristotle Canvas for Organizations

	WHY	WHAT	WHERE
WHO	**VISION** What is your organization's purpose? What is the world it wants to help create?	**MISSION** Who are the organization's stakeholders? What value will the organization create for them?	**PEOPLE** What kinds of people does your organization need to create value for its stakeholders?	**MINDSET** What kinds of behaviors by those people are rewarded in your organization?
HOW	**PROBLEMS** What are the key challenges your stakeholders have?	**SKILLSET** What core skills does your organization need to solve problems and create value?	**VALUES** What core values define the way the organization conducts its activities?	**TOOLSET** What key technologies and techniques does the organization use to enable it to create value?
WHEN	**GEOGRAPHY** Where in the world does the organization do its work?	**ENVIRONMENT** What kind of working environment helps the organization's workers to do their best work?	**STRATEGY** What scenarios will allow the organization's workers to continually deliver value to its stakeholders?	**ALIGNMENT** How does the organization continually align everyone with the organization's goals?

SOURCE © 2021 Charrette LLC. Used by permission. A blank version of this canvas is available at gbolles.com/canvas.

stakeholders of the organization—customers, workers, partner suppliers, the communities in which the organization operates, the planet, and shareholders—in order of their priority to the organization. (The mission may be achievable in your lifetime. But if you *did* accomplish it, by that point you'd have a new mission.)

WHAT

Problems: What *specific* problems does your organization solve for its stakeholders listed in the mission, and what value does it create for them?

Skillset: What is your organization good at? What core skills does the organization use to create value and conduct its activities?

WHO

People: What kinds of people does your organization need to create value for its stakeholders? (Remember that these people are themselves stakeholders of your organization.) Include whatever consistent characteristics stand out to you.

Mindset: What are the two or three ways of thinking and acting by those people that are most rewarded in your organization?

WHERE

Geography: Where in the world does the organization do its work? In what communities does it operate, and what communities benefit from its offerings?

Environment: What kind of workplace(s) does the organization provide to help its workers do their best work?

WHEN

Strategy defines the top two or three steps the workers of the organization take to solve problems and deliver value for stakeholders. The strategy can and should change as the organization continually understands the needs of its current and future customers.

Alignment: How does the organization continually align everyone with the organization's goals, and with the goals of teams and individuals? What practices ensure everyone knows how they contribute to solving stakeholder problems and creating value? (If you don't know what those practices are, leave it blank. Future work to be done.)

HOW

Values: What core values define the way the organization conducts its activities? What are the key anchors of the culture of the organization?

Toolset: What key techniques and technologies does the organization use to enable it to create value?

Depending on your role in the organization, you may not know the sanctioned answers for all the questions. That's fine. Just "assert" what you think the answers should be, and you can later get others to "respond." (I'll explain this at the end of the next chapter.)

> **Try This #1: Your perspective on the organization.** Print out the Organization Canvas at gbolles.com/canvas. I urge you to take a few minutes to do that now. Jot down brief answers from your perspective.

> **Try This #2: Make it a team sport.** Ask others in your team, or throughout the organization, to do the canvas. Compare notes. What do the differences between each of your perceptions mean, and what should you collectively do about those differences?

Whether you choose to do the canvas alone, or with others, answer the questions in one very important context: what you believe to be the authentic truth. That is, *what do you believe is actually true* for each of these characteristics? Don't think about the "corporate values" on the cafeteria wall, or the marketing speak on the organization's website. What is authentically true about your organization, today, from your lived experience?

Each of the dozen canvas characteristics has a deep legacy of literature and thinking behind it. That gives you many resources to help you dive in deeper on any of these issues that you think are critical for your organization. If *why* draws your attention, then Simon Sinek's *Start with Why*[12] is a great place to, well, start. Sinek offers simple but actionable advice for steps to follow in getting consensus on the rationale for actions the organization takes. And if *how* interests you, I highly recommend *How: Why how we do anything means everything*, by Dov Seidman,[13] the founder of The HOW Institute for Society. I've learned a lot from Dov about the need for a deep connection between our actions and our authentic selves.

You'll find links to more suggestions for organizational deep dives at gbolles.com/canvas.

You can also upload one or both of your canvases to my website if you'd like to offer them as examples to others.

Once you have done your own canvas, and one for your organization, place them side by side. Where are they aligned? Where are they not aligned? What do you think about those connections? Is there someone you'd like to talk to about those connections? And is there action you need to take, either personally or inside your organization, to increase their alignment?

Looking through the Lens of Mindset, Skillset, and Toolset

The next three parts of the book cover mindset, skillset, and toolset, with two chapters on each.

Now that you are armed with the Aristotle Canvas for Organizations, you can explore the enterprise mindset in Chapter 3, skillset in Chapter 5, and toolset in Chapter 7. And with your canvas for you as an individual, you can dive into the mindset for individuals and teams in Chapter 4, skillset in Chapter 6, and toolset in Chapter 8.

Before we do that, though... What exactly are the differences between mindset, skillset, and toolset?

Picture this.

I wave a magic wand, and suddenly you and I are standing at the bottom of a tall mountain. Looking up, you realize that you have magically been given all the skillset of a mountain climber. You have climbed mountains dozens of times before. You can picture all of the techniques you would need to climb the mountain above you. You can even picture the route you would follow, and in your mind you can solve every potential problem you would likely encounter.

But when you see the top of the mountain, you say: That looks too cold. That looks impossibly high.

You have all the *skillset*, yet none of the *mindset*. Will you climb the mountain? No, you won't climb the mountain.

Now, I wave a magic wand again, and suddenly, you have none of the skillset for climbing a mountain, but all of the mindset. You have never climbed a mountain before. But you look up at the top of the mountain, and you think, "How hard could that be?" You take one step. Two steps. You encounter problems. You solve them. Eventually, you are standing at the top of the mountain, looking down. And you say: "How hard was that?" And then, you look up toward the next mountain.

You started with all of the mindset, and none of the skillset. You developed the skillset as you climbed, just in time and just in context.

(One of my favorite related quotes is from Caterina Fake, the co-founder of the Internet's first large successful image site, Flickr, who today hosts the *Should This Exist?* podcast. "Sometimes you

FIGURE 2.8   Mindset, Skillset, Toolset

climb the mountain, and you fall and fail," Caterina has famously said. "Maybe there is a different path that will take you up. Sometimes a different mountain.")

Of course, there is a third leg of the stool, and that's your toolset. If you're wearing sandals and shorts, and staring up at a forbidding wall of ice as freezing winds whip around you, a toolset that includes spiked boots, insulated clothes, an ice pick, pitons, and rope would probably all come in pretty handy.

And since mindset alone can't solve every problem, the experience from learning the skillset of climbing an ice wall would also be quite useful.

CASE STUDY

A Real-World Example of Mindset, Skillset, and Toolset

Matthew Corcoran Anders was a 16-year-old living in the San Francisco Bay Area who had just completed his junior year of high school. He thought he would spend the summer working like his friends at Jamba Juice, especially liking the idea of free smoothies. But his father had other ideas, encouraging him to work at a relative's pest control business across the Bay. Matthew was placed on the customer service phone line, working beside people two to three times his age, answering calls from angry customers whose bug-ridden homes hadn't yet been sprayed.

A problem with an office computer prompted the office manager to call an IT consultant. Matthew observed the consultant doing some perfunctory tests, then declaring the PC fixed. Seeing how easy the work seemed to be, Matthew instantly declared himself "the IT guy" for the office and began solving computer problems.

The first big problem was that the office had purchased a VOIP system that hadn't been fully installed. Not even knowing what VOIP was, the teenager went home and began researching online. He discovered that VOIP is voice over IP, which means phone systems that run on the Internet. By scanning helpline forums and reading user manuals, he was able to learn how to migrate the office's computers to the latest version of Windows and get the VOIP system up and running.

After having made himself rapidly indispensable to the office throughout the summer, before he headed back to finish high school, he wrote a guidebook so the office workers could manage the systems after he was gone.

Mindset, skillset, toolset.

Matthew had little of the *skillset* when he started the job, but he had the *mindset*, and he created the *toolset* as he went along. He could have continued doing the stressful work answering phones. But he saw a problem he thought he could solve. And he knew he could learn *just in time* and *just in context*.

Just in time means that he only had to gather the information he needed to solve the problem, and no more. He didn't tell the office manager, "Listen, I'll go get an IT degree, and I'll be back in four years to install the VOIP system." He focused on learning the specific *know* skills he needed for the tasks in front of him.

Just in context means that the teenager was able to learn *as he was solving problems*. He didn't learn about the history of security software, or about the hundreds of different kinds of security programs. He focused on that specific application, and just for the specific needs of his hirer. And he did it in a practical working environment.

When I tell this kind of story to educators around the world, I get one of two responses. Educators with more of a traditional mindset display what we call in the US a "deer in the headlights" response, envisioning an onrushing tsunami of learner-driven education, and feeling completely unprepared. But educators with a Next Mindset are tremendously excited, seeing new possibilities for making learning relevant to anyone.

Think of mindset, skillset, and toolset as three facets of the diamond of your work, in a variety of contexts. Take, for example, "networking." Thinking of yourself as a "networker" is a mindset. Networking with a range of people around the world is a skillset. And using an online network like LinkedIn is one toolset to do that.

Often, though, there is no bright line between mindset, skillset, and toolset. Mindset can be reinforced by skillset, and vice versa, depending on the problems you're trying to solve. You may think of a strategic practice like a problem-solving methodology as part of your toolset (a technique), or as part of your skillset (a *know* skill if it's problem-solving for, say, software testing, or a *flex* skill if it's usable in many situations).

Effectiveness, Growth, Involvement, Alignment

As we dive into perspectives and practices, it's important to remember that there is no perfect approach to adopting the Next Rules. Your goal will be to **empower effectiveness, enable growth, ensure involvement,** and **encourage alignment.** But you and your organization will have your own priorities for which of these is most critical for your immediate focus.

Developing mindset, skillset, and toolset to implement the Next Rules is a journey, not a single achievable destination. You will need to try, adapt, and iterate. Something that works for another organization may not work for you and yours.

One final note on mindset. Remember that the goal in learning the Next Rules is *always* to create the conditions for more human-centric work. The robots and software will be just fine. Our mantra needs to continually be: no human left behind.

Now: What is mindset in the context of the overall organization? That's our focus in the next chapter.

PART TWO

Mindset

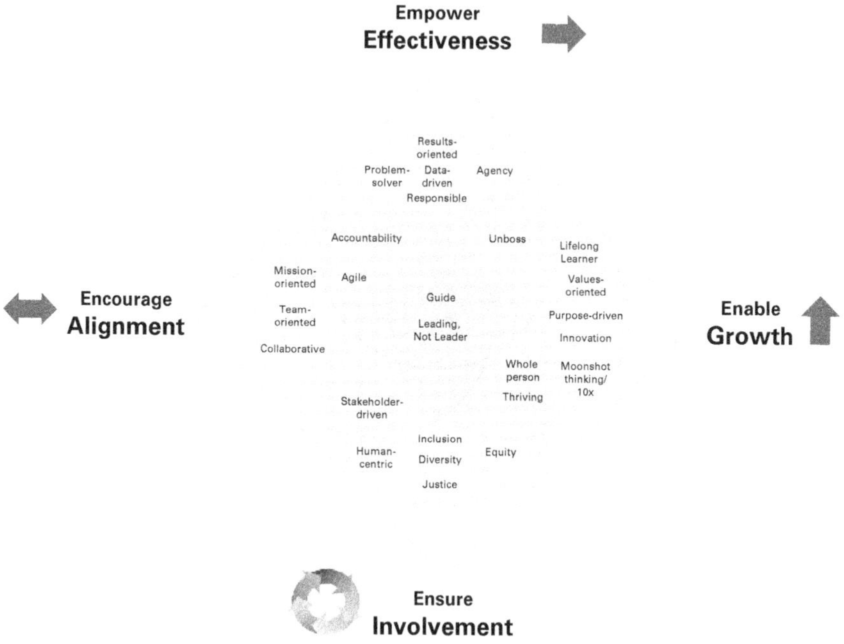

Empower
Effectiveness →

Results-
oriented
Problem-   Data-   Agency
solver   driven
Responsible

Accountability   Unboss   Lifelong
                                                    Learner
Mission-   Agile   Values-
oriented   oriented

Encourage   Guide
Alignment   Team-   **Enable**
              oriented   Leading,   **Growth** ↑
Collaborative   Not Leader
                                    Whole   Moonshot
                                    person   thinking/
                         Stakeholder-   10x
                         driven   Thriving

                         Inclusion
              Human-   Diversity   Equity
              centric
                         Justice

Ensure
Involvement

FIGURE P2   The Next Rules: Mindset

03

Your Organization's Culture
Is Its Mindset

Next Organizations commit to developing an aligned mindset. But many of those who lead don't know what consistent mindset the organization actually has. That's the first problem to solve.

The next most common question by those who lead organizations is: How can I *change* my organization's culture? Those who lead need to guide an inclusive co-creation process to determine which of the possible Next Rules mindsets is most appropriate for the organization.

Though organizational change initiatives have a dismal failure rate, those that are successful point to a set of consistent factors for an effective transition. The mindset of those who lead, though, must be that transformation is an ongoing journey, with no final destination.

Sitting in front of you is a pair of augmented reality goggles. This disruptive technology will give you a completely new perspective on your work and your organization.

Put them on.

You look around, and suddenly you see your organization in completely new ways.

You realize that you used to act as if your organization was a box. Because there was an abundance of talent outside the box, and a limited amount of work opportunity inside the box, you felt that you had to manage a limited pool of talent. But now you see that there is no box. Your organization is really a *network* of talent. And what you once thought of as a workforce is really a *worknet*. And rather than having only a limited amount of talent available to you, like the tip of an iceberg, now you see the entire iceberg, and the *nearly unlimited amount of human potential* in your organization.

You also realize that you used to see workers with a binary perspective. People were either employees, or they were not employees. But now you see that each person involved with your organization, ranging from traditional employees to cloud-based gig workers, is part of your worknet, the fabric of human abilities that collectively help your organization to solve problems and create value for stakeholders.

If your company is public, or a venture-backed startup, you thought the *purpose* of your organization was primarily to generate value for shareholders. Now you realize that your organization is *an engine for channeling human energy to solve problems and create value for the organization's stakeholders*. If you thought the core strategy of your firm was simply to make a happy customer, now you see that your organization needs a *stakeholder mindset*, with the customer at the center of an expanded set of stakeholders.

Finally, you realize there are four core mindsets that are like building blocks for your organization: empowering effectiveness, enabling growth, ensuring involvement, and encouraging alignment.

These goggles have helped you to see with new eyes the Next Mindset. See how easy that was?

What's a Mindset?

Of course it's not that easy.

The most frequent question I hear from those who lead organizations is, how can I change my organization's culture? My typical response is another question: How hard and how collaboratively are you willing to work?

Encouraging mindset change can be extremely difficult, because an authentic mindset shift requires a dramatic shift in behavior. Few of us wake up in the morning and say, "I'm going to think and act really differently today," and actually do it, authentically and sustainably. A mindset shift often means as much unlearning as it means learning. And changing your mindset means you will need to give yourself permission to take new risks, which can often be more challenging than we think.

As we'll see in later chapters, you'll also need to continually develop a Next Skillset to solve new problems. And you'll have to choose your Next Toolset to provide you with the techniques and technologies you'll need to be successful.

Finally, even if you have fully adopted a Next Mindset for yourself, you still need to help others in your team and your organization to see the future you see, and to change their own mindsets.

Think of mindset as the *cognitive framework you use to approach the world around you.* In her influential book *Mindset: The new psychology of success,*[1] author Carol Dweck talks about two basic mentalities toward change:

- A *fixed* mindset means you see yourself as a static creature. You liked yesterday, today was pretty good, and tomorrow will be just great if it's like yesterday and today. You don't think of yourself as being deeply curious about much, and you certainly aren't interested in this "lifelong learning" thing. After all, you can't teach an old dog new tricks, right? We all are pretty much born who we are, and nothing really changes us throughout our lives.

- But if you have a *growth* mindset, you see yourself as a constantly changing person. You're curious about a range of topics. You're doing something completely different for work now than you did years ago, and you think it's pretty likely you'll be doing something different in a few years. Even if you've been at the same organization for a long time, your role has continued to change. To keep yourself learning and growing, you are unfailingly curious. You read, or watch online courses, or talk regularly with people who think differently than you, or attend local classes, or all the above.

A fixed mindset is obviously anchored in the Old Rules of Work. After learning a trade or getting a degree, you worked in the same field for years or decades. But as you've already intuited, the Next Rules of Work encourage you to have a growth mindset, because you will need to continually adapt.

If you have a fixed mindset, and still follow the Old Rules of Work, you're doing nothing wrong. But the world may have changed dramatically around you. You might have worked in a factory, or a mine, or in a retail job. Then that business closed, and perhaps you were unable to find work in that profession. It's not your fault. But a fixed mindset is part of what keeps you from being able to readily adapt.

Why does mindset matter so much?

The research company Gallup conducts an annual survey of worker engagement in the US, asking people how connected they feel to their work—a pretty fundamental mindset question. In 2020, Gallup found[2] that *only about a third said they were engaged in their work*. The other nearly two-thirds of workers were not connected to their organization or their work. And those workers said they would leave for a deal only a little better than what they have now.

That's a stunning statistic. Everyone who leads in an organization should be deeply concerned. If on average far less than half of your workers have an engaged mindset, how much of themselves are they bringing to bear on solving problems and creating value for the organization's stakeholders—including themselves?

What Mindset Does Your Organization Actually Have?

There is an enduring myth that large organizations have a consistent mindset.

Think of mindset as *the aggregate beliefs, values, and behaviors of the organization*, sometimes called the organization's culture. Your organization probably already has a list of values that those who lead talk about frequently. That list is likely included in the new-hire packet provided by the HR department and posted on the walls of company micro-kitchens.

But many who lead in organizations don't really know what behaviors are consistently exhibited outside their view, nor do they understand just how widely varying those behaviors can be. And they can easily misinterpret the behavior they do see, because their presence is a behavioral distortion field, encouraging workers to warp their actions to conform to some expected norm.

Try This #1: A flash survey of your organization's mindset. Here is an exercise you can conduct in the hallway, or on a series of video calls. In separate conversations with any random half-dozen workers who don't know you well, ask them to answer the question: What are the three things someone needs to do in this organization to be successful?

If the consistent answers are, (1) Make customers and other stakeholders happy, (2) Follow agile practices, and (3) Treat everyone as a collaborator, then congratulations are in order. (If indeed those are some of the mindset characteristics you've prioritized.)

But if the consistent answers are, (1) Keep your head down, (2) Do what your boss tells you without question, and (3) Don't challenge the status quo, then you have a pretty good idea about one of the strong mindset threads that runs through your organization.

Those who lead are often behavioral distortion fields, encouraging workers to warp their actions to conform to some expected norm.

Try This #2: A comprehensive survey of your organization's mindset. If you're truly committed to a substantial shift in the organization's mindset, you'll need a comprehensive understanding of its current mental and behavioral state. That means a broad survey of what workers throughout the organization believe, the values they hold dear, and the values to which they believe the organization is committed.

There are numerous software tools or services you can use. Just make sure to guarantee worker anonymity, or else you will erode worker trust. And if you are someone who leads in the organization, for bonus points, ask what values that workers believe are held by those who lead. You may maintain that you personally embody those widely cited values. But you may find that others don't actually see those behaviors exhibited authentically and consistently. You should be willing to take the risk of finding out.

What's likely, either from your anecdotal survey, or from an organization-wide scan, is that you will hear inconsistent answers. If the organization has multiple geographical locations in multiple countries, hires from a variety of cultures, organizations, and colleges, or is a "rollup" merger of several other organizations, then a consistent mindset is usually an illusion promoted by those who have a vested interest in an inauthentic narrative of organization-wide harmony. You are far more likely to find out that different divisions, departments, and teams will have a range of beliefs and behaviors. And you might not like all that you find.

Where you do find a consistent mindset, you may find that much of it is anchored in the Old Rules of Work, and therefore has deep-seated challenges. A performance mindset is obsessed with putting "high performers" on a pedestal *but* can send demotivating messages to others that they are "low performers," when in fact it may be the organization's failure to help them achieve their potential. A quality mindset is focused on repeatable processes and continuous improvement *but* may dampen innovation and risk-taking. A resilience mindset may continually anticipate threat-based competitive and environmental challenges *but* reinforce a process of protecting existing assets and market share rather than creating new value. And a shareholder mindset may ensure the organization's stock price remains elevated *but* force the organization into the short-termism straitjacket of quarterly earnings reports and constrict innovation to the margins.

Perhaps one or more of these is the Old Rules mindset you actually want. That's great. There are plenty of books and processes to help you hone them.

But I'm guessing you see a range of potential mindset challenges appearing in the key metrics of your organization. Perhaps the rate of organizational innovation is slowing dramatically, with fewer new product ideas. Maybe customer satisfaction ratings are dropping. It could be that worker engagement ratings are in the basement, and complaints on Glassdoor.com are rising. You can't retain existing talent, or attract new talent, the way you used to. People who used to frequently take quick action have started cc'ing an endless list of people on email threads so they can deflect responsibility, and their out-of-office email notifications are perpetually on.

Or perhaps the problem is existential. A nimble competitor is starting to eat away at your core market. Your most profitable division took a nosedive. You see nothing in the product pipeline that will let you satisfy the needs of your "future customer", as Charlene Li calls them in *The Disruption Mindset*.[3] Or, a pandemic forced you to shut down a major part of your organization.

Or perhaps you are simply worried that any of these things *could* happen. Whatever the impetus, you realize you need to catalyze a new mindset.

What Mindset Do You Need?

Suppose you could have a consistent mindset practiced by everyone in your organization, in the blink of an eye. What are the top mindset characteristics you want?

There are numerous "cultural characteristics" you could choose for the key aspects of the organization's mindset. You'll find a seemingly endless list of books and consulting models defining the most important four, six, ten or more kinds of corporate culture. The most important thing to know about these models isn't so much what the possible cultures are. It's the opportunity to create a common language in the organization about what the core mindset characteristics need to be.

I'm not going to tell you what kind of mindset your organization needs. Defining that needs to be a co-created process with your stakeholders, anchored in the organization's vision, mission, and strategy. But the four core Next Rules provide us with useful categories for grouping together some of the most popular options.

Here is a list of some of the most frequently cited mindset aspects, in the context of the four core Next Rules.

Effectiveness Mindset

Organizations that embrace an effectiveness mindset are often focused on results. They want workers to be accountable for their commitments. They encourage workers to be adaptive and agile. They encourage accountability through tools like objectives and key results (OKRs), which we will explore in subsequent chapters. They want people to take responsibility for solving problems, to be results-oriented, and to adapt quickly. They are unfailingly data-driven, encouraging people to make decisions based on objective information, but not so reliant on data that they miss critical human factors. They prize speed of decision-making and action. They encourage agency, the mindset of the team guide, and "unbossing."

The Russian online marketplace company Avito is a good example of an organization with an effectiveness mindset, which you will read about later.

Growth Mindset

Organizations intent on a growth mindset reward those who are constantly growing and learning. They want the organization to be dedicated to maximizing human potential. Every worker needs to commit to developing a growth mindset, with their own personal learning path, so the organization itself will be a learning organization. They are frequently purpose-driven, helping people to understand and support the values of the organization, because it matches their own individual mindset toward purpose. Growth-oriented organizations work to embrace the whole person, committing not just to wellness, but to mindfulness and other practices intended to encourage thriving. These organizations often prize innovation, encouraging people to generate dramatically new ideas and to take new risks. They often encourage "moonshot thinking" and a "10× mindset," so workers will co-create products and services that are 10 or 100 times faster/better/cheaper than existing alternatives.

I asked Adam Grant, best-selling author of books like *Think Again*[4] and host of the popular podcast *WorkLife*, to describe the single most important mindset to encourage throughout the organization. He responded without hesitation: "Build a learning organization. Replace 'that's not how we've always done it' and 'that will never work here' with 'I wonder what would happen if…'"

Lisa Kay Solomon, author of *Design a Better Business*,[5] calls the end-to-end growth mentality "full-stack learning," infusing learning processes into virtually every aspect of work in the organization.

Novartis, the pharmaceutical giant, is a good example of a company that has a commitment to a growth mindset. We'll hear from their global head of talent, Markus Graf, in Chapter 4.

Involvement Mindset

Organizations with an involvement mindset are human-centric. They want everyone in the organization to treat co-workers with empathy, decency, and integrity, in the most diverse and inclusive ways possible. They infuse diversity into all of their core people processes, from how they envision work roles, to how they hire, connect people to work opportunities, develop, and promote people. They commit to equity in power dynamics, from the ways that people are compensated, to whose perspectives are sought on key issues "in the room where it happens." And they remain aware and intentional about inclusion, from decisions about who is involved in meetings, to how the voices of stakeholders are continually included in products and services. Many benefit corporations, and nonprofits, non-governmental organizations (NGOs), and foundations think of themselves as involvement-first organizations.

The software and website testing company Ultranauts is an organization that was designed from its founding with an involvement mindset. You'll learn from them in Chapter 7 how this can be done by a for-profit company, by making its authentic involvement philosophy *the reason it is highly competitive and makes money.*

Alignment Mindset

Organizations focused on alignment as the key mindset are authentically committed to strategies that deliver on the company's mission and vision. They also use mechanisms like OKRs to ensure that projects and worker output are connected to the strategy, but they have processes that ensure their often-distributed teams remain connected and aligned throughout every project phase. They are often customer-obsessed, encouraging workers to wake up thinking about new ways to make stakeholders happy. They can be relentlessly collaborative. Companies with an alignment mindset are often the best at managing their distributed worknets because they have a commitment to maintaining continuous connections between workers, teams, and the organization's purpose.

I think of Asana, the workgroup collaboration software developer, as the "alignment engine" company. Their chief operating officer, Chris Farinacci, offers a variety of insights later on about continuous bottom-up and scaled alignment.

The four core Next Rules are not mutually exclusive. You can and should encourage all of these mindsets. But one of the critical steps in implementing mindset shift (see the Spiral Up Approach in Figure 3.1) is prioritizing. You can't be all things to all people. If your organization's purpose, its vision and mission, are authentic and consistent, you'll know what your mindset priorities need to be.

When You Need a Mindset Shift in Your Organization: The Great Reset

Until early 2020, the global narrative for discontinuous change came from the constant drumbeat of headlines about disruptive technologies transforming industries, evaporating jobs, and dramatically changing the work that technology hadn't already destroyed.

Then along came a virus.

Many organizations with an Old Rules mindset were suddenly at a tremendous disadvantage. They had not invested in digital transformation, so they had to scramble to acquire the technologies they needed to keep their workforce communicating. Their rigid hierarchies kept them from easily redistributing work. Their box-centric hiring processes made it challenging for them to find new skillsets. Their investment in massive corporate headquarters in urban areas left them with hugely under-used assets.

If I had told you in January 2020 that you needed to prepare your organization with a new mindset to deal with the pace and scale of change, you might have agreed, but felt little urgency to catalyze a dramatic shift in your organization. This is an entirely human response. It often doesn't matter how much arm-waving might be done by strategists pointing to the risks of impending disruption. We know that economic downturns, the appearance of disruptive tech-nologies, the emergence of disruptive competitors, freakish weather, and war and terrorist events can each have a dramatic impact on individuals, organizations, industries, communities, and economies. But when these seismic events continue to wash over us like rogue waves pummeling a beach, we have less opportunity to recover and prepare for the next.

The mathematician and author Nassim Nicholas Taleb calls these "black swans,"[6] seemingly unpredictable events that hit the reset button for industries, organizations, and human lives. What has become clear in recent decades is that while the exact source and timing of black swan events is often hard to predict, the likelihood that some disruptive event will occur becomes increasingly more predictable.

As the global response to the modern pandemic began shutting down industries and human work around the planet in early 2020, I looked back at prior whacks to the side of the head for our econo-mies and societies, such as the Great Recession. I realized that each seemed to follow three phases: an initial "falling off the cliff" phase with 100 percent uncertainty; a "riffling along the bottom" phase that looked like a fever chart of on-again/off-again economic activity; and an eventual "recovery" phase.

In late March I wrote the article "Welcome to The Great Reset,"[7] posted on the Techonomy.com website in early April, pointing to the seismic impact on work, organizations, and communities, and suggesting strategies for "flattening the slump" of job and business loss. A few months later, the World Economic Forum chose "The Great Reset" as its theme for the year, and WEF founder Klaus Schwab co-wrote a book[8] by the same name (happy coincidence, I'm sure).

Those who lead their organizations need to treat the pandemic as a wakeup call. Today it's a virus. Tomorrow, it's a technology and a business model from a competitor that disrupts your entire business, the Uber or Amazon or Google of your industry. Or it's a breakthrough technology like artificial general intelligence or quantum computing or nuclear fusion that will upend entire economies. Or it's the next pandemic.

You don't need any new impetus to catalyze dramatic change in your organization. The combination of a global health crisis and the recurring blows to industries and economies around the world should give you plenty of examples to serve as a wakeup call for your organization to co-create its Next Mindset, Skillset, and Toolset.

How Do You Catalyze Mindset Change?

One of the most common questions I hear is: Can you actually sponsor large-scale mindset change in an organization? Is it actually possible to change an organization's culture so that the new values and behaviors are practiced by everyone?

The answer is: yes, but.

In the past, an Old Rules Organization would hire a consulting company to articulate a set of "corporate values," defined in a workshop by a small number of "top" executives in an offsite retreat. The consultant would conduct more workshops with "management" to promote the new values. That list would be posted on the cafeteria wall and dutifully cited by hiring managers and HR advisors.

But those who lead the organization would have little incentive to change their behavior. After all, the old behaviors helped them to get to the level of success the organization has today. Why should they change? Change is hard. Change can hurt. Besides, nothing changed in terms of their own compensation or new opportunities. What incentive do the "leaders" have to change? And if those who lead don't change, why should anyone else? Just keep your head down, give lip service to the list of values, and a new CEO will eventually come in, and start the next culture-change kabuki.

There also are many barriers to individual behavior change. People who believe themselves to be adequately effective at their current work are often not immediately open to change. When the opportunity for a mindset shift is introduced, there is an explicit or implicit message that the old way of doing things is no longer valid, which must of course mean that those who are best at it are now suddenly wrong.

"You're introducing a pathogen into the corporate environment," says Samantha Liscio, chief technology and innovation officer for Canada's Workplace Safety and Insurance Board, and the country's CIO of the Year for the public sector in 2020. "All the antibodies want to get rid of that."

So what kinds of strategies are actually effective at changing an organization's mindset? There are three schools of thought and practice: edge strategy, incremental strategy, and core strategy:

- **Edge strategy:** John Hagel, former co-chairman of Deloitte & Touche's Center for the Edge, and now founder of Beyond Our Edge LLC, has extensive research and experience that shows how challenging it is to catalyze cultural change at the core of the organization. John knows that few of those who lead organizations may actually sign up for changing their own behavior, which makes it nearly impossible to get others in the organization to sign up for transformation. John's recommendation is to follow an "edge strategy." Start a new initiative or division composed of people who are selected, or who self-select, because they are already aligned with the new mindset. Especially if there is any question about the dedication of those who lead the organization to the initiative, an edge strategy may be necessary, focusing on transforming one part of the organization that's far outside the core area of focus. Scale those edge initiatives rapidly, and they have the potential to swallow the rest of the organization.

- **Incremental core strategy:** Another approach to mindset change is to pick one or more influential groups in the core of the organization and focus on behavior change for that specific group. Using digital tools, the desired mindset and behaviors are made explicit to workers and teams, incentives put in place, and tracking mechanisms used to help people see their progress. Again, this kind of approach may be most appropriate if those who lead the organization aren't committed to their own behavior change. Or it may be that there is a tactical problem to solve with a specific group, division, or subsidiary.

- **Large-scale core strategy:** If you believe those who lead the organization can make the appropriate commitment, widespread transformation may be possible. Microsoft CEO Satya Nadella was able to take the company's famously competitive culture and catalyze a transformative initiative to promote a growth mindset. Since Nadella himself already had a growth mindset, he was able to authentically and consistently embody that approach.

Of course, most people want to go big or go home, so they want to try large-scale mindset change. Unfortunately, the vast majority of the time those core initiatives fail.

In 2019 i4cp, the Institute for Corporate Performance, conducted a study[9] of over 7,000 global professionals, about two-thirds of whom had been involved in some kind of cultural transformation initiative. The results were predictably dismal, with respondents reporting an 85 percent failure rate.

Imagine catalyzing an initiative you knew would fail 17 out of 20 times. Perhaps you've even done that already and seen just how challenging it can be.

Cultures solidify and calcify over time. There are very human reasons for this, many the result of the mental marriage of "the innovator's dilemma" and a fixed mindset. An organization that has been successful encourages behaviors that are assumed to have contributed to that success, whether or not that correlation is true. And behavior change for many requires an exceptional amount of work and dedication.

There is hope. By following the practices of the 15 percent of organizations who say their efforts *were* successful, i4cp says that transformation is possible. But the organization suggests a different mindset about that process. Rather than "transformation," it's "renovation."

To me, that sounds a little like a house-building reality TV show. I prefer "journey," because I don't know of any culture change that isn't a continuous work in progress. But you may feel that "renovation" is an appropriate metaphor for your organization (especially if it includes re-architecting the workplace).

Whether it's transformation, renovation, or a journey, the goal in any mindset shift isn't "conformity," which is an emotion-coded label that implies penalties for those who aren't seen as falling in line. It's not mind control, or a mandate for groupthink. Catalyzing successful mindset transformation is a co-created process that helps people throughout the organization to see the challenges created by the old ways of doing things, agree on the goals for what transformation entails, and sign up willingly not just to become part of the process, but to help drive it.

Who Should Catalyze Mindset Change?

One of the greatest barriers to catalyzing change is the potential lack of commitment by the team leading the organization. Few are often willing to commit to the time and behavioral consistency needed to spark a large-scale and sustainable mindset shift. If you are an influential executive in the organization, and you want to catalyze a new mindset, your own mindset and behavior must change first. And you must involve a variety of others in the organization, with special care given to choosing those who will help to lead the charge.

Who should lead? I've asked that question to "chief everything"—chief executive officers, chief human resources officers, chief operating officers, chief innovation officers, and chief information officers. Who is in the best position to catalyze a mindset shift in the organization?

I've received three consistent answers.

First, there is absolutely no question that the sponsor of the initiative must be the CEO or other leading executive for the organization, division, or department. That person must be personally committed to participating in the program and exhibiting the mindset and behaviors to which they and other leading executives have committed. That executive also needs to put the organization's skin in the game, committing to what may be a substantial financial cost for training and revamped work roles, as well as giving air cover to the board of directors, investors, and any others with the power to challenge the investment of time and money.

Second, all those who work directly with that leading executive must also be committed to the program and demonstrate the behavior change themselves. By holding each other *and the leading executive* accountable for that change, they will send the strongest signals possible to the rest of the organization.

Finally, if their role is outside that team of leading executives, the person charged with leading the initiative must have unfettered access to the main executive team, and the ability to leverage that team's collective involvement to reinforce participation and commitment.

That person's role in the organization can vary widely. Sometimes it is the Chief Human Resources Officer (CHRO) or other leading HR executive who can influence policy and practice. Sometimes it's the chief innovation officer, who can leverage new product development to assemble agile teams that can more rapidly adopt the Next Mindset.

And sometimes it's the chief learning officer (CLO). Because they are often committed to the development of every worker in the organization, the CLO has broad reach. There is often a budget for learning and development, especially for what are considered hard-to-hire skillsets, so the CLO already has experience directing funds to change initiatives. And the CLO can have credibility with the leading executives of the organization, especially if it's within the CLO's mandate to source and direct coaching resources for those leading executives.

Whether it's the CHRO, the CLO, or someone else with a C title, they can only be successful with the unbending support of the CEO and other C-suite occupants—and the budget to make it happen.

CASE STUDY

Mindset Change through "Unbossing": Novartis

Markus Graf is the global head of talent for Novartis, a 110,000-employee pharmaceuticals company based in Basel, Switzerland. The company's stated mission is "to reimagine medicine to extend and improve people's lives."

"Unbossing" is the company's initiative to develop self-aware, inclusive leaders throughout the organization who are able to empower their teams by creating clarity and accountability, removing obstacles and empowering and supporting others to reach their full potential. Its "Unbossed Leadership Experience" program takes workers through a personal growth journey. It enables behavioral shifts and self-awareness on how others see them, and how as a leader each can make a different impact on others in their daily work.

Novartis also introduced a flexibility policy that they call "Choice with Responsibility," which shifts the responsibility from "manager-approved" to "manager-informed," empowering workers to choose how, where, and when they work. Novartis's intended goal is for everyone to feel able to be their best selves at work and at home, and to be committed to supporting and enabling them to be inspired, curious, and unbossed. Novartis sees the global pandemic as accelerating its organizational need to explore new working models, as its workers expressed a strong desire for more flexibility in how, where, and when they work.

The scale of the process is breathtaking. Markus says that the CEO has signed off on a substantial financial commitment to training every single employee, and the top 300 executives in the organization are on board for the new mindset. "We have circa 20,000 managers who also role-model the change," said Markus. He says the company tracks its efforts in real time through metrics like its employee engagement score, and so far is well above industry benchmarks.

Whoever is chosen or volunteers to lead the mindset transformation, it's important to ensure that they have the long-term mandate and resources to be successful. However, a mindset alignment initiative also needs to be broken down into short-term steps so that progress can be made continually visible.

Insights on Successful Mindset Alignment

When i4cp looked at the practices of the 15 percent of the survey who claimed they were successful, three major steps stood out that were highly correlated with success—plan, build, and maintain—and within those steps, a total of 18 actions were consistently found to contribute to positive results. *Plan* included surveying to understand what kind of culture you actually have, getting commitments from those who lead the organization, and gaining agreement on what the transformation needs to be. *Build* included story-telling, and the involvement of influencers. And *maintain* required the adaptation of existing processes to align them to the desired mindset.

For example, performance management, which I group under effectiveness rules, must be aligned with the new hoped-for mindset. If you don't change the context for conversations about work-related effectiveness, and back those agreements with appropriate incentives and compensation to reinforce behavior, little is likely to change at scale.

Tellingly, four out of five companies reporting successful "renovations" said the CEO both committed the resources and time needed, and modeled the new behaviors embedded in the plan. I'm not a fan of "CEO as hero" narratives. But as we know from our own experiences with families, if we don't see authentic behavior modeled by those we look to for our behavior cues, there is little reinforcement for our own change.

You'll find a complete discussion of the techniques from the i4cp study in *Culture Renovation*[10] by Kevin Oakes, i4cp's CEO and co-founder. Another great resource is Charlene Li's book for organization transformation, *The Disruption Mindset*.[11] Charlene highlights the difference between organizations that have a "stuck culture" versus a "flux culture." She points to the need to create a foundation of trust throughout the organization to truly guide mindset transformation.

CASE STUDY

Microsoft's Cultural Transformation Journey

In 2014, few industry pundits gave Microsoft any chance of engineering a cultural transformation for its 128,000 employees. The much-touted rollout of Windows 8 had cratered, and the culture inherited from the Steve Ballmer era was one built on contention and internal competition. Its frequent competitor Apple was ascendant as an innovator. (I don't love market cap numbers, because a stock price is a myopic way to judge an organization's success. But suffice to say shareholders of the time liked Apple much more than Microsoft.) In the critical new paradigm of cloud computing, Amazon had a dominant 27 percent market share, and Microsoft was an also-ran with 10 percent.[12]

New CEO Satya Nadella had a massive task before him. He decided he needed to revamp its culture. As he details in his book, *Hit Refresh*,[13] Nadella quickly established a cultural transformation journey for the company that he said began with him.

By the end of 2020, Microsoft had nearly doubled its cloud computing market share to over 19 percent, while Amazon grew its share more incrementally to 32 percent.[14] And in early 2021, Nadella announced that his company's revenue rose 17 percent for the previous quarter, and profit ascended a stunning 33 percent.

Why is Microsoft such an important example? Scale and pace. There are very few examples of large organizations that have made successful mindset shifts, and in such a comparatively short period of time.

Assuming you're going to catalyze this journey, what steps should you follow? Whether you decide on an edge, incremental core, or large-scale core strategy, here are the common steps I've found by analyzing different models of organizational transformation. These include:

- **Inventory:** What is the organization's current mindset? What are the cultural anchors? What behaviors are encouraged, and which are discouraged? How consistent are these behaviors throughout the organization? What subcultures exist and where, and how do those subcultures differ from each other? Conducting an inventory isn't a design exercise. It's a process for determining what actually exists today.

- **Impetus:** What is driving the need for a mindset shift? While it may be tempting to use a threat-based narrative—"Our competitors will eat our lunch if we don't eat theirs"—think instead about a positive narrative that excites people about the opportunities for the future. How can you make that possible future tangible so that it is seen by everyone within the organization as being deeply relevant to their future success?

- **Envision:** What is the mindset that you and other stakeholders believe the organization should have? How is this mindset and related behaviors connected to the purpose, vision, and mission of the organization? This co-creation process must be collaborative, involving not just those who lead throughout the organization, but also line workers, customers, and partners. Use design thinking or a similar toolset that guarantees the envisioning process begins with empathy. And be sure to use this exercise as an opportunity to determine if you need to modify the organization's statements about its purpose, vision, and mission.

- **Prioritize:** No organization can be great at everything. What is the shortest list of mindset, behaviors, and values that will allow the organization to achieve its purpose? If you do those high-priority things, are you likely to get the results that you want?

- **Prototype:** What's the smallest thing you can do to test out your hypothesis for your Next Mindset? Are there already parts of the organization that exhibit the mindset you are working toward, which you can use as an iconic example? Test out your mindset model over just a few days or weeks with one or more small groups, assessing whether your approach actually does change mindsets. Don't just ask people what they think. Watch what they do.

- **Commit:** Those who are seen as leading the organization must take the first steps by embodying the Next Mindset through their own consistent and authentic behavior and communications. They must be vulnerable and transparent about their efforts. This is hard stuff. Let others see your efforts.

- **Communicate:** Get everyone on the same page through relentless communication. Write a manifesto. And develop compelling narratives.

In his book, *The Journey Beyond Fear: Leverage the three pillars of positivity to build your success*,[15] John Hagel makes the distinction between narrative (a vision that has no conclusion) and story-telling (which has a beginning, middle, and end). The organization needs an authentic narrative as to *why* it is going through its transformation. Examples of iconic customers and other stakeholders, stories about workers who embody the Next Mindset, and narratives about the organization's mission and vision are all fodder for the initiative. Also, authentic rituals such as recognition for breakthrough achievements and dramatic personal development are needed to send strong signals to others about the need for new ways of thinking and acting.

CASE STUDY
Your Mindset Manifesto: Learning from Avito

In 2020, Avito was the top "secondary market" platform in Russia, with online marketplaces enabling other businesses to resell everything from cars to jobs. A subsidiary of the global classifieds OLX Group, which is itself a subsidiary of Naspers, the Dutch retail giant, Avito has consistently delivered new services that have cemented its market-leading position. With 2,500 workers and $400 million in annual sales, any objective analysis would tell you that this was a nimble and adaptive company.

Yet Avito CEO Vladimir Pravdivy wasn't satisfied.

Vladimir charged his team with creating a manifesto that described the kind of mindset transformation they were hoping to catalyze. Here is a company that by many measures was already a Next Organization. It was already the leader in its field. It was already deeply digital in its products and processes. It was already moving up-market to add more services to its transaction offerings.

And yet here also was a persistent focus on continuing to push forward. The company wanted to ensure that a Next Mindset was spread widely throughout the organization. So the company catalyzed a cultural change initiative to ensure it was continually encouraging the Next Mindset. As you'll see if you download it from my website, the manifesto answers questions like: What organization do we build? What are our values? What is leadership behavior to us? And, what environment would we like to create?

One of the most encouraging signs was the level of commitment by Vladimir's direct reports. In Chapter 6, I'll talk about the amazing range of psychological diversity among the Avito executive team. I could have spent hours exploring their fascinating backgrounds. Suffice to say, this was not the traditional MBA-fueled executive suite.

The Avito manifesto is an excellent example of the kind of mindset statement that leading executives need to co-create and communicate for cultural change initiatives. You can find a PDF of the manifesto at gbolles.com/mindset, provided with Avito's permission.

- **Action:** Encourage specific actions by specific groups to embody the new mindset. If your journey begins with a commitment to a learning plan by every worker in the organization, have the team of those who lead publish their own learning plans, and post updates on their progress. When that team follows through, reinforcing behavior signals ripple throughout the organization.

- **Align:** Conduct workshops to help people practice the new mindset and behaviors. Change hiring, onboarding, review processes, and promotion processes so they're aligned as well. And, perhaps most importantly, ensure that incentives and compensation are aligned to the new values, especially for team guides (whom you may call managers) throughout the organization.

- **Measure:** If you're successful, how will you know? What data-driven insights will help you to track your progress? Surveying attitudes is fine, but as with prototyping, focus on what people actually do. Make sure this data is kept in the light of day, where all stakeholders can see it. If you need some suggestions, i4cp maintains a "healthy culture index" against which you can bench-mark yourself.

- **Iterate:** Successful mindset transformation is not some change manage-ment exercise. It's a perpetual process.

Think of this as a "spiral up" approach. In practice, these usually aren't linear steps. You will develop your own scenario with your team to determine how you will execute these steps.

One warning: If yours is the kind of organization that has gone through repeated "transformation" exercises, a mindset shift toward

FIGURE 3.1   The Spiral Up Approach for Mindset Change

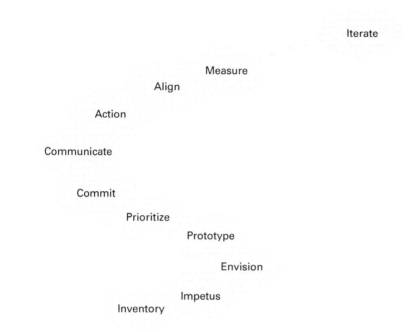

SOURCE © 2021 Charrette LLC. Used by permission.

the Next Rules will be seen as yet another useless process. As the American author Charlton Ogburn Jr. once wrote,[16] "[W]e tend… to meet any new situation by reorganizing; and a wonderful method it can be for creating the illusion of progress while producing confusion, inefficiency, and demoralization." Instead, treat your transformation process as an opportunity to create clarity, effectiveness, and re-engagement.

Correction: Maybe Anyone Can Help Catalyze Mindset Transformation

The insights from i4cp make it clear that those who lead the organization must be advocates for mindset change. But what happens if you can't get the commitment of those who lead the organization?

The answer: Assert and respond.

In the long history of organizational alignment strategies, the modern turning point was in 1990, when the Balanced Scorecard approach was popularized by Harvard Business School professor Robert S. Kaplan and David P. Norton, co-founder of the management consultancy Nolan-Norton. The balanced scorecard offered a set of consistent metrics for performance across the organization, involving every function in its development and tracking. I was involved in a project with the Balanced Scorecard team when I was the editor-in-chief of *Network Computing Magazine* in the early 1990s, working closely with companies that had used the scorecard like Capital One, the financial services giant. What impressed me most was the mindset that pushed the understanding of and responsibility for aligning to and implementing strategy throughout the entire organization. Kaplan and Norton eventually published in 2001 *The Strategy-Focused Organization*,[17] with detailed case studies of organizations that had used this approach.

A few years later, as an independent consultant I was asked by the manager of a small bank's innovation team to help craft his group's strategic goals and plan for the coming year. I suggested that we use the balanced scorecard, and asked him what the organization's strategic goals were. His response: He didn't know.

That wasn't his fault: The organization's strategic goals weren't widely discussed throughout the company. But without that information, how could he define his group's goals?

In the scorecard project, I had learned from the Capital One team that one of their widespread cultural practices at the time was called "Assert and Respond." I was told that it worked like this:

> You, as a project leader, inevitably have a series of dependencies on others throughout the organization.

> Sometimes those other executives are on the critical path for your project. If you need something from them, but they don't respond, your project is stalled. For example, if your project depends on someone from Accounting to sign off on your budget before you can proceed, and they are radio silent, you are roadblocked.

The practice of "Assert and Respond" allows you to send your budget to the decision-maker in Accounting. You get to "assert" to them that you think they'll say the budget is just fine. If they don't "respond" in a week, you'll go ahead and act as if they'd signed off. And the organization's culture made that kind of assertive action okay.

A week goes by. You notify Accounting that you are proceeding with the project, and you continue as if you had received signoff.

I suggested that my client use "assert and respond," so he could get his plan done. He "asserted" what he thought the company's strategic goals for the year were, aligned his own group's goals with the company's perceived goals, and submitted his plan to his boss.

I checked in with my client a few months later to see how things were going, and he told me I should talk to the HR department. An HR executive told me that my client had submitted his plan to his boss, who immediately wondered, "Well, what *are* the company's strategic goals?" The same question continued up the food chain, until a top executive decided this was a company-wide vacuum. So the entire organization had implemented the balanced scorecard process for continuous alignment.

This is why I rarely accept someone's contention that they are "just a cog in the machine," or that they don't have any personal power in the organization. Sure, you probably don't have *100 percent* of the power to achieve the change you desire. But use what percentage you believe you do have, and do it in an involving and authentic way. That's how change is catalyzed, by someone who leads from anywhere within an organization.

Now that we've explored mindset change across the organization, it's important to deconstruct what that process looks like on the ground level, for individuals and teams. As you'll see in the next chapter, it turns out that there is one key element in the mindset shift at the personal level: the mindset of the problem-solver.

04

The Problem-Solving Mindset of Workers and Teams

You're a problem-solving engine. That's good, because Next Rules-based work will increasingly become more problem-centric and project-based.

The way you solve problems is through your *cognition*, a set of mental functions that help you to process information and make decisions. Those complex cognitive mechanisms are actually guided by a few basic motivations. The more you can understand your own motivations, the better you can solve the challenging problems of today and tomorrow. You can hack your own cognition to become a better problem-solver—and you can teach others to do the same.

A team is a band of problem-solvers, with a set of common characteristics. Increasingly, the way you will gain new problem-solvers is to double down on the organization's purpose.

Magic Wand Time

I wave a magic wand, and suddenly you and I are microscopic in size. We are about to embark on a breathtaking tour through the human brain.

We journey through the spinal cord into the brain stem and the brain. The largest part is the cerebrum, and its outer layer, the cerebral cortex, is where we do our complex thinking. One lobe, the occipital, processes visual information, while the temporal lobe manages sound

THE PROBLEM-SOLVING MINDSET   113

and language. Next to the brain stem is the thalamus, which diligently regulates our consciousness, while the hypothalamus coordinates through the pituitary gland to the endocrine system, which produces our hormones.

Positive motivation at work can come from the influences of those hormones, behavior-reinforcing *neurochemicals* spurting around our brains. *Dopamine*, little jolts of hormone and neurotransmitters sent along four major pathways in the brain, can be triggered when we have a goal that we need to push toward, with the promise of a bigger spurt of dopamine when we achieve it. (Unfortunately, we probably also get dopamine hits with experiences such as getting lots of "likes" on social media.) *Oxytocin* is triggered in trusted environments, reinforcing feelings of safety. That's an early-human survival response that likely told us when we could let our guard down when we knew a saber-toothed tiger couldn't get us. *Serotonin* is triggered when we feel important, which we see in animals when they dominate a resource, such as becoming the alpha in a social pack (and likely also when we dominate others in meetings, or on social media). And *endorphins* are triggered when we feel stress or physical pain, or push our physical limits, generating an opioid-like source of euphoria. That response might be useful, for example, when you push your physical limits by pulling all-nighters to complete a project.

Unfortunately, our time is limited, so we can't journey down the body to the gut biome, which has a surprising amount of influence on our mental processes and behavior. Next time.

This tour through the physical part of the brain is crucial to understanding mindset—because the meta-physical functions of the mind are built on top of the physical functions of the brain. And the mind is where we solve problems.

You Are a Complex and Adaptive Ecosystem

Now that we're back to our normal sizes, take a few moments to marvel at the creature that is you.

You have about 30 trillion cells in your body. About 100 trillion bacteria[1] occupy the ecosystem that is your microbiome, the legion of microbes inhabiting your body in complex symbiosis. You have about 86 billion neurons in your head, which is in the vicinity of the low-end estimates for the number of stars in our galaxy.[2] Your eyes see at a resolution of about 576 million pixels,[3] about 70 times the density of a 4K TV screen. Your body secretes around 50 hormones, regulating a broad range of your mind and body functions. And all of these elements interact in complex ways to enable your mind to function, and therefore how you behave, in the context of work and life.

From the time you were born, your developing young mind worked very hard to try to learn about your complex adaptive system, and to process information from the world around you. You had to figure out what you were seeing, what things were called, and how things worked. You went from having other humans feed you and change your diapers, to learning the rules for functioning independently in a complicated world.

Along the way, you tried things. You made mistakes. We don't call it trial-and-success: We call it trial-and-error. We all make mistakes, *lots* of mistakes, when we're young.

The good news is that, as a child, we're pretty much okay with making mistakes. It's called learning. In fact, according to my favorite cognitive neuroscientist, artificial intelligence expert, and self-described "professional mad scientist" Vivienne Ming, we actually learn better when things are a little hard. It's only as we get older, and as others influence our feelings about mistakes, that we begin to lose the mindset of error-as-learning and start substituting a mindset of error-as-failure.

Over time, you interacted with other people more and more. Some of those—your peers—joined you on your learning journey, in something called school. Since we all are testing and learning as we go along, you found that solving problems and reaching goals could also be a team sport. Unfortunately, what usually *doesn't* get taught in school is *how* you solve problems, and how your unique cognition works to help you do that.

You, Problem-Solver

In other chapters, we have focused on all four of the Next Rules. Because problem-solving and *effectiveness* are so fundamental, we're going to spend the majority of this chapter on a range of insights for improving our mindset for solving problems, and how to get more diverse problem-solvers into the organization, especially those driven by purpose.

Not everything in life and work, of course, is about problem-solving. Having fun doesn't usually come from a need to solve a problem, except to make sure you're enjoying yourself. But in the context of work, frequently there is a problem to be solved. Whether you simply want to be more effective in your own work, or you help to guide the efforts of a team, understanding the ways your marvelous mind functions can help improve your ability to influence your own mindset, and to help others to influence their own as well.

Those functions are known as *cognition*. (And when I ask your human mind to think about cognition, that's called *meta-cognition*. Rather circular, isn't it?)

Remember that work, mechanically, is just three things: our human skills, applied to tasks, to solve problems. That's why people pay us, and why we pay others. To solve problems. That's how we create value for the organization's customers and other stakeholders.

If you work on an assembly line, performing repetitive tasks like assembling a set of components, you are a problem-solver. Every time you assemble those components, a problem is solved. And then along comes the next one. If you are in a leading executive role, you help others to resolve key challenges ranging from whom to hire to determining how the organization makes money. Decision made? Problem solved.

Years ago, when my father was doing the research for *What Color Is Your Parachute?*, the world's enduring career manual, he realized that people were far more likely to get hired at a job if they positioned themselves as problem-solvers. He suggested that job-hunters conduct extensive research on the organization they most wanted to work for, so they would be prepared to tell the person who had the power to hire exactly what problems they understood the organization to be facing, and how the job-hunter was exactly the person to help solve those problems, whether a job opening existed or not.

That's why problem-solving is such a fundamental mindset for the Next Rules of Work. It's the key to *effectiveness*, the first core Next Rules skill. We all want to feel that we are effective in our work, because it helps to create the value each of us is contributing, and leads to so many of the rewards that we seek.

This Is How Your Mind Solves Problems

A problem-solving mindset starts with the stunningly obvious premise that many problems have a solution. Just as with the mountain climbing analogy from Chapter 2, if you have the mountain climber's mindset, you are mentally prepared for the problems you will encounter.

When you walk into a room with a problem-solver's mindset, you are prepared with a mental framework for dealing with potential challenges. It doesn't daunt you that you may not initially have the ideal amount of information, resources, or time to solve a problem. (Those are the three things that startups always lack.) Your mindset is that the first thing to be determined is what the problem is, then to determine the most effective steps to iterate toward its solution.

Of course, the opposite mindset is also obvious and inevitable— because if you think you can't solve a problem, you're probably right, as well.

Our guide through the problem-solving steps of our cognition is Chaim Guggenheim, the former CEO of the Feuerstein Institute in Jerusalem, Israel, and co-founder of the educational technology startup Cognitas, which develops training for thinking and learning skills. The Institute was founded on the breakthrough work of Professor Reuven Feuerstein, a psychologist who demonstrated that intelligence is actually fluid and modifiable, and who developed a deep understanding of the mechanisms of "learning how to learn," especially in the context of solving problems.

Building on Feuerstein's work, Chaim points to four steps or phases we follow when we encounter a unique problem or conceive of a goal. Below is Chaim's model of those cognitive building blocks, which offers some very practical ways to improve our problem-solving mindset (see Figure 4.1).

First, there is a sort of "pre-problem-solving" step that comes when we encounter a new problem, and we have to decide if we are going to engage with it. That can be a split-second decision, or can be a more involved process that itself is a problem to be solved. Finding that a door in an unfamiliar building is locked might be met with a shrug. Or it might be a barrier to something you really need, like going to the bathroom.

Once we've decided to engage with the problem, we need to **collect information**. If it's a physical problem right in front of us, we may be able to collect information by poking and prodding. If it's an information-based problem, there may be enough available information, such as an overview by a co-worker in an email message. Or we may need to begin gathering from a variety of sources to try to understand the problem. We also check our memory banks to determine if we've encountered the problem before, and if we've solved a similar one, we may be able to jump ahead to apply that solution.

We also try to make sure we're using credible and relevant information, out of the swirling tsunami inundating us every day. It's hard to do that deliberately and thoroughly, but it's the mission-critical process each of us must do to develop accurate and effective solutions.

If it's still a novel problem we haven't encountered before, next we **process the information** we've gathered. We use flex skills such as defining, analyzing, grouping, comparing, and synthesizing, so that we can mentally sculpt the information into some digestible form.

The third step our problem-solving cognition goes through is to **abstract the information**. Most of us can't keep a huge amount of data in our heads, so we distill information, create new rules and concepts, and link different chunks of information in useful ways. We look for patterns. We come up with hypotheses. We test those hypotheses to see if the information we've gathered supports them.

FIGURE 4.1   The Cognitas Cognition Model

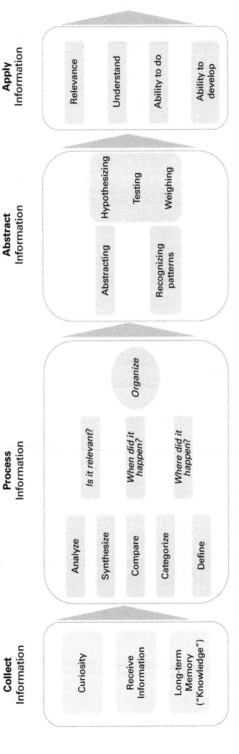

SOURCE © 2021 Cognitas Thinking Solutions Ltd. Used by permission.

Now we are ready to solve the problem.

Finally, we **apply our learning**, using it in some real-world way, and ideally repeat our learning process so we can solidify our understanding into a well-developed skill. And if we want this process to help us change our behavior, we need to ask ourselves, "Where else in my work or my life could this apply?"

Note that, depending on the complexity of the problem, this isn't necessarily a linear step-by-step process. We keep cycling back and forth between these phases as we work to understand the problem and develop potential solutions.

What is critical is to be aware of the process, to continually hone and improve the ability to solve problems, and keep working toward achieving mastery that will help us solve increasingly difficult and complex challenges in the future.

In your head, all of these functions work together in a process that's a lot more like a network than a single linear thinking engine. Much like the Pixar movie *Inside Out*, we typically make decisions as a networked process, with various parts of the brain contributing information and impetus, ultimately resulting in a decision (or in a decision *not* to decide, which is also a decision).

Let's look at a mundane example in the real world:

Suppose you hear there is a sudden drop-off in customer usage of your product or service. That sounds like a pretty important problem to solve, so it's a no-brainer that it's one with which you want to engage.

You first need to **collect information** to see if you can determine the cause. Because there have been usage blips before, you have some experiences in your long-term memory banks that you can pull from to help guide your information-gathering. As you gather information, you begin to process it and organize it, analyzing various forms of information like raw numbers and graphical charts, separating the information into categories like customer behavior and general economic trends, determining what information is relevant and what may be irrelevant to the problem, adding labels to data sources like "reliable" and "questionable," synthesizing the information sources into groupings like "behavior" and "product availability," and comparing all of that with past problems in your memory banks that were similar.

Now you're starting to shift gears to **abstract information**. It seems there is a pattern of customer usage drop-off in New York, Amsterdam, and Dubai. What is similar about those three locations? You take a stab at a hypothesis, wondering if there is a problem with the cloud computing servers that serve them. You test that hypothesis, but can't find any difference in the data, so you weigh that hypothesis, find it unsupportable, and discard it. You run through a dozen other hypotheses. Did a competitor launch a marketing campaign? Could there be different reasons in each location for the drop-off? You test against the data you have. If one of your hypotheses looks like it's supported by the data—yes, it does seem that a competitor had a big marketing push in those three markets a month before the drop-offs began—you gather more information and compare it against the hypothesis.

Okay, now you think you understand the problem. It was because of a competitor's marketing campaign. You **apply that information** to a new solution, modeling out what it would take to do a new marketing campaign yourself. You look at your budget, determine you can afford it, and send off a note asking for approval.

The next time you are confronted with a major problem in your work, whether it's to figure out why a piece of software isn't working the way you want, or it's a social problem rising from a complex dynamic between a group of people, watch your own *process* for solving that problem, rather than just the solution. Did you approach it with the mindset of a problem-solver, confident you were going to figure out a solution? What steps did you follow? Could you have done anything differently to collect, process, abstract, or apply information?

And can you teach those same steps to others?

Optimizing Your Problem-Solving Engine

If the first solution you devise works, great. But what if it doesn't? As I said earlier, you are a trial-and-error engine, through processes you learned when you were very young. Your cognition is *designed* for making mistakes, determining what didn't work, adjusting, and trying again. But when those mistakes are viewed and reacted to by others, we may get a new set of inputs that tell us why failure is "bad," and we build an aversion to making mistakes, at least in the light of day. Old Rules organizational cultures bake that aversion into their DNA, to the point where risk-taking isn't just avoided, it's shamed and shunned.

This is why startups talk frequently about "embracing error" as a critical part of the innovation process. If you aren't ever allowed to make mistakes, you will constrain your solutions only to those that have the greatest possible chance of success, which means you'll likely never take big risks. Just remember the famous line of Esther Dyson, the iconic investor and founder of health startup Road to Wellville: "Always make *new* mistakes."

Remember Esther Dyson: "Always make *new* mistakes."

Throughout your work day you are continually encountering and solving a portfolio of problems, ranging from the simple ("What am I eating for lunch?") to the complex ("How do I solve this problem I've been working on for a month?"). You'll probably solve the lunch choice issue because it's a low-risk proposition. But the weight of pressures at work might encourage you to continually kick the can down the road for that big problem.

CASE STUDY

Thinking Like a Problem-Solver

I learned the basics of problem-solving in my early twenties. At the time, I was rather aimless in my work life. I had little interest in college, so after high school, though I took a few courses, I worked at a series of random jobs. (One of them was being trained as a career counselor in my father's methods at the age of 19. But I eventually found that wasn't my path.)

Since the first class I had taken in high school taught typing on manual typewriters, I could find temporary office work at businesses in the San Francisco Bay Area. In the early 1980s, few people in management roles knew how to type, so that meant a lot of low-paying work for those familiar with a keyboard. Temporary agencies such as Manpower and Kelly would receive work orders from clients, and people like me would work on a project for a day, a week, a month, or longer. Today we call this gig work. It allowed me to do a countless series of projects to pay the rent. But the work was often mind-numbing and demoralizing.

Increasingly, though, what I was typing on was this disruptive technology called a personal computer. Many small businesses bought those early PCs because they were inexpensive. But they didn't have the slightest idea how to use them effectively. It turns out that was a problem I knew how to solve.

I began approaching temp agencies for computer-related work. I would go to the client's office in the morning, read the computer's software manual, and by the afternoon I'd be showing them how to use their PCs more effectively. Some of these office productivity programs had rudimentary programming languages known as "macros," so sometimes I would automate basic tasks by creating simple macro programs that office workers could use once I had moved on.

I considered moving from the east Bay Area down to Silicon Valley. I assumed, though, that I had missed the hi-tech boom. Here it was, 1984, and Microsoft and Apple were already huge companies. It seemed that all the big innovation had already been done. How could someone possibly come up with new ways to use a computer?

But I decided I didn't want to keep on typing other people's work. I needed a bigger challenge. I moved to the San Francisco peninsula at the cusp of Silicon Valley, and went to find work through a local temporary agency. I asked the placement representative, "What's the hardest project you have that has to do with computers?"

The rep paged through a binder of listings and stopped at one work order. "There's this company called TeleVideo Systems, and they're looking for a quality assurance test engineer." She looked up at me. "We don't know what that is. We keep sending them people that they reject."

My response: "I'll take it."

I drove my beat-up Chevy Nova down to the company's office in Sunnyvale, and presented myself to Dawn Griffey, the company's QA supervisor. Dawn was a rarity in Silicon Valley, a young black woman in a management role. That's still too much of a rarity today.

I told Dawn that I could do the software testing work, but that I couldn't live on the low pay rate they were offering. So I suggested an alternative. Pay me double the offered rate, and if after a week I wasn't doing the work she wanted, she could fire me. (I had never done anything like that before. But what did I have to lose? If it didn't work out, I'd just find another mind-numbing typing job.)

It worked out. Dawn's gamble on an aimless, college degree-less young person gave me entry to the hi-tech world. And I learned some of the most fundamental methods of problem-solving.

It turned out that we were testing one of the earliest software programs for managing networks of personal computers, Novell's NetWare software, which TeleVideo was going to relabel, repackage, and resell. Months later when the testing was done, the software was to be released on TeleVideo's hardware. But the company's training department had recently lost several of its managers and trainers, and there was nobody who knew the software anywhere near as well as I did.

Ah. A new problem to solve. I suggested the company hire me to create and deliver the training classes. I ended up becoming the supervisor of the sales training department, which helped to cement my start in the world of hi-tech. (And it's also how I met my future wife—who happened to attend one of my training classes when she worked for our ad agency.)

What Motivates Problem-Solving: Pleasure or Pain

Much of that "pre-decision" process is opaque to us. In fact, we often come to some decision from all of that mental activity, taking certain action, but convince ourselves afterward the reasons why we did it. That's according to my favorite behavioral economist, Dan Ariely, who is the James B. Duke Professor of Behavioral Economics in the Fuqua School of Business at Duke University.

As a high school student in Israel, Dan was preparing for a traditional evening ceremony when an accident started a fire that burned 70 percent of his body. While recovering in the hospital, he wondered why nurses followed certain instructions for burn victim care from doctors—which often meant more pain for patients—rather than having the nurses follow their own knowledge and instincts. Why, he wondered, do we continually do things against our own best interests?

Dan eventually became one of the top behavioral economists in the world, with TED talks viewed over 15 million times, and the author of books like *Predictably Irrational: The hidden forces that shape our decisions*.[4] One of the reasons Dan's work is so compelling is that he doesn't just posit the way human cognition works. He conducts real-world studies with actual tests of human behavior. His results are often surprisingly counterintuitive, because they don't fit the comfortable narrative of humans as rational creatures.

Dan distills down human motivation into just two factors: We are drawn toward pleasure, and we avoid pain. That's it. The entire complexity of human achievement, defined in just two fundamental drivers.

Part of that calculus is what psychologists call the *calculation of effort*, our pre-decision guess at how much work an activity may take us. Procrastination is often a response to a mental calculation that balances the potential pain of doing something now versus later (often overestimated), and the likelihood of the pain that such a delay might cause (often underestimated), and concludes with an "answer" of how much work it might be to do something now. The frequent result is a decision to delay. And, as Dan has also said, we often make up a completely bogus reason why we did what we did (or didn't do), after the fact, to ensure it meets our personal internal narrative.

We each have different kinds of motivation to solve different kinds of problems. You can generally classify motivation into positive and negative (pleasure and pain), and internal and external. When we're young, we're initially driven by intrinsic motivations such as curiosity, or extrinsic motivations such as pleasing a parent or teacher. As we age, more complex sources of motivation can come into play, such as positive motivations ranging from a salary to a desire to improve ourselves, and negative motivations such as worries about repercussions if we don't perform at work.

Do you often convince yourself to do something because of your own motivations, or because you want to please or avoid displeasing other people? Are you more motivated by positive incentives, or by avoiding negative incentives? Your impetus to take any particular action (or not) comes from a complicated Venn diagram of elements that includes your beliefs and values, your history and experiences, and your in-the-moment calculations about the aggregate amount of pleasure or pain you'll experience.

FIGURE 4.2   Quadrants of Motivation

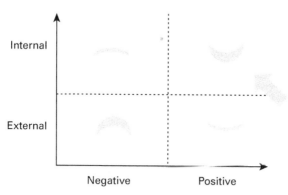

SOURCE © 2021 Charrette LLC. Used by permission.

This is one of the reasons that infusing game mechanics into learning and working can be so effective. Games are not only problem-solving situations; they also have the incentives for solving the problem baked into them, delivering pain (for losing) and pleasure (for winning) in a range of contexts.

CASE STUDY

Hacking Your Own Cognition: Tiny Habits

If you help guide the work of another person who regularly procrastinates, you may find it helpful to suggest ways they can overcome that recurring calculation of effort that allows them to repeatedly kick the can down the road.

As we grow older, we build habit patterns that may either work really well for us, or that may continually work against our own best interests. If you find yourself experiencing more of the latter than the former, the most useful methodology I've found for convincing your brain to solve problems to your own benefit comes from the work of BJ Fogg and the Stanford Behavioral Design Lab.

BJ developed a model of human motivation for developing positive habits. A habit is essentially a default behavior that we develop that reduces the cognitive load for making a decision to take action. We each have plenty of actions we know are good for us, ranging from healthy eating to regular exercise. When we *don't* do those things repeatedly, the cognitive network in our heads is typically making decisions to avoid pain (exercise), or to embrace pleasure (that second piece of chocolate cake). Because so many actions throughout the day are small ("Just one more bite..."), the human mind rarely makes the frontal cortex add up the impact of all those little decisions to assess the true cost to us.

BJ found that we tend to make decisions to do certain tasks through the combination of how *easy or hard* we think a task will be, calculated against what kind of *reward* we think we will receive. If we think a task is easy, but the reward isn't very valuable to us, we won't take an action, or repeat that action enough to develop a habit. If a reward is very valuable to us, but we have to work too hard to get the reward, we won't take the action or develop the habit, either. BJ offers a free course to experiment with his methodology at TinyHabits.com.

These are all "cognitive hacks," actions we can take to influence our own mindset and behavior. We are constantly performing cognitive hacks to others around us, as well. As we grow into social beings, we learn how to get things we want, starting with getting fed and having diapers changed: Crying often results in someone coming to our aid. Our cognitive hacks get more sophisticated as we crack the code on the behavior of humans around us, learning how to encourage pain ("I'm telling Mom") or pleasure ("I'll give you my toy") to get what we want.

That's your trial-and-error engine humming. If you want some exercises to take you through an explicit learning process, I have a variety of activities in my learning-related courses on LinkedIn Learning.

No particular motivation is "right" or "wrong." But it's important to know the kind of motivation you typically default to, and how effective that motivation is in helping you to achieve your goals. And the more you can develop your own *internal* motivations, the more control you'll have over your own decision-making.

A Team Is a Band of Problem-Solvers

Now that we've seen what makes for an effective problem-solving mindset for an individual, we can delve into the mindset of effective teams. Happily, there is a growing body of understanding about just what enables a team to be consistently effective.

Notice that I don't say "high performance." You may believe that a high-performance mindset is most appropriate for your organization's culture. I prefer to focus on *effective* teams (Next Rule #1) whose mindset is to create value for customers and other stakeholders.

One of the most influential studies on team effectiveness was conducted by Google in its Project Aristotle[5] (no relationship to the Aristotle Canvas). Google's research showed five key characteristics of *effective* teams. They are, in order:

- **Dependability:** Team members are mentally committed to following through on their commitments to each other. (In the Next Rules, that's also *alignment*, as well as *growth*, so that each team member is competent in their role.)

- **Structure and clarity:** Clear roles, well-defined plans, and well-articulated goals serve to give great clarity to the work of the team (*alignment*, through strategic tools like objectives and key results, which we'll explore in Chapter 8).

- **Meaning:** Team members each believe their work has value and purpose (*alignment*).

- **Impact:** What the team is working on will create value for one or more of the organization's stakeholders (*alignment*).

- And, perhaps most important, **psychological safety**. Team members feel safe to take risks, offer crazy ideas, and to be vulnerable with each other (*involvement*).

To this list, I'd like to add one more mindset factor, which was included in an earlier Google study ("Oxygen"):

- **Psychological *diversity*** (*involvement*, on steroids): If everyone in the room looks like you, and has a similar background, your team is likely to have a similar set of biases and mental framing. Having a broad range of backgrounds, perspectives, and socioeconomic status and history can dramatically increase the team's collective mindset to solve new problems. (A frequent challenge cited by those who are able to achieve psychological diversity in teams is that there is often a lack of trust, which of course means psychological un-safety. That's why it's critical to design for a trusted environment.)

The importance of each of these team mindset practices is amplified with distributed teams. The more that workers regularly function outside the same geographical location, the more *intentional* the team must become to continually align its problem-solving mindset.

EMPOWERING YOUR BAND OF PROBLEM-SOLVERS

Here is a thought exercise that I use in one of my LinkedIn Learning courses to help team guides to empower their teams.

Suppose you lead a team. (That may not be much of a stretch.) You come into the office Monday morning, and you tell your team, "I'm not sticking around today. I want you each to take a stack of sticky notes, and write down a problem that you, personally, regularly solve in a given week. Write down one *problem* per note, and put your initials on it. Put up as many problems on the white board as each of you can think of." (Of course, if you lead a distributed team, do it with an online brainstorming tool like a Miro board.)

"Wherever you see patterns, group together the problems that each of you solves. Try to agree as much as possible on the groupings, but don't work too hard at it, or fall in love with the way you group them, because it may change."

First thing Tuesday morning, you tell the team, "I'm not sticking around today either. Take a different colored sticky note than you used yesterday, and I want you to each write down a *task* that you perform in a given week to solve a particular problem. Write one task per note, with your initials. Make sure you assign tasks to every problem you've listed. Write down as many tasks as you can think of, and put them all on the board. Again, group them where it makes sense."

Wednesday morning rolls around, and you are probably way ahead of me by now. You tell your team, "I'm leaving again. But today I want each of you to take a different colored sticky note, and write down the *skills* you use to perform those tasks and to solve those problems. One skill per sticky note, plus your initials. You don't have to use the same language that others use. Put all those skills up on the board, next to the related tasks you perform. But don't worry about grouping the skills together."

On Thursday, you instruct the team, "Today, I want you all to work together to reorganize all the problems, tasks, and skills.

"Place the problems at the center of the whiteboard, and group them together where it makes sense. If you get new insights about what any of the problems really are, redefine them.

"Take all of the skills and link them to specific problems. Are the people with the most effective skills focused on solving the right problems? If you realize that some essential skills are missing that are critical to solving certain problems, put up some red sticky notes describing the skillset. Those may be skills that someone on the team needs to learn, or for which we need to hire.

"Now you can sync up tasks to those problems and skills. But toss out as many unnecessary tasks as you can. Only add new tasks that are really important. And be sure to move around the tasks to see if there are better ways to organize them."

After giving those instructions, you can take off.

Friday morning arrives. You tell the team, "Now, put this all into practice. Agree on your goals. Self-assign roles and responsibilities. Determine when you need to be together onsite, and when you don't. Make sure everything aligns with the organization's mission, vision, and strategy. And be sure to agree how you, the team, will continually align throughout the project."

Of course, this is just a thought exercise. Or is it?

In a session during the Business Insider Workplace Evolution virtual conference[6] in early 2021, Karl Preissner, Procter & Gamble's HR Director of Global Equality and Inclusion, said that P&G was shifting to a model where teams throughout the company would decide when and where they would work, based on their individual and collective work and personal needs. Along the way, Preissner said, the company was redesigning systems like parental leave to ensure that any bias was removed that could disadvantage workers trying to leverage the new model of flexibility.

By focusing the team on problem-centric work, team members are encouraged to demonstrate the agency needed to continually self-realign their efforts on an ongoing basis.

One way to rapidly encourage psychological diversity in your organization is to build cross-functional problem-solving teams. Bridge across the silos in your organization, pull together people from very different divisions and roles to focus on new and difficult problems, and see what sparks you can catalyze.

Why Young People Want to Solve Problems with Purpose

Let's look at the problem-solving mindset from a completely different lens: that of purpose. I'm often asked by those who lead organizations: Why do all these young people walk in the door of my company and start asking about purpose?

Under the Old Rules of Work, when you first enter the world of work, your goal is usually to make money. So the problem you most want to solve is to find out **what you can be paid for**. After a while, you realize you get paid better if you do **what you are good at**. In the Old Rules, that might have been enough to give you meaning. So what if you didn't love it? It's work.

As my father talked about in *Parachute*, there are problems that you love to solve, and skills that you love to use. So in addition to being paid well and being good at it, you also want **work that you love**. And again, for many people, that might be enough.

> "Why do all these young people walk in the door of my company and start asking about purpose?"

But there is a fourth element. Often much later on in their careers, perhaps even when they're retired, some people get a sense of purpose or meaning if they are also doing **what the world needs**, if they are solving problems that benefit other people or the planet. And in the latter half of the 20th century, *work you love* and *work the world needs* were New Rules.

The entire four-part model is known as *Ikigai,* and is usually represented (of course) as a Venn diagram. Ikigai is widely practiced in Japan, and especially on the island of Okinawa. In fact, as author Dan Buettner detailed in his book *Blue Zones,*[7] the people of Okinawa are some of the longest-lived on the planet. And they believe that a life is not well lived unless all four of these work mindsets are practiced.

But waiting late in a career to go full Ikigai means a lot of delayed gratification. So many young people around the world are flipping the sequence. They leave high school or vocational school or college, and they want to do **what the world needs.** If they can do that, it will be **work that they love.** If they can do work they love, they will keep working at it until they get **good at it.** And if they can get really good at it, they will be **paid better for it.**

Since in Silicon Valley we tend to see many sets in a group of functional layers known as a "stack," Figure 4.3 shows what that would look like.

This is why many young people walk into your organization, and immediately want to know its purpose. It's because they want

FIGURE 4.3 Ikigai as a Stack

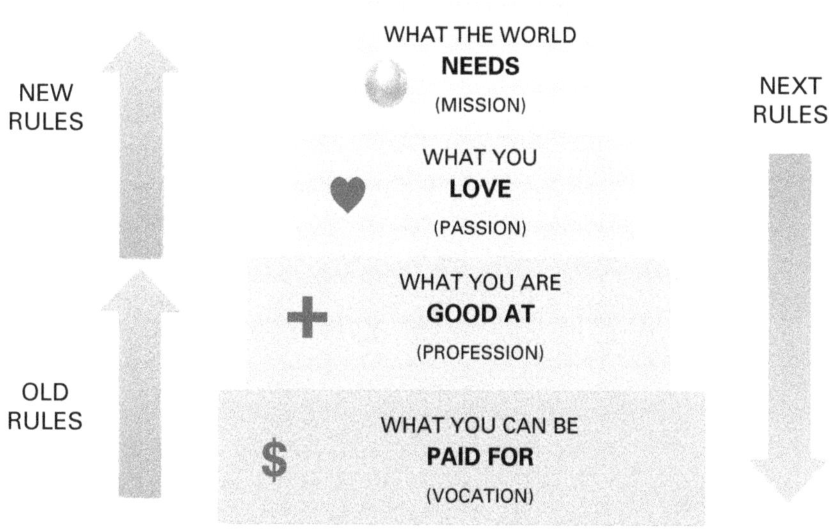

NEW RULES
OLD RULES
WHAT THE WORLD NEEDS (MISSION)
WHAT YOU LOVE (PASSION)
WHAT YOU ARE GOOD AT (PROFESSION)
WHAT YOU CAN BE PAID FOR (VOCATION)
NEXT RULES

SOURCE © 2021 Charrette LLC. Used by permission.

to do what they believe the world needs, and they don't want to wait for it.

When it comes to purpose, there are actually two completely different kinds of problems that people solve: the problems you choose, and the problems that choose you. If you were born into poverty, or with a physical or cognitive challenge, or in a refugee camp, you didn't choose to have those problems. Those problems chose you. So some people decide that what the world needs is people to help those whom the world has chosen for special problems.

This mindset offers a new framing for the problems that young people increasingly want to solve. If your organization allows them to fulfill what they feel is their own mindset toward purpose, they will be focusing on the problems they are most obsessed with solving.

SOLVING THE BIGGEST PROBLEMS: "MOONSHOT THINKING" AND A 10X MINDSET

Once you accept that purpose is an increasingly important part of a worker's decision to work for your organization, there's an obvious next step: How big is that purpose?

As innovators in organizations work together to solve problems and create value for customers and other stakeholders, they will invariably envision solutions designed to solve the problem at a reasonable scale. After all, we tend to bias results by dialing down our expectations so that a solution is "realistic." It's a natural response, since that default mindset potentially reduces the risks of failure, minimizing potential pain.

Yet our problem-solving processes define the range of potential outcomes. By setting your sights low, you can serve to simply dial down the likelihood of a breakout success. That's as true for personal career decisions as it is for developing solutions to complex problems for your organization's stakeholders.

But what if instead your mindset was to continually scale your solutions? What if you could focus on solving bigger and bigger problems?

Suppose you and your team work with a set of stakeholders to define a problem, like helping a group of a dozen customers who regularly need to get from one location to another a few hundred miles away. In a world of disruptive technology, you might envision a self-driving bus that could run a predefined route. That might already seem like a pretty mind-blowing solution.

But once you and the team go through that kind of design exercise, what if you turned to the team and said, "How can we '10x' this?"

Your team might return to the whiteboard with a stack of sticky notes, and start thinking about alternatives, such as a *flying* autonomous bus that would cut the travel time by 75 percent. That may sound like a science-fiction solution. But dozens of manufacturing companies, from large-scale airplane manufacturers to nimble startups, are all working on exactly this kind of product.

A "moonshot mindset" continually pushes to expand the pace and scale of a solution in the design phase, temporarily ignoring what is "possible" given current knowledge, and instead working to envision solutions without traditional constraints. Aiming lower inevitably means you'll scale to a smaller solution. That may be necessary once you understand the constraints of time, money, and information. But don't bias that result by limiting it to what you know about today.

Moonshot thinking approaches the problem from a completely different mindset. Elon Musk didn't ask, "How can I make existing government contractors make better rocket ships?" Instead, he envisioned what it might take to make private space flight a reality.

Think of this approach as dramatically expanding the organization's "portfolio of innovation." We'll explore the toolset for this kind of scaling in Chapter 8 when we cover techniques like inclusive design thinking and rapid prototyping.

For more on moonshot thinking and the 10x mindset, check out Peter Diamandis's book *Abundance*,[8] as well as *Exponential Organizations: Why new organizations are ten times better, faster, and cheaper than yours (and what to do about it)*,[9] by ExO Works CEO Salim Ismail and co-authors.

As we'll see in the next two chapters, organizations can dramatically increase mindset and skills alignment by changing the process of connecting people to the problems of the organization, and to the value to be created for stakeholders.

PART THREE

Skillset

Empower
Effectiveness

Problem-solving

Competence Decisiveness

Speedy Sense of Follow-
urgency through

Guiding Inspiring Unbossing

Collab- Curiosity
orating Humility

Perceptiveness Communicating Learning

Adaptive Coaching **Creative**

Encouraging Empowering Teaching

Group Leading Self-
brain- Supporting knowing
storming Synthesizing Mentoring

Analyzing

Compassion

Connecting Listening

Using insight Including

Empathy

Encourage
Alignment

Enable
Growth

Ensure
Involvement

FIGURE P3 The Next Rules: Skillset

05

The Skills of Next Organizations

The word "leadership" is losing its meaning. Thinking of *leading* as a skillset helps to better prepare people throughout the organization to take charge to solve problems and create value. That means anyone can, and should, lead.

There are specific skills for those who lead to *empower effectiveness, enable growth, ensure involvement,* and *encourage alignment.* There are excellent examples of Next Organizations that excel at each of these skillsets.

Those who lead in the organization must dedicate themselves to maximizing human skillsets by increasing the understanding of the range of human skills in the organization and reducing the friction of movement within its worknet. The best way to increase the power of its worknet is to hack the hiring process. And remember, every talented worker is a multifaceted human who needs the conditions necessary to thrive.

Magic Wand Time

I wave a magic wand, and suddenly you have the power to start an organization of 100,000 people. From scratch. Overnight.

Who will you hire? *How* will you hire them? What skillset will you hire for?

What you're trying to figure out, of course, is how to manage risk. How could you know if the people you want to hire actually have the skillset you need? To factor for that risk, would you simply hire people who look and think like you? Is that likely to lead to the success you want?

After deep thought, you gain the insight that you have approached the problem with the wrong mindset. You realize this isn't about you.

Instead, it's about the first people you will bring in. Together, you will define the organization's core values, and its key stakeholders, starting with customers or other core constituents, which should include workers, partners, suppliers, the communities where you will operate, and the planet. And, yes, shareholders, but not to the exclusion of the others. You will also define the sustainable value to be created for those stakeholders.

Now you can define the skillset you need. By defining the anchors of the organization, the skillsets you'll need become far more obvious.

All of these founding principles are *fractal*. Without those anchors, your process is untethered. The risk of hiring people who aren't aligned with the organization explodes. Fault-line fissures inevitably spawn fatal fractures. Your efforts to hire the skillsets you require will be deeply hampered.

But with these processes, your "first principles" will echo in every hire, every promotion, every training class, every major decision, every meeting. It will send all of the signals needed to help all stakeholders to understand what successful behavior means to this organization—and, most critically, the skills the organization needs to achieve its goals.

Redefining the Role of Those Who Lead in Organizations

I've already pointed out that there is a growing and justifiable backlash against the "leadership industry," the global business infrastructure dedicated to creating the leaders of today and tomorrow. It isn't that we don't need leadership. It's that we need to throw away the mindset that leadership is binary, that you are either a leader of an organization or you are not. That's why I try to avoid talking about "leaders of organizations," and instead talk about "leading *in* organizations." That's the mindset whether you sit at the "top" of a traditional hierarchy, or in the people fabric of a "leaderless organization," or somewhere in between.

Every organization has structures defined by two kinds of power: positional power and personal power. Positional power comes from an explicit or implicit hierarchy, a slot in an organization chart. When you walk into a meeting, you know pretty quickly who has the most positional power, because everyone else continually watches them for social cues, and repeatedly defers to their decisions.

But those who lead *in* organizations often have far less positional power and far more personal power. Their insights are frequently sought, but not considered to be holy writ. They often embody the culture of the organization, reinforcing its values. They can make decisions, of course, but often only when a consensus process fails or when urgency requires it.

That's the *mindset* of those who lead in organizations. Now let's talk about the *skillset*.

Rather than teaching a flexible skillset that could help to empower and amplify the work of team members, Old Rules Organizations often took the industrial-era command-and-control model of supervision and simply updated it to function in the modern office. That model included obsession with process over results, treating workers as resources owned by the manager, and prioritizing performance and productivity over maximizing human potential. The inevitable result was a systemic lack of trust, inspiration, and engagement.

I know that sounds harsh. But remember that Gallup says only about a third of all US workers are engaged in their work. And in its *State of the American Manager*[1] report, Gallup found that the vast majority of the difference in engagement scores—70 percent—*comes from the worker's relationship with their direct manager*. So if you believe that your workers are disengaged, you probably don't have to look farther than the way your organization crafts the role of the typical manager.

Perhaps even more concerning, Gallup said that only about a third of US managers are *themselves* engaged in their work. It's disengagement, all the way down.

For a clear example of the state of trustless management, look at how few organizations had work-from-home policies before the global pandemic. I mentioned before that companies like IBM and Yahoo that once had those policies often cancelled them, or limited them to a small number of roles and workers. But the Great Reset of 2020 forced managers to trust, overnight. Result: the head-slapping insight that people are for the most part responsible and committed. It turns out the failure was often in the way we trained managers to help lead those teams.

So what is the Next Skillset for someone who guides the work of a team? You guessed it: empowering effectiveness, enabling growth, ensuring involvement, and encouraging alignment. The four core Next Rules, each as flex and self skillsets.

A Skillset for Empowering Effectiveness

- Flex skills for effectiveness include *communicating* clear expectations, *guiding* workers and teams to solve problems, *coaching* to improve effectiveness, and *leading* when clear direction is needed.

- Self skills include *competence* to model professionalism, *courage* to provide honest and constructive feedback, *consistency* to exhibit the behaviors you suggest, *decisiveness* to model leading, and *urgency* when people indicate they need a kickstart.

Here's an example of a company working to empower effectiveness:

Remember that in Chapter 3 we talked about **"unbossing"** as a mindset. Novartis shows how it also appears as a skillset.

As he talked about Novartis's cultural transformation, Markus Graf, their global head of talent, told me that "if we continued as in the past, we wouldn't be successful in our mission." So the company committed to drive large-scale cultural change for three new core skills: inspiring, curiosity, and unbossing.

Inspiring and curiosity were necessary to ensure that people could be self-motivated and continually develop new abilities. "We need to recognize that a lot of skills will become redundant very quickly," Markus says. "We need to double down on creativity, and coming up with new ideas." And unbossing is actually a skill family that includes empowering workers to make decisions and encouraging individual and team problem-solving.

As part of the initiative, the company removed its former performance ratings system, focusing on learning journeys and personal growth. "People are greater than numbers," Markus said. "They showcase the cultural change."

WHY CALL IT "EFFECTIVENESS," AND NOT "PERFORMANCE"?

"You guys failed," said the Silicon Valley CEO. "You're a B team. B players. Too many people here are B or C players, so today we are releasing some of you to have the opportunity to work at our sister companies here in the valley."

"Performance." "High-performing team." "Low performer." Each of these terms can be divisively emotion-coded.

In its most appropriate use, "performance" can simply refer to the ability of a worker to meet their own and others' expectations. With a positive mindset, performance metrics offer workers clear goals and can encourage healthy competition. A sales team angling for a bonus knows exactly the target it's shooting for. Mild pressure to perform can be channeled into good-natured jockeying for rewards, especially when everyone hired into the organization knows the culture they signed up for.

But an obsession with performance can just as easily create a toxic culture. The language of the organization becomes binary, separating teams and workers into "high performance" or "low performance." Several Silicon Valley companies famously promoted their practice of regularly laying off the "bottom 15 percent" of their workforce, like bilge water jettisoned from the back of a boat. Relentless focus on performance can also enforce a "short-termism" mindset tied to quarterly reporting, placing the organization's shareholders in sole control of the driver's seat.

Enron was a "high-performance" company, until its toxic culture was exposed.

"Effectiveness" provides a different lens on goals and achievement. It's anchored in a set of constantly updated agreements about what each worker and team is trying to accomplish, which should include not just near- and long-term goals, but explicit alignment to the organization's strategic goals, as well as personal development and human thriving. An internal free-agent innovator who sparks creativity anywhere they go in the organization can be just as effective in their own right as a salesperson who exceeds a quarterly target.

Incidentally, the quote above is from Walter Isaacson's book, *Steve Jobs.*[2] It's in the text of Jobs' announcement of a 25 percent layoff at an Apple company division. Throughout the years there have been frequent micro-kitchen conversations in Silicon Valley companies as to whether Jobs encouraged breakthrough results because of, or despite, his famous high-performance pressure tactics.

I'd rather ask a different question: How can someone who leads help other people to be just as effective as someone like Jobs was—without the side effects of toxic, performance-obsessed leadership?

A Skillset for Enabling Growth

- Flex skills for enabling growth include *supporting* people in their growth journeys, *teaching* new skills and perspectives, and *intuiting* when people need help.

- Self skills include *perceptiveness* to see the potential in others, *supportiveness* as others learn, and *patience* to help others achieve their potential.

Many of those who lead say they want theirs to be a **learning** organization. But learning isn't just a mindset. It's also a specific skillset.

Vidya Krishnan is the chief learning officer for the 100,000-employee communications giant Ericsson. Born in Bangalore, India, and growing up in New Jersey as the daughter of engineers, Vidya told me that she first saw the power of education to change lives as a teenage camp counselor. At Ericsson, that translates into a deep commitment to learning throughout the organization. "We are building tomorrow's technology today," she said. "Our expertise is everything."

Ericsson's inspiring mantra: zero tolerance for zero learning.

In fact, the company has an inspiring and positive mindset statement: zero tolerance for zero learning. Every worker must have a personal learning plan, and if they don't, that failure is treated as the responsibility of the worker's manager. That's key, because it bakes commitment to the growth process into the incentives of each team guide.

"Every employee establishes a personal learning development plan each year," Vidya told me, "and empowering this development is treated as the responsibility of the manager, company, and employee—called the 'partnership of three'—emphasizing leaders as learning drivers."

RESKILLING, UPSKILLING, OUTSKILLING, AND OTHER OLD LABELS OF WORK

There's no denying we all need to be lifelong learners. The pace and scale of change mean that the shelf life of information in many fields is shrinking. As a 2012 article[3] in *Harvard Business Review* by John Hagel, Bill Eggers, and Owen Sanderson of Deloitte showed, the shelf life of information was already decaying rapidly. They cited research showing the average value of a four-year degree was five years—in other words, about one year longer than it took to learn it. That doesn't mean that everything you learned in college will be out of date that quickly. But the *know* skills you gained in your field are likely to keep changing so rapidly that you must continually gather more information, simply to remain current. Think of it like a milk carton: Your college degree has a sell-by date.

In hi-tech, the shelf life of information can be even shorter. Sebastián Espinosa, managing director of San Jose, California-based programmer camp Coding Dojo, told me an example of just how fast. Sebastián said that Coding Dojo can take someone who has barely touched a keyboard, put them through a week-long intake program, teach them three full-stack web programming languages in four months, and within six months after graduating, 90 percent of his graduates will have found a job that pays $90,000 a year or better. However, Sebastián says that if a graduate doesn't keep on learning, the knowledge they gathered in the camp will be out of date within 15 months.

The result of such rapid change is the need for constant retraining. But that can be especially difficult in the face of the scale of change, as workers with older skillsets may need to make bigger and bigger leaps to their next work. Think of all the skills required to repair mechanical assembly line equipment in a factory. Now think of all the skills needed to become an artificial intelligence programmer. The skills overlap is extremely small. So someone repairing mechanical equipment might need significant schooling to become proficient at developing AI software. It's not that it's impossible. But it might not even be a good use of their talents, especially if they truly enjoy working with their hands.

Now think instead of the skillset between factory hardware repair and, say, a wind turbine repair technician. There is actually a significant skills overlap, meaning that the training could be done in a reasonably short time, and the worker could be making money much more rapidly than attempting to become a programmer.

Many call this training process reskilling (if the new job seems similar), upskilling (if the new job seems like a "higher" set of skills), sideskilling (if it's in a different division but a similar job level), or outskilling (if the learner is likely to go to another job or company). I've even heard "de-skilling" used to signify unlearning the Old Rules of a work role so newer rules could be learned.

I'm not a fan of any of those labels. They sound like the industrial-era mindset we need to leave behind us, things that are done to you, not by you. They sound painful. And they also betray bias. Who decides if a learning process is "up" or "down"?

There is nothing wrong with calling it training or retraining. We've been doing training for a long time. Most people don't mind training, which can either be something you proactively seek, or something provided to you. "Learning" isn't bad, either. But "skilling" someone at best sounds like a poorly balanced dynamic.

What will inevitably happen is that training will increasingly shift to just-in-time and just-in-context learning. Workers will gain new skills as they need them, and they will learn those skills in the context of problem-solving in real-world situations, such as apprenticeships and project-based learning.

A Skillset for Ensuring Involvement

- Flex skills for involvement include *inspiring* others to become engaged and achieve their goals, *connecting* with people who have widely varying mindsets, *listening* to understand the lived experience of others, and *empowering* workers to have agency.

- Self skills include *insightfulness* about the motivations of others, *responsiveness* to the needs of others, and *compassion* for the challenges of others.

There is substantial focus on the skillsets needed to encourage diversity, equity, and inclusion in organizations. And if there is one skill for those who lead that stands out here, it's **compassion**.

Leading compassionately may sound like a nicety. But human-centric management is a logical response to the increasingly dehumanizing effects of the mechanization of work. Some think the goal is simply to care about workers. But as Jeff Weiner, the former CEO of LinkedIn, has put it, "Compassion is caring plus action."

Jeff is a passionate advocate for compassionate leadership. Unique to the social media industry, LinkedIn has largely avoided the negative press received by its peer companies. As a testament to his ability to lead, Jeff was ranked in the top 10 CEOs on Glassdoor.

In a 2018 commencement speech at the Wharton School of the University of Pennsylvania,[4] Jeff said that he had an epiphany when he realized he had been leading the organization with a style that actually disempowered people:

> I vowed that as long as I'd be responsible for managing other people,
> I would aspire to manage compassionately. That meant pausing,
> and being a spectator to my own thoughts, especially when getting
> emotional. It meant walking a mile in the other person's shoes;
> and understanding their hopes, their fears, their strengths and their
> weaknesses. And it meant doing everything within my power to set
> them up to be successful... I've now been practicing this approach for
> well over a decade. And I can tell you with absolute conviction that
> managing compassionately is not just a better way to build a team, it's a
> better way to build a company.

That perspective was seconded to me by best-selling author Adam Grant, who frequently is rated the most popular instructor at the same school. When I asked him about the three most important characteristics for someone who leads an organization, his response was, "Confident humility, mental flexibility, and compassion."

You can train workers to develop the skill of compassion. But it must be practiced by those who lead the organization, and it must be linked to people processes ranging from regular management conversations to the compensation of those who lead.

A Skillset for Encouraging Alignment

- Flex skills for aligning include *inspiring* others by the mission and vision for the organization, *analyzing* to understand disparate needs in a team, *synthesizing* to help bridge together those perceptions, and *building trust* to help team members work together.

- Self skills include *perceptiveness* to understand disparate and potentially conflicting points of view, *diplomacy* to balance emotional and ego needs, and *objectivity* to ensure that all voices are heard.

When two or more people work together, they can rapidly get out of sync. So it's no surprise that as organizations scale, opportunities for misalignment abound. They stop communicating effectively, they stop agreeing on consistent goals, and they can actually start working against the strategic goals of the organization. Especially as a workforce becomes a worknet, with soft walls and fluid teams, **aligning** must become a natural and automatic practice for any Next Organization.

I think of the workgroup software company Asana as the poster child for aligning.

To remain continuously aligned, Asana's chief operating officer, Chris Farinacci, told me that the company runs six-month sprints it calls Episodes. At the end of an Episode, the majority of Asana's workers conduct a rapid company-wide strategy review. What were we trying to accomplish for the past six months? How did we do? What do we need to do in the next six months? Go.

Taking so much time out of the year for strategy alignment for so many workers may seem like a high cost. But imagine the same process in any relationship, whether it's a marriage, or a large group of voters. Alignment is about a set of agreements on what matters, and how stakeholders all will do their part to achieve what matters, on an ongoing basis.

That process is best done if it's performed "bottom up," with teams and workgroups responsible for alignment and real-time clarity. "Our founding principal was, if this is going to work, it can't be top down," Chris says. In the past, "the tools were never for the whole team. We're providing value for the whole team, and then scale from there."

Chris says that Asana focuses on three simple practices: purpose, plan, responsibility. What is the purpose of the activity we're doing? What is the simplest plan we need to design to succeed? Who will take responsibility for which aspects of the project? In fact, virtually every area of focus in the company has someone who takes the lead as a decision-maker on that topic. Rather than the continuous overhead of jockeying for political position, or trying to figure out who in the room can make a decision, the lead on each issue is sought out for a decision—a great example of personal power.

Think of this approach as an alignment engine. Rapid review cycles, constant communication, and aligning every initiative with the organization's strategic goals, together ensure continuous alignment, even at scale.

There is a complementary toolset to this skillset. In Chapter 8, we'll talk about one of the increasingly common ways to manage performance through alignment, OKRs (or objectives and key results), and how these kinds of tools can be adapted to the varying needs of Next Organizations, as well as KPIs, the key performance indicators that provide data about results.

> **Try This: Flash problem-solving camp.** If you want to practice your Next Rules skillset, find an important but relatively "boxed" problem in your organization, a problem on which nobody is currently focusing. Send out a call through the organization to find four or five people willing to spend a few hours in the next few weeks to solve it. Don't spend much time defining the problem, or even the skillset needed to solve it. Let the "coalition of the willing" dive in. Empower them to ask for help on anything—methodology, additional skills, etc. Just keep the timeframe short, a few hours at most, and be sure the team debriefs on the process afterward.
>
> If a project succeeds in launching, replicate it, and publish why it worked. If a project fails to launch, celebrate and publish those learnings, too. The insights will help others to avoid any errors in the future.

Maximizing the Skillset of the Organization: The Inside Gig

We have focused so far on the skillset of those who lead, from those who guide teams to those who guide the entire organization. Those who lead also have the responsibility to empower the most effective use and development of the skills of all the workers across the organization's worknet.

Kelley Steven-Waiss is the co-author of *The Inside Gig: How sharing untapped talent across boundaries unleashes organizational capacity.*[5] She is the former CHRO of HERE Technologies, a

9,000-employee "location cloud" company that offers geographical data and mapping services, and is the founder and CEO of Hitch Works, Inc., an enterprise software company focused on human skills, which Kelley incubated at HERE before spinning it out.

Kelley realized that there were two major challenges with the way that organizations historically have managed human skills. First, most organizations have few effective methods for inventorying all of the skills, experiences, hobbies, and interests of their workers, so they don't actually know all of the human potential of their worknets. As we will see in Chapter 8, that's partly because few of us know our own skills, so the organization is likely to know even less about us. But few organizations are actually committed to conducting that inventory. They usually take a worker's skillset at face value, looking only at the skills for which the organization believes it hired the worker in the first place.

This is why I tell those who lead in organizations that their worknet is "an iceberg" to them, with only a tiny portion of worker skills visible above the waterline.

FIGURE 5.1   The Skills Iceberg

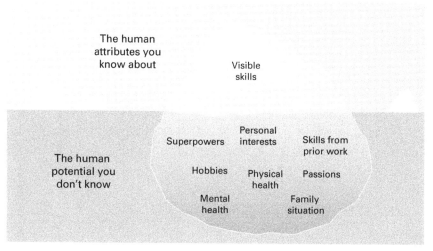

Suppose you run a manufacturing company, and you've decided you want to create new products for artists and musicians. You could spend a lot of money doing expensive market research to find potential customers to participate in design thinking exercises. But what if you knew that you already had dozens of artists and musicians working for your organization, in roles that had nothing to do with music or art? You could conduct "flash" design thinking exercises at a moment's notice, speeding your time to market, designing better products, and giving your workers the chance to use more of their human potential.

"The first deliverable is to get visibility to your skills supply chain," Kelley told me. "That's the first step to understanding. Are we going to have a build or a buy strategy?" That is, can you get the skillset you want solely through inventorying and developing your current group of talent? Or do you need to hire that skillset? For example, when she was at HERE, Kelley said, "We needed more artificial intelligence and data visioning people. The only way we could understand how we could build [that capacity] is to understand what skills we already have."

The second problem Kelley identified is that managers in organizations often treat people like personally owned assets. If you hired someone into a well-paid position, you probably worked very hard over a period of weeks or months to find, hire, and onboard them. Ideally, that worker's skillset should be usable anywhere they can solve problems for the organization's stakeholders. But if you "lose" that worker to a new project or job in another group, you've "lost" the time you invested in them, and you have to start the hiring process all over again. Because of that anticipated pain, you do everything you can to "keep" the worker under your domain.

Yet remember that the new mindset for Next Organizations is no longer that you have a workforce, but a *worknet*. Workers need to be able to continuously and dynamically bind around problems, throughout the organization, wherever there can be an optimized fit. If you have metaphorically chained a worker to a desk, you're the only one who wins. The worker loses, because they can't grow and learn from that new opportunity. And the organization loses, because that worker's skillset can't be applied to what could potentially be a more important problem. That's a poor optimization of skillsets and problems, for all involved.

How do you solve it? "The number one hurdle is leadership mindset. There has to be a commitment to say, we're going to have a new way of working, called talent sharing. Talent is owned by the company, and not by the manager," Kelley said. "When I talk about the [internal] talent marketplace, you visualize all the talent on one side, and the work on the other side. It's all buyers and sellers. It's about opening leadership mindsets." As we'll see in Chapter 7, it's also a toolset: software like Hitch that helps to ensure involvement across the organization.

The opportunity to maximize skillset involvement and alignment extends beyond the borders of the organization. In *The Human Cloud*,[6] authors Matthew Mottola and Matthew Coatney detail the advantages from sourcing through online work markets, as well as the opportunities for "changemakers" to find project-based work. Some think of this as the Hollywood model, where teams of independent workers are brought together on a project basis, then disband and re-band for a new project.

Organizations that already function the most like worknets are large consulting firms. They have a portfolio of talented people with a range of skills, and a portfolio of client problems. Consulting firms are continually honing their understanding of client problems, creating flash teams that dynamically bind around those problems, and continually optimizing that changing landscape. Organizations in other industries can take away valuable lessons about maximizing self-driven matching between skillsets and projects.

Hiring Is the Key to the Next Skillset

Where and how will you find the skillsets for today and tomorrow? By completely rethinking the hiring process.

There is no more important inflection point at the intersection of the worker and the team with the organization than how, when, and who you hire. So let's treat hiring as a problem to be solved, based on the four core Next Rules: effectiveness, growth, involvement, and alignment:

> You are a team guide for a dozen workers, each of whom is also working on a project for at least one other team around the organization.

> You ask one of your team members (not you) to lead a design thinking exercise to look at the problems that the team needs to regularly solve—anchored, of course, in an alignment process directly connected to the organization's strategy and purpose. It becomes clear to all of you that there is a set of problems that are not being addressed, and that the bandwidth and skillset of the team is not currently sufficient. You collectively brainstorm the ideal characteristics for a candidate, including the kind of aligned mindset, ideal existing skillset (flex, self, and know skills), and ideal toolset proficiency. You prioritize those requirements (mindset comes first, of course) then run an anti-bias software scan of those characteristics, redesigning requirements that could have advantaged candidates with the same backgrounds as the team.

> The team breaks the problem set into several micro-projects—the most important being, of course, a micro-project to ensure the team really understands the problem to be solved in the first place. You then leverage the organization's worknet, placing the micro-projects into the fabric of internal and external connections. You get back a series of responses, continually feeding them through anti-bias filters. The team (not you) chooses three candidates to take on three different paid micro-projects, two of whom it turns out are based in developing economies halfway around the world. That works well, because it means they can be working when you're not.

> It so happens that one candidate is a phenomenal talent that one of your team members met through a community organization they were mentoring. The candidate is so good at the micro-project, the team immediately decides to increase the contractor's project load. You also ask the worker to complete their own Aristotle Canvas, so you can see how you align. It becomes clear that the worker's personal development path is highly aligned with your team and the organization.

Within a few months you, your team, and the new worker are co-creating a work role. You all agree that a full-time committed work relationship makes sense for all, and the new worker shifts to a commitment agreement with a flexible set of terms that benefit the worker, the team, and the organization. They continue working from their home country.

By this process, you have ensured *involvement* by following an inclusive process; *alignment*, by sending strong signals about what the organization's stakeholders and your team need; *effectiveness* by co-creating a work role where the worker can be successful; and *growth* by ensuring the worker's own development path and the team's role and needs are aligned.

(Of course, the appropriate worker might have been sourced from within the organization itself. That also means, of course, that your team workers are themselves available to work on other projects throughout the organization—an opportunity you welcome, because it enhances their skillsets, expands their worknet connections, and identifies new problems to solve.)

What did we just do? We reduced risk, and increased opportunity, for the worker, for the team, and for the organization.

Old Rules hiring is mainly about risk management. If you had 100 percent certainty that the first candidate you spoke with would meet every expectation, you would look no further. Risk reduced to zero. Hire the first person to walk through the virtual or physical door.

> Let's face it. Hiring is really all about reducing risk.

Of course, no such certainty exists. A frequently cited US Department of Labor study suggests a poorly aligned hire commonly costs at least 30 percent of the worker's annual salary. Organizations respond to that risk by reinforcing the Old Rules of Work, requiring a two-year, four-year, or advanced degree, or a mythical number of years of experience. In *Parachute*, my father called the hiring process "reading the tea leaves," with the hirer as a fortune-teller trying to guess the possible future if they hire the candidate (though it may actually be more like palm-reading, anticipating what the candidate will actually do). That's why an inclusive hiring process must be deliberately designed to reduce the risk of misalignment, both for the hirer and the worker.

Hiring Mindset Over Skillset

Let's say you don't have this kind of inclusive hiring process in place. What's the Next Rules solution? For many work roles, concentrate more on hiring for mindset than on hiring for skillset.

In the iconic management fable *The Five Temptations of a CEO*,[7] author Pat Lencioni devised a number of insightful suggestions to help those who lead in organizations to understand their own challenges and opportunities, and new ways to articulate how to get the best out of those who work in those organizations. My favorite was a simple construct of his. Pat called this cultural fit versus performance fit. I've taken the liberty of adapting this to mindset alignment versus skillset alignment.

FIGURE 5.2   Aligned Skillset and Mindset

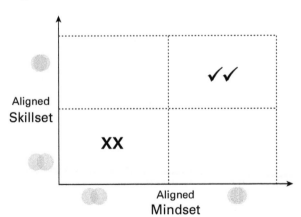

SOURCE © 2021 Charrette LLC. Used by permission.

In the Old Rules of Work, hiring is often focused on *performance fit.* Does a job candidate have the experience that would lead the hiring manager to believe the worker will be successful in the role? In that context, the worker is being assessed for "fit," as if the job is a hole for which the peg-shaped worker is being assessed.

Yet a relentless focus on performance leaves out the most important factor: the worker's mindset, and alignment with the mindset of the organization and the team. When mindsets are aligned, everyone has clear agreement for what constitutes success.

Notice I don't call this "fit," which is often seen from the perspective of the organization. If you don't "fit," you are the problem. But "alignment" is a balanced table. If the worker's and the organization's values, needs, and abilities align, you have a good match. If they aren't aligned, nobody is at fault. But it's not a good idea for either the worker or the organization if they continue to be out of alignment.

To paraphrase management guru Peter Drucker, "Mindset eats skillset for lunch." If you have the skillset, but not the mindset, it's very likely there will be a substantial cultural mismatch. If you have all of the mindset, but not yet all of the skillset, you'll crawl through broken glass to develop the ability to solve the problem.

We will talk more about tools to enable that alignment in Chapters 7 and 8. For now, think of skillset alignment as the perception that a worker has the capacity to execute the work for which they are needed *or can learn them rapidly*; the organization can offer the opportunity for the worker to use the skillset the worker most loves to use and is best at; and the worker has the capacity to continually develop those skills.

Beyond Skills: Human Thriving

Our focus on skills shouldn't blind us to the fact that there is far more about us as humans than just our abilities. According to Brian Kropp, group vice president at the Gartner research firm:

We used to think about our employees as the people who happened to be working for us. If we paid them, everything was fine. Now there are *human beings* who happen to be working for us. Employees and people are separate things. Our employees have a life, and work is a sub-component of that life. How do we help them have a better life, not just "a better work"?

Until the global pandemic, the mindset of the Old Rules of Work simply reinforced the iceberg model in many organizations. Those who lead organizations had little incentive to know much about the whole person working with you. As workers were suddenly forced to become distributed, it was an epiphany for many for the first time who could peer into their peers' homes and lives. "You have kids?" "What's the cat's name?" "You have a sick parent living with you?"

> As Brian Kropp of Gartner asks, "How do we help people have a better life, not just 'a better work'?"

Of course, some workers following the Old Rules may prefer the anonymity of the iceberg model, where the organization is only aware of the worker's known skillset, and nothing more. Just show up, do your work, keep your private life private. That's certainly their prerogative. But what will they do when something bad happens, and they need a co-worker to cover while they visit a sick parent in the hospital? How can they ask for time to go to a kid's soccer game, if the team doesn't even know they have kids?

Another breakthrough insight of the modern pandemic era is about our health. Many organizations don't go any farther than providing mandated contributions to health insurance. But workers will only come to a healthy workplace, and only if they themselves are healthy. That demand forced many organizations to completely rethink everything from work-at-home policies to redesigning workplaces, cafeterias, and even elevators.

Our collective takeaway must be that Next Organizations have to engage in a holistic model of human work, committing to every individual's well-being, and understanding the circumstances of their lives. This includes:

- **Physical well-being:** Pre-COVID-19, many organizations could simply provide some kind of healthcare benefits, and leave it at that. It took a pandemic to show many who lead organizations that without physical health and safety, workers can be deeply affected.

- **Mental well-being:** The stress of isolation and lack of human contact during the pandemic led many to realize that mental health needed to be focused on directly, rather than simply being assumed.

- **Emotional well-being:** Your co-workers might never have known in the past if there was something affecting your family, such as a sick loved one. The pandemic made it clear that such a toll could have a significant impact on a worker's ability to do their job.

- **Financial well-being:** If a worker's compensation doesn't allow them to cover their bills, their life—and therefore their work—is compromized. Workers who have their hours significantly reduced, or their shifts constantly changed, will be at a constant disadvantage.

- **Spiritual well-being:** That doesn't mean intruding into a worker's beliefs. What it requires is the concern that workers feel fulfilled in their work and their lives, which often comes from alignment around meaning and purpose.

As we also discovered in the pandemic, each of us also has a set of circumstances that influence our well-being. We should all have family, a home, and friend groups. If we have children, we need childcare. If an elderly parent becomes sick, we may need more flexible work hours. We may have huge challenges dealing with the stress of isolation and constant health worries.

Next Organizations will see these issues not as a problem, but as an opportunity. By committing to the whole person, those who lead organizations have the chance to dramatically increase worker engagement and loyalty. In an era when the social contract between many employees and employers is rapidly eroding, a hirer dedicated to providing meaningful, well-paid work to every worker will gain from increased productivity and reduced turnover. You'll find you can dramatically increase the value of your organization's brand, reducing hiring costs and increasing your reputation with customers.

As Gartner's Kropp says, "It's not just about making your employees better off; it's about making your company better off."

These are all logical arguments. But treating everyone who contributes value to your organization as a whole human being is simply the right thing to do.

We Must Co-Create the New Management Together

I've called this new skillset of those who lead in unbossed organizations "guide management." I don't know of any organization that uses that label as yet. What I want to encourage is a process of co-creation to define that empowerment mindset and skillset.

When it comes to the skillset of leading, I would love to jettison the word "management" altogether, and simply focus on the work of "team guides," no matter their formal role in the organization. I have no quarrel with "managing" *projects*. "Managing" other humans, though, is where things get gnarly. But I suspect the weight of history will continually drag us back into the management realm.

There are certainly many people who crave others to tell them what to do. In my own experience, that's usually because they don't have the combination of *information* needed to solve problems, the *permission* to solve problems, and the *self-confidence* that encourages them to solve problems.

You can solve the *information* problem by referring back to the Cognitas problem-solving cognition model in Chapter 4. In a world of just-in-time and just-in-context learning, you can provide workers with the necessary toolset to rapidly and effectively collect, process, abstract, and apply critical information.

You can solve the *permission* problem by continually empowering workers and teams to make their own decisions, take risks, and always make *new* mistakes. Unboss yourself.

And if you reinforce every worker's ability and agency to solve problems, you'll have helped to solve the *self-confidence* problem.

As you'll see in the next chapter from "leaderless" organizations, many of the actual practices of guide management aren't new. But the practice of management-by-surveillance is an all-too-common default behavior when humans are suddenly placed in the role of guiding the work of other humans. It takes intentional training and coaching in a new skillset and mindset to help team leads to become team guides.

We can do that together.

From the Guide, to the Individual and the Team

Now that we've set the table for the skillset of those who lead in organizations, we can dive into the skillset of individuals and teams. These will provide many of the important building blocks for developing the critical skills of the Next Organization.

06

The Skills of Tomorrow for Workers and Teams: PACE

Which skills should workers and teams focus on developing? Four flex skills are the most important for dealing with a world of uncertainty and change: Problem-solvers who are Adaptive and Creative, with Empathy (PACE). These skills are the building blocks for functions like entrepreneurship and agency, and especially for innovation.

Key insights for your own skills, and the skills of those around you, include your portfolio of skills and their intersections, your superpowers at the intersection of what you love and what you're good at, our frequent blindness about our own skills, and the need to *learn how to learn* new skills.

Skillset is also a team sport. There are four key characteristics of skillful teams, which are especially important as teams will become increasingly distributed.

It Is the Day You Were Born

Imagine if on that day you entered the world, the hospital nurse had presented you to your parents. "Here is your beautiful child." As your proud parents hold you close, the nurse adds, "And here is your child's user manual."

Your parents look up quizzically.

The nurse holds up a book. "This manual will be the guidebook that will help the child learn Why, What, Where, When, with Who, and How they will do their best work."

The nurse begins to thumb through the manual. "You'll find here described all of the ways that your child can maximize their human potential.

"Here is the way your child's mind will work. The manual shows them what is unique about their cognition.

"Here are all the things your child will be good at throughout their life. Here are all the problems your child will love to solve. Here are the child's favorite skills.

"This part describes the kinds of people who will help the child to do their best at work and at learning. And here is a description of the kind of workplace the child will most enjoy, as an adult.

"Oh, and here is a section that talks about the meaning your child will find as an adult, the purpose your child will follow, and the fulfillment your child will find through work and throughout their time on the planet."

Your parents are amazed. What an incredible life you are going to have.

The Four Flex Skills of Tomorrow: PACE

Okay, so that probably didn't happen.

But why not? Why shouldn't there be a "user manual of you"? When you buy a digital distraction machine (also known as a mobile phone), you get a user manual. It says what the device is good at, and what it isn't. Why don't you have the same reference for you?

Since nobody gave you a user manual, you had to just go ahead and develop skills. I hope you got lots of help along the way, from family and teachers and friends and co-workers and mentors. But for many of us, we were never explicitly shown *how* to develop skills, nor which skills would best help us to navigate a world of uncertainty.

All that has changed. Welcome to the Age of Human Skills.

A cottage industry of consultants and researchers has appeared suggesting what the most in-demand "future skills" will be. Many of these studies focus on know skills, and point to bodies of knowledge like machine learning/artificial intelligence programming and neuroscience. These may well be highly sought after in, say, 20 years. But just as Tom Friedman pointed out the unpredictability of the number of jobs in the future, the same uncertainty is true about specific fields.

Parents ask me all the time: What field should my adult kid go into that will be safe from disruptive change? I honestly can't offer them any guarantees. Maybe plastic surgery. Probably not.

What *is* predictable is the need for flex and self skills. It seems everyone has an opinion about what those "21st century" or "future" skills should be. In its *The Future of Jobs Report 2020*,[1] the World Economic Forum listed analytical thinking and innovation, active learning, complex problem-solving, critical thinking, creativity, leadership, digital skills, resilience, and reasoning—all flex and self skills, and not a single know skill among them.

But though all are useful, we need to prioritize, to identify and train for the skills that will matter the most. After digesting every study on future skills I could get my hands on, and talking to numerous chief learning officers and educators, I've found that four skills continually rise to the surface.

Every single worker needs to become *a problem-solver who is adaptive and creative, with empathy.*

FIGURE 6.1   PACE

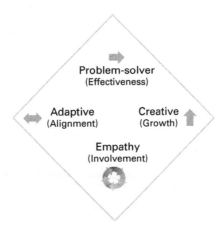

SOURCE © 2021 Charrette LLC. Used by permission.

Happily, in a world beset by the increasing pace of change, these spell PACE. And they line up quite nicely with the Next Rules.

Problem-Solver (Part of the Skillset for Effectiveness)

As we have seen repeatedly, in a world of uncertainty, the most consistently important mindset *and* skillset for any worker is to think of themselves as a problem-solver. That's why people hire you, and why you hire others: to solve problems. As we saw with the analogy of climbing a mountain, if you approach new problems with the mindset of a problem-solver, you're far more likely to be able to either leverage or develop the skillset to solve the problem. And our cognition gives us problem solving skills like gathering and synthesizing data, constructing theses, envisioning and testing solutions, and challenging assumptions.

Adaptive (Part of the Skillset for Alignment)

Adaptability is really a skill family, including thinking flexibly, rapidly iterating, and taking manageable risks. It's driven by a growth mindset that says you can continually learn new skills and methods to solve new problems.

In *The Adaptation Advantage*,[2] authors Chris Shipley and Heather McGowan offer a variety of strategies for continuous adaptation. One key is what they call the agile learning mindset, which they say includes agility, adaptability, and awareness (all flex skills), culminating in agency (a self skill). I highly recommend reviewing their book for insights into ongoing adaptation.

Creative (Part of the Skillset for Growth)

This is one skillset that will keep us ahead of the robots and software. Abilities like envisioning novel but useful solutions, integrating problem-solving strategies from disparate arenas, and designing new products in creative ways are all deeply human skills. Software can only mimic some of these processes, but we are a long way from general-purpose software that can emulate the broad range of human creative functions.

Empathy (Part of the Skillset for Involvement)

Another uniquely human skill is our ability to understand the lived experience of another human. That's critical, whether we are empathizing with a customer's problems, or with our teammates' ideas and perspectives, or with the challenges of someone who is disadvantaged in our society. Brain research studies show that empathy is typically learned (or not learned) very early in child development. It can and should be taught in later years, but ideally children receive positive reinforcement for empathetic behavior as early as possible.

Those are the four core building block skills. Here are several contexts where a PACE skillset becomes extremely valuable:

- **Entrepreneurship,** or inside the organization, intrapreneurship: What does an entrepreneur do in a startup? They first *empathize* with a customer's lived experience, then they do *creative problem-solving* for that customer's problems, and continually *adapt* as their understanding of the customer's needs changes. PACE, over and over again.

- **Agency:** The *mindset* of agency is best encouraged through the *skillset* of PACE. Since agency is *the belief that taking an action could have a positive outcome* (sometimes called "hope"), you are far more likely to believe you can climb to the top of the mountain if you've already demonstrated the skillset. By developing skills for problem-solving, adapting, creativity, and empathy, a worker's positive mindset will be reinforced, and they will be far more likely to take action to solve future problems.

- **Resilience:** In a time of continuous disruption, some people are extremely resilient, able to cope with frequent setbacks, barriers, and discontinuity. PACE provides a mindset *and* skillset that can help workers to continually understand challenges, respond to problems with a positive mindset, and solve them as effectively as possible under the circumstances. Resilience is both more critical and more possible with teams that are committed to PACE.

- **Young learning,** often occurring in school: Project-based, collaborative learning *is* PACE. Young people are coached to develop problem-solving skills, develop their creativity, continually adapt, and have empathy for those they are co-creating with—and starting the younger, the better.

- **Underadvantaged:** Workers who are differently abled, or who were born with significant socioeconomic challenges, or who are formerly incarcerated, are empowered through developing PACE skills.

And, most important to many organizations:

- **Innovation:** While some organizations think of innovation as a skillset, I think of it more as an *output* of PACE. If you have PACE workers, you'll have a more innovative organization, as they continually use their creative problem-solving skills to solve new problems.

These four core Next Skills are the key building blocks for the skillset of tomorrow. But you have many many other skills. How can you understand and develop that portfolio, and especially your "superpowers," both for yourself and for others?

Building the User Manual of You: Four Key Insights

Here are four important insights about your skills.

Insight 1: You Have a Portfolio of Skills, with Many Possible Intersections

You have a broad range of skills that you are continually developing. Some came to you naturally, while others took time, commitment, and hard work to develop. Some were useful in your prior work and are no longer skills you use regularly. Others are still in development and may provide you with new capabilities in the future.

That's a portfolio of skills. Just as an investment manager would advise you, it's important to have a set of skills you know people will reliably pay you to use. And there are others that may be more rooted in your passions, which either are not yet developed enough to make you money, or which you are just fine keeping as hobbies and interests, without the slightest motivation to provide income.

Increasingly, demand for new skillsets will be at the intersection of multiple interests. Think of this as a Venn diagram of skills, with a unique overlap between them defining a unique skillset. (In fact, remember the skills intersections of John Venn, the diagram's inventor.) If you can conceive of an overlap in your interests, no matter how esoteric, there is always a possibility that someone will pay you to do that work. Here's a real-world example.

CASE STUDY

A Nobel Prize–Winning Intersection: Sir Harry Kroto

In the mid-1980s, Harry Kroto was a talented artist in the United Kingdom who dreamed about opening up his own studio for scientific graphic design. But he was also a gifted young chemist and researcher. His team at the University of Sussex was doing some promising research about the properties of carbon atoms, which they thought could be fused into a mesh, and the resulting molecule might be able to take on a range of different shapes.

Harry was conflicted between his two loves, and thought seriously about quitting academics for art. But he decided to continue with his chemistry research to see if it might lead somewhere. That research team was subsequently credited with discovering what is now known as a *fullerene*, a chemical structure named after Buckminster Fuller, because one form of the molecule looks something like Fuller's famous geodesic domes. And in 1996, Harry's research team was awarded the Nobel Prize in Chemistry.

In 2013, Harry was invited by Google to serve as a judge for its international Google Science Fair competition. Our company, Charrette LLC, was asked to produce a Google Hangouts show to excite teens around the world about science and technology, and we invited "Sir Harry"—who by then had been knighted by the Queen—as a guest. He said during the show that at one point in their research, he had decided to create an artist's model of a fullerene molecule, and that seeing the physical conception of the atomic structure led to new insights about the molecule's properties—a skills intersection if there ever was one.

Harry passed away in 2019. But his team's Nobel Prize–winning discovery has helped fuel a range of applications in the creation of nano-materials, including the sci-fi-class material graphene, which is 100 times stronger than steel.

Intersections of skills will increasingly create new opportunities. Because skills intersections deliver such a specific set of abilities, not only is there less competition for this work, there is often far more flexibility to adapt the work to you, rather than the other way around.

Insight 2: Some of Your Skills Are Superpowers—the Intersection of What You Love and What You're Good at

One of the most important parts of your portfolio of skills is your set of abilities that sit at the intersection of the skills you're most proficient at, and the skills you most love using.

As I found out when I was trained as a career counselor in my late teens, it turns out that if we love using certain skills, and solving certain problems, we have far more motivation to improve our skills. And if we continually practice and hone those skills that we love, eventually we will not only love using those skills, but we'll be extremely proficient with those skills as well.

That's a superpower.

Of course, few people do work that is *always* the combination of what they're good at and what they love. Pretty much every work role has some aspects that aren't perfect. But our greatest satisfaction comes from developing and using our superpowers. And if you have the power to hire, you can gain great satisfaction from hiring others who can do the same.

Using your superpowers can be the time when work is the most fun. That's not usually a word people use about work. "After all,

FIGURE 6.2   What You're Good at, and What You Love Doing

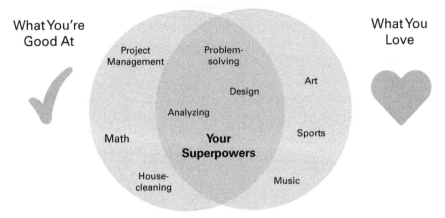

SOURCE © 2021 Charrette LLC. Used by permission.

work is work, right? It's not supposed to be fun." I hope that sounds as much like an Old Rules mindset to you as it does to me. Of course work can and should be fun, as often as possible. And when it's not, you can use your creative problem-solving skills to make it more fun.

CASE STUDY

Superpower Story: Dean Kamen, Master Innovator

Dean Kamen was born on Long Island in New York. He discovered in high school that he was a gifted innovator and inventor, and as an adult he went on to create breakthrough inventions ranging from the Segway personal transporter to a prosthetic arm. When our group Charrette LLC produced a Google Hangouts interview show for the international teen competition Google Science Fair, we invited Dean to talk about his philosophy of life to young people around the world.

We asked Dean the same question we asked all of the guests on the show. "If you could go back and give one piece of advice to your teenage self, what would it be?"

Dean responded that he would give the same advice his dad had given to him. He said that his father Jack was a gifted artist and illustrator who inspired Dean to be different. Jack encouraged his son to follow his passions, to do work that he loved, but to make sure he was proficient enough at that work so that people would pay him.

Dean obviously took his father's advice. As Dean's Wikipedia entry will attest, in the mid-1970s he was making $60,000 a year—before he graduated high school.

Insight 3: You Are an Iceberg, and Probably Blind to Many of Your Skills

In *Thinking, Fast and Slow*,[3] psychologist Dan Kahneman quite rightly points out that we are "blind to our own blindnesses." That is, we don't even know what we don't know. And, I'd add, we don't even know what we *do* know. These are both especially true for our skills. In fact, others often see our skills far better than we do.

Psychologists have had a way of thinking about this for decades. In 1955, psychologists Harrington Ingham and Joseph Luft developed the Johari Window, a "magic quadrant" image to illustrate the interaction between our own self-awareness and how others see us. Luft and Ingham said that there are characteristics that are (1) known to us about ourselves, and (2) that we don't know. And there are things that (A) others know about us, and (B) things they don't know. Your "blind spots" include skills and behaviors that others see, but you don't, and skills and behaviors that *nobody* sees, not even you—what is often called "hidden potential." You didn't know you were good at math or drawing, and neither did anyone else, until you stumbled onto it. And even then, you might have thought, "Well, anybody can do that."

Actually, no, many people can't.

CASE STUDY
Blind Spot: The Boat

In 2017, our company Charrette LLC, including our managing partner (and my wife) Heidi Kleinmaus and I, conducted a "future of work" workshop for a group of native New Zealand teens from a Maori tribe who came from the country's North Island to an innovation journey through Silicon Valley. In a workshop at Stanford University's Hasso Plattner School of Design (also known as d.school), Heidi and I led the teens through an exercise to help them understand their own skills.

We went around the room asking them to talk about a time they had solved a problem, and to explore the skills they had used. But one teenager—we'll call her Kali—simply couldn't think of an example where she had demonstrated some kind of skill. She didn't think she'd accomplished anything. (If you're a parent of an adolescent, you know the drill: Teenagers either think they know everything, or nothing. Thankfully, you and I weren't like that. Right?)

Finally, I asked her to tell a story about a time when she had done something fun, but that took a little work. Shy at first, Kali began talking about a time when she wanted to go visit a friend of hers on a neighboring island, but her parents didn't want to pay for the ferry trip.

So Kali built a boat.

My stunned response: You built a boat? How?

Showing mild exasperation at my obviously stupid question, Kali explained: You cut down a tree, you hollow it out, you treat it with resin, and so on.

Incredulous, I asked: Did it float?

Of course it floated.

To Kali, this was no big deal. Doesn't everyone know how to build a boat? But to several other teens in the workshop from a Bay Area inner-city youth program, the young woman showed a set of skills that were superpowers.

The same analogy of the iceberg that we used in Chapter 5 for the organization applies to each of us as individuals. The small amount of the iceberg sticking above the waterline are the skills you see. But there are so many skills and interests and experiences and motivations and hopes that you have either forgotten, or can't see, that are below the waterline. How can you bring them into the light?

The key to understanding your own skills is what we call self-inventory. (The Old Rules label is "assessment." But you're the only person who should be "assessing" you.) Self-inventory comes from the mindset that self-discovery allows you to understand your own strengths, interests, and goals. Yet it's necessary to do at least part of that self-discovery process with one or more other people, so you can leverage the insights of others who may be able to see a lot more of your skills that are under the waterline than you can.

We'll explore some of the toolset for self-inventory in Chapter 8.

Insight 4: You Can Learn How to Learn *Skills*

One of the greatest opportunities for our systems of childhood and adult education is not just to help people to learn, but to *learn how to learn.*

We've explored some of that process in our journey in this chapter through cognition. That complex set of functions in our heads includes a series of mechanisms that can reinforce learning, so it sticks with us for a long time. By learning *how* to learn, we can collect, process, abstract, apply, *and retain* information far more effectively.

These insights are directly useful for the process of learning and developing skills. Unless a new skill is something you find you can learn effortlessly, you will inevitably hit speed bumps on your learning path. Understanding your own reward system can help you to better craft the combination of incentives and disincentives you need to get over the bumps, and to build those longer-term memories that allow you to retain more skills.

Sometimes, of course, that process also includes *unlearning.* Guide management is a good example. If you were taught that being a manager meant you had to be the one in the room with the best answers, it may take some time to unlearn that part of the role, so you don't continue some of the less-effective behaviors, and then learn how to be the one in the room with the best questions.

Skillset as a Team Sport

Now let's apply the PACE skillset to a team.

Think of the members of a team as a group of people who all have superpowers. Just like in a superhero movie, each time the team encounters a problem, the person on the team with the most appropriate superpower should be the one to solve that problem.

Remember the key characteristics of a team, from Google's research in Project Aristotle: psychological safety, dependability, structure and clarity, meaning, and impact, to which I've added psychological diversity. These factors all establish the *context* in which a team does its work.

But what does a team actually *do*? My favorite definition of a team's actions comes from Rachel Dzombak, a research fellow at the Blum Center for Developing Economies. She points to three main characteristics for a team:[4]

- They are committed to **a common purpose**. That may be a short-term deliverable or a long-term mission.
- Their interdependence requires **coordination of their work**. That includes a responsibility for regular communication and synchronization.
- They hold themselves **mutually accountable**. They make commitments to each other, follow through on those commitments, and challenge and support each other if someone doesn't do what they say.

To these, I add a fourth for the disruption era:

- They **dynamically bind around problems**. Team members work together to understand the problem they are trying to solve, align the tasks to be performed with the most appropriate skillset on the team, and co-create the solution to the problem.

CASE STUDY

Band of Minds: Those Who Lead at Avito

I mentioned earlier that Vladimir Pravdivy, CEO of the Russian online marketplace Avito, has one of the most psychologically diverse sets of leading executives I've met. Imagine having a team where:

- The head of organizational development is a former management consultant.
- The general manager of the automobile business unit is a trained mathematician.
- The chief people officer is a sociologist from Siberia.
- The CTO has a PhD in computer science.
- The head of corporate development has a master's degree in literature and a PhD in philosophy, and speaks five languages.

"We encourage the clash of opinions," Vladimir told me. "When two different opinions collide, they produce a thought that is much better."

It's a rare person who leads an organization that will assemble that kind of diverse thinking. But those who do will ensure that a broad range of mindsets and skillsets are continually brought together to solve the problems of the organization's stakeholders.

What are Vladimir's recommendations to others like him who lead an organization? "Keep an open mind toward the voices on your team. Embrace the diversity of their thoughts. Be hungry for new ideas, and constantly search how [you] can become better."

The PACE skillset aligns well with the characteristics and actions of a highly effective workgroup:

- Remember that **a team is a pool of problem-solvers**. (This is how teams are *effective*.) Everyone in a high-function team is an individual problem-solver. Sometimes the team will be solving a problem it knows well, but in many cases they will be approaching a new problem. If they pool their complementary problem-solving skills together, they will be far more likely to dynamically and effectively bind around the problem and solve it.

- **A team is continually adaptive.** (This is one way teams stay *aligned*.) They continually work together to understand and solve the next problem, especially when it's a unique challenge they haven't encountered before.

- **A team uses their collective creativity.** (This is how teams continually *grow*.) Even in some of the most repetitive work situations, a psychologically diverse team that practices psychological safety will have endless opportunities to use their collective creativity to solve problems more effectively, and to create a more stimulating and fun work environment.

- **Empathy.** (This is how teams continually *involve*.) Another unique human skill is our ability to understand the lived experience of another human. That's critical whether we are empathizing with a customer's problems, or with our teammates' ideas and perspectives, or with the challenges of someone who is disadvantaged in our society.

Note that I haven't used the phrases "high performance" or "high productivity" workgroups. Remember that at its worst, a performance focus can become an enabler of toxic behavior that polarizes workers into "high performers" and "low performers," disenfranchising those who don't measure up to the metrics without guaranteeing the support to improve. And also, at its worse, productivity is a set of shareholder-driven metrics that guarantees a future end-game of roboticized work maniacally focused on squeezing the last drop of energy from a worker.

That's why I use adjectives like "highly effective," "high function," and "highly aligned" teams. A team should be able to establish its own metrics, aligned to the goals of the organization, and to the goals of each individual worker in the team.

When "Remote" Is the New Normal: The Skillset of Distributed Teams

As much of the work of teams becomes distributed, the PACE skillset shifts from important to critical.

Though visionaries like Upwork chief economist Adam Ozimek told me in December 2019 that distributed work would someday soon become a growing trend, until early 2020 organization-wide "work from home" policies were relatively rare. The widespread practice of management-by-surveillance encouraged managers to mistrust workers they couldn't see working, and few organizations had taken the risk of allowing workers to operate remotely.

And then, along came a virus.

In the virtual conference mentioned above, P&G's Preissner predicted that the average worker would only be onsite in the office three days a week. The new mindset: Every worker is "remote," even if they are onsite in the office. With the default mode of untethered work, a completely Next model of work is far more possible.

Of course, it's important to balance the good and the less good of distributed teams from different perspectives. If you are highly intro-verted, distributed work is awesome. But if you are highly extroverted, it might seem like banishment. If you have had trouble finding talent, hiring workers from anywhere in the world is potentially game-changing.

But if it's your job to figure out how to rapidly find, hire, and compensate that worknet, you may feel that life has gotten very complicated.

In a post-pandemic world, many workers who got a taste of distributed work will want more flexibility for when they need to be onsite at the office. An early 2021 study[5] by LiveCareer.com found that 61 percent of the 1,000 workers surveyed wanted to continue working from home at least part of the time. That means that enabling distributed teams is a new skillset for Next Organizations, requiring a technique and technology toolset that will ultimately enable the organization to include far more diverse talent than it could before.

What are the most important skills for distributed teams? You guessed it. Empowering effectiveness, enabling growth, ensuring involvement, and encouraging alignment.

An excellent resource for coordinating your distributed work-group comes from San Francisco Bay Area author John O'Duinn. I've called John's book, *Distributed Teams*,[6] "the distributed worker's bible." There are few resources that were as timely—John released it over a year before the global lockdown—or as useful.

Like John, I try to avoid using the phrase "remote work," because it implies a disenfranchising work hierarchy that shouldn't exist. The workers onsite at the mothership office aren't "local," and the workers at other locations aren't "remote." To truly be involving, the group's mindset has to be that the team is distributed, even if only one worker is at a separate location.

LEARNING FROM HIGHLY DISTRIBUTED AND AUTONOMOUS ORGANIZATIONS

When is an organization not an organization? When it's distributed, autonomous, digital—or all of the above.

Strategies for changing the traditional roles of those who lead in organizations, and coordinating highly distributed organizations, are actually not new. There are many examples of organizations that are either some form of *holacracy* (leaderless or autonomous), fully distributed (no central office), or both:

- **W.L. Gore**, the company that makes outdoor clothing products using its Gore-Tex fabrics, has functioned as a leaderless company since the mid-1970s. Gore also famously, for years, aimed to cap the size of offices at 150, a number estimated by British anthropologist Robin Dunbar as the maximum number of names and faces the average person can retain. Gore has followed practices such as encouraging new hires to find their work role by walking around the company and interviewing co-workers to find unaddressed problems, and letting workers devise their own job titles. (My favorite: "Grand Empress of the Universe.")

- **The Morning Star Company**, a $700 million business that processes a quarter of all tomato production in California, has 400 workers who function without traditional managers. (Adam Grant, host of the WorkLife podcast, has a great conversation with fellow author Dan Pink, "A World Without Bosses," talking about insights from Morning Star's approach, on TED.com.[7])

- **Basecamp** (formerly 37signals), creator of the popular team collaboration tool, has been a fully distributed organization without a single office since its inception. Co-founders David Heinemeier Hansson and Jason Fried co-authored a book on distributed work[8] back in 2013 to help others learn their distributed-management strategies. Basecamp also famously suggests that workers limit their weekly work time to 40 hours, a practice that strongly encourages people to set guardrails around their work lives.

- **Automattic**, developer of the WordPress content publishing service, with 1,200 workers in 77 countries, has also been distributed since its 2005 founding. And **GitLab**, creator of the GitHub project and software repository, has 1,300 people in 69 territories.

- **Upwork**, the gig platform company, has 2,000 workers, but only a quarter of them are full-time payrolled employees. The other 1,500 are actually distributed workers operating on its platform, some of whom have been working with the organization for more than 10 years.

- **Valve Software**, founded in 1996, is one of the most visible examples of a company with no explicit management hierarchy or C-suite leadership team. The organization has posted its HR manual online, and the images of the company's "hierarchy" look like node graphs and network charts—a worknet if there ever was one. New workers are often hired for a cultural profile and a set of competencies, but rarely for specific job roles.

- **Ethereum** is an example of the mind-blowing new form of distributed and leaderless company known as a decentralized autonomous organization, or DAO. Ethereum is a set of software tools that power a marketplace for a digital currency, also known as Ethereum, similar to Bitcoin. But Ethereum is also a software service for creating DAOs, and Ethereum the organization is itself a DAO using its own software to organize its distributed workers and owners. Ethereum is a poster child for the kind of next-generation company that inspirational author Salim Ismail talks about in his book *Exponential Organizations*.[9]

Here are three key insights we can take away from these organizations following Next principles:

1 There is a consistent skillset exhibited by those who lead in these organizations, such as embracing ambiguity, relentlessly adapting, exhibiting vulnerability, and continually aligning, all of which are reflected in the Next Rules skillset, especially growth and alignment.

2 At their best, fully distributed and autonomous organizations empower individual workers, prizing skills, solving problems, creating value, and offering opportunity and wealth in new ways. But an organization still has humans, with all their strengths and flaws. A scan of Glassdoor.com posts on these companies may show that "leaderless organizations" sometimes aren't. Personal power takes the place of positional power, and those with strong egos and clear goals often dominate decision-making. These may be design flaws in the social structure of those organizations, or they may be the inevitable dynamics of human interaction. That's a great reinforcement of the need to "involve" people in the organization with an aligned mindset.

3 We need to be increasingly intentional about the very nature of an organization, from how it creates value, to how it channels the work of humans. Entirely new forms of organizations are possible in a world of exponential change.

The Third Leg of the Stool: Toolset

We've explored the successful mindset and skillset for the organization, as well as the mindset and skillset for individuals, teams, and team leads. Next we'll dive into toolsets, the techniques and technologies to help individuals, teams, and organizations leverage the Next Rules.

PART FOUR

Toolset

Empower
Effectiveness →

Objectives and
key results
Flexible   Reducing
rewards   work-about-work
Flex workplace
practices

Agile   Personal
process tools   effectiveness
Team   tools   Online
Team   Distributed   learning   learning
alignment   teams   services
techniques technology
Internal
innovation   Just-in-time
marketplaces   and
Organizational   just-in-context
alignment   learning
software   Internal work
marketplaces
Rapid   Self-
Culture   prototyping   knowledge
surveys   Inclusive   Inclusive   tools
promotion   personal
Inclusive   development
design   programs
thinking

Worker
Worker   collective   Effective
health   practices   bias
practices   removal
Inclusive   software
hiring

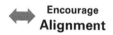

Encourage
Alignment

Enable
Growth ↑

Ensure
Involvement

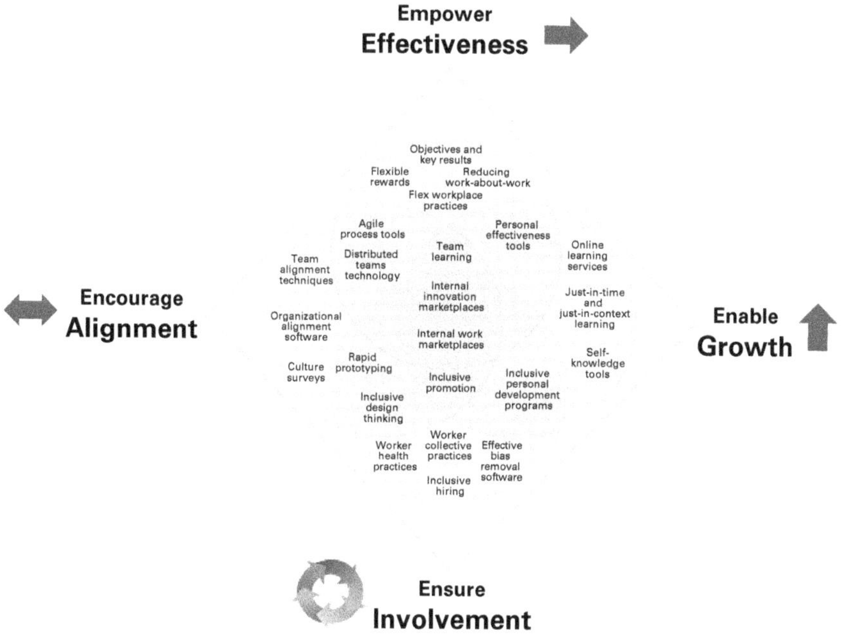

FIGURE P4   The Next Rules: Toolset

07

The Next Toolset for Organizations

There is a seemingly endless list of strategic techniques and technology tools. As we shift increasingly to the Next Rules of Work, we need to evaluate our tools by how much they help us solve problems and create value for our core stakeholders.

You can evaluate the efficacy of many of the tools intended to enable speed and alignment by a few simple principles. And you can assess specific techniques and technologies by their ability to power the four core Next Rules:

- **Growth tools**, helping every human in the worknet to continuously maximize their human potential, and to continually thrive as a whole person.

- **Effectiveness tools**, helping people to continually innovate to solve problems and create value for stakeholders, and matching incentives and rewards that appropriately and inclusively compensate workers for their contributions.

- **Alignment tools**, helping the broad range of independently innovating and widely distributed people to continually stay aligned with each other, and with the strategic goals of the organization.

- **Involvement tools**, enabling the organization to hire, develop, and promote inclusively, encourage individual- and team-driven growth, effectiveness, and alignment across the ecosystem, and remain anchored in the needs of stakeholders, especially communities and societies.

Many of those who lead in organizations are heavily focused on the tools of digital transformation. But it's important to remember that digital transformation often has far more to do with empowering workers than with any specific technologies.

Magic Wand Time, Again

I wave a magic wand, and suddenly you are sitting in a beautiful park with six other people, each of whom is seated on a small individual bench.

You turn toward the first person, on your left. "Who are you?" you ask curiously.

"I'm your customer," they reply. "If you meet my needs, I'll be using the products and services your organization creates and delivers."

Fascinated, you begin asking about the most important problems with which your customer is faced. You probe to understand the value they need to have created for them. The customer doesn't, of course, tell you how to solve those problems and create that value. So you brainstorm solutions, prototype your ideas verbally, and co-create with them.

You then turn to the second person. "May I ask who you are?"

"I'm a worker," they respond. "If you hire me, I'll help you to solve problems, and to create value for the customer here." Your customer smiles and nods.

You're also fascinated by the opportunity to talk to the worker. You explore what they believe are their superpowers, their best-loved and most effective skills, as well as what they need most to be effective in their work, and to have a full and productive life. You probe to understand their mindset.

Then your attention turns to the third person. Before you can ask, they say, "I am your potential partner and supplier. I can provide you with some of the resources that you need, so you and your worker here can deliver value to this customer. And I also deliver value to the customer directly, so that means you and I are also collaborators." You discuss with the partner supplier what their organizational purpose is, the kinds of problems they're most optimized to solve, and the value they're most effective at delivering.

The fourth person, clearly agitated, waits until it seems that discussion is almost done, then blurts out, "I'm sorry to interrupt. But I'm the community in which you will operate. I'm sure you'll bring a lot of value to us. But honestly, it's not all good news. I don't think you're going to hire in a way that reflects our community. I don't think you're going to take responsibility for some of the, what do you call them, 'negative externalities,' the problems that your offerings can create in society. In fact, I don't think we are anywhere near as in sync as we need to be. I have a lot of challenges, and I don't think you realize that you may actually be contributing to the *creation* of those problems, rather than their solution."

You listen carefully, digesting their words for a moment. "I hear what you are saying. I know I need to do a lot more to reflect your needs. And I also will have some of my own challenges in leading an organization, especially if I can't hire the skillset I need from your community. Let's talk about how we can better understand and meet each other's needs, and to continually stay aligned." You talk together about a series of actions you each can take, and you make firm commitments to follow up.

Then you turn to the fifth. "As you may have guessed," the fifth says, "I am the planet. You, and many others like you, have functioned for some time without considering me as a stakeholder, except in the most minimal way. But we're at a point where that can't continue. So it's time to talk about some very concrete ways to go forward." In some ways, this is the hardest conversation. But it becomes clear to you that there are some big, authentic steps you can commit to that can have real impact.

It's been an exhausting and exhilarating series of conversations. But there is one more discussion to be had. "Last but not least," you say with a smile to the sixth.

The sixth waves a hand, almost dismissively. "I'm your share-holder. And we don't really need to talk. If you meet the needs of each of these…"—the sixth gestures to the others in the park—"I know you'll be successful. And then, so will I."

You take a deep breath, and you realize that this session has been a gift. How often do you get to hear directly from your stakeholders? And for them to hear from each other? From now on, your strategy as an organization, and the tools you choose to execute that strategy, will have far more clarity. And you resolve to have this discussion on a regular basis, so you continually stay in alignment with all of your stakeholders.

Organizational Techniques and Technologies to Deliver Value to Stakeholders

That vision of a connection to your organization's stakeholders provides the context for the techniques and technologies in the organization's toolset.

In previous chapters, we've focused on mindset and skillset, the what, who, when and where from the Aristotle Canvas. Now we'll focus on *how* your toolset can enable the Next Rules.

As with climbing a mountain, there are certainly many problems in your work and your organization that can be solved purely by humans, using their aligned mindset and skillset. But many problems can be solved far more effectively with the appropriate toolset. When you're standing on a mountain looking up at that wall of ice, a para-chute probably isn't going to be much help. But we know an ice pick is the right tool for the problem.

The third leg of the stool for organizations is the toolset of tech-niques and technologies that can enable the organization to solve problems and create value for stakeholders. The goal here is not to explore every strategic technique related to business strategy and execution, nor to cover every major technology used throughout the organization. We'll focus specifically on the techniques and technolo-gies that enable organization-wide practices supporting the four core Next Rules: effectiveness, growth, involvement, and alignment.

Of course, a tool is only effective in the context of the problem it helps to solve. Whether you're considering a technique or a technology, be careful to avoid "the law of the instrument." That's the concept offered by the American philosopher Abraham Kaplan, who is quoted as saying in 1962, "Give a small boy a hammer, and he will find that everything he encounters needs pounding."[1] (The meme is more commonly linked to American psychologist Abraham Maslow's famous quote, "I suppose it is tempting, if the only tool you have is a hammer, to treat everything as if it were a nail,"[2] which came four years later.) Using a tool that doesn't match the problem you're trying to solve is at best a waste of time, and at worst it will point you toward a poor outcome.

As with all tools, the main assessment is simple. Does it work? You'll need to be aligned with other stakeholders and collaborators as to what "work" means. We'll talk about how to think of that as well. But if throughout your organization you are aligned, you're in good shape to determine if a tool is useful. If it's not working, either adapt the tool to your situation, or toss it and find or create another.

THE "SNIFF TEST" FOR TOOLS: THE STARLING PRINCIPLE

The starling is a mid-sized bird with cousins living on six continents. Because it tends to be invasive, the starling isn't particularly loved by many ornithologists. I wouldn't normally suggest admiring the starling for much of anything, except for one exceptional property: real-time alignment.

A flock of starlings is known as a *murmuration*, an evocative word that should gain them some respect. But it's the behavior of the birds in a murmuration that is so remarkable. Watching the undulating movements of the flock is like seeing a sentient fabric in motion, a Northern Lights configuration of living creatures in flight. Murmurations can count in the hundreds of thousands, blotting out the sky. Yet even with so many in a flock, they continue to move in concert together. How is this possible?

Researchers have built computer models of the movements of starlings, and found they can replicate the birds' movements based on just a few simple principles. Scientists call this "rapid transmission of local behavioral response to neighbors." (Sounds like mindset alignment.) There are three basic strategies:[3]

- Watch the birds around you, and match their speed and direction.
- If you're too near a bird, move slightly away, heading toward open space.
- If you start to drift too far away from the birds near you, start moving toward them.

How many fellow murmurers does one starling watch? The magic number is around a half dozen. You watch your six or seven closest neighbors and follow the three basic principles. (Sounds like the ideal size of a Next team.)

There is one other important factor: Starlings respond *fast*. In a wingflap or two, they adjust in real time to their neighbor's movements. Again, and again, and again.

So what can we learn from starlings? In keeping with the Starling Principle, just four words: simplicity, synchrony, speed, scale:

- Tools must be **simple to learn and use**, without being simplistic, so long as they are sufficiently sophisticated to enable people to make consistent and authentic decisions and take effective action.
- Tools must encourage **synchrony**, to help people stay in alignment with each other.
- Tools must enable **speed**, without encouraging knee-jerk reactions. Rapid movement in concert with other team members ensures that a team will respond quickly to solve problems.
- Tools must **scale** across the organization. A tool that's only usable in a corner of the organization can help solve a focused problem. But to be broadly useful it must be broadly applicable.

One insight from this metaphor is useful for *innovation*: heading for open space. Innovators in organizations don't go back over the same issues repeatedly, nor do they use the same thinking that's been used before. They head for open space, taking risks, and looking for ways to 10x solutions.

Design Requirements for the Organizational Toolset for Work

What kinds of techniques and technologies help to enable the mindset and skillset needed to support the Next Rules, to solve problems and create value for the organization's key stakeholders?

I'll express these as a set of requirements and offer suggestions for the kinds of strategic processes (techniques) and software (technologies) that are needed. Some of these exist, and many of them don't. Yet. Because the landscape changes so quickly, I've maintained a set of specific examples for some of these tools at gbolles.com/toolset.

Tools to Empower Effectiveness across the Organization

The organization understands each worker's uniqueness, including their cognition and learning style. The software works seamlessly with other technologies, such as virtual reality and augmented reality headsets and glasses, neural sensing headsets, and online learning platforms. An artificial intelligence coach supplements their existing skills with tools to augment their abilities and helps each worker to rapidly learn new skills.

The organization helps workers to continually understand their effectiveness in their work and to see the connection between their work and the value being created for stakeholders. It anonymously gathers input from other team members, infusing that information into a set of suggestions for worker-led discussions with team leads. Conversations between workers and team leaders about effectiveness (which used to be called "performance") are supported seamlessly by software, and it also helps those who lead teams to do effective coaching.

The organization tracks how all workers prefer to be rewarded, including pay versus specific benefits. It traffics in micro-benefits to ensure that even contract and gig workers are compensated appropriately. It also tracks worker needs for supportive services, such as needing help with childcare, and when their priorities change, such as when a child is born, or leaves the house, the worker's compensation changes appropriately. And it does this for everyone from full-time employees to gig workers and apprentices.

The organization's purpose principles also drive incentives. Those who lead teams are rewarded when all team members follow learning plans, and when team members take their planned time off, such as vacation and learning micro-sabbaticals. Those who lead teams also receive rewards when they encourage team members to contribute to cross-disciplinary projects, and when they make projects available to others throughout the ecosystem. The organization helps those who lead teams to easily find needed talents from elsewhere in the organization, making any of the traditional "talent ownership" mindset unnecessary. And those who lead teams are rewarded whenever they deliberately create meaningful, well-paid, stable work roles, since this is one of the purpose principles that is dedicated to creating "good" work for its community.

CASE STUDY

Cross-Functional Innovation Toolset: ExO Sprints

A frequent mantra at Singularity University (SU) is the need to think and act exponentially. One process for catalyzing an exponential mindset and skillset is through a toolset known as an ExO sprint.

Salim Ismail is a Canadian entrepreneur who was the founding executive director of SU, the former head of Yahoo's Brickhouse incubator, and is co-author of *Exponential Organizations*.[4] Today, Salim's organization ExO Works knits together a global network of catalysts trained to guide innovation exercises intended to shift mindsets, accelerate innovation, and fuel organizational growth.

Salim and others have guided sprints for corporations and governments around the world, helping sets of stakeholders to co-create actionable plans to catalyze transformative change. The sprints guide collaborative groups through a series of exercises to apply moonshot thinking and 10x techniques to amplify and scale the best ideas for solving complex problems. Sprint steps include *prepare* (plan, awake, align), *execute* (discover, disrupt, build, launch), and *follow-up*.

You can read more about the techniques for ExO sprints in Salim's book, *Exponential Transformation: The ExO sprint playbook to evolve your organization to navigate industry disruption and change the world for the better.*[5]

Tools to Enable Growth across the Organization

Every worker can manage their own portfolio of work. Workers know their own best-loved skills and have a continuous process for identifying their priorities for how they would like to work, such as the kinds of problems they most like to solve, where they want to be geographically, what kind of work environment helps them to do their best work, and what shifts they prefer.

The organization helps each worker to have a holistic but completely private view of their own thriving, including their mental, physical, emotional, and social health. It makes gentle and helpful suggestions for continuous improvements, ideas for techniques such as mindfulness, and gives each worker easy ways to gain access to non-judgmental support services.

The organization enables every worker to manage a portfolio of learning. Every worker has a comprehensive and up-to-date inventory of their own skills and other characteristics and interests. Each person has a North Star or Southern Cross of meaning or purpose that guides their work and their learning. Today the software tools for coordinating learning activities are often called learning management systems. But the Next Toolset will look a lot more like an AI-driven coaching system with deep knowledge about each worker's skills and aspirations.

The organization coordinates innovation processes, such as internal hackathons, process-a-thons, "fail camps," and innovation competitions. It ensures that good ideas don't fall through the cracks, but instead move through a value chain that hones and tests ideas with actual stakeholders. The organization continually recognizes and rewards making new mistakes.

Tools to Ensure Involvement across the Organization

The organization enables inclusive and collaborative hiring processes. Whether it's for a brief project or a long-term work role, the organization walks team guides and teams through the process of articulating the problems to be solved. The organization is seamlessly connected to online talent marketplaces, ranging from gig to full-time work, as well as the networks of its workers. The organization ensures that the hiring process is inclusive, and that teams will gain the best talent available. These processes are designed to eliminate bias, avoiding the mistakes of early machine-learning applications that actually reinforced old biases. The organization also ensures that workers will receive the most appropriate compensation possible by continually indexing not just against real-time industry standards, but through the organization's own purpose principles, such as encouraging the hiring of under-represented workers. And the organization ensures that hiring is a team sport, with co-workers co-creating work roles with team guides and candidates.

The organization continually sends strong demand signals throughout the worknet ecosystem, identifying the problems that are going unsolved, the projects that need human energy. The software tools the organization uses aggregate the information about the skillsets used and that are needed, and make that information available throughout the worknet, including to schools, colleges, and learning platforms. The organization's own training materials are made available to these populations so that they will be far better prepared to help meet the needs of the organization, today and tomorrow. These market signals are aggregated with those of other organizations, including competitors, and used by communities, educators, and government to determine societal needs and opportunities. Your organization shares anonymized information about its skills ecosystem and ontology into an open global fabric. (For more, see "Cracking the Code on Human Skills: We Need a Work Genome" in the Appendix.)

The organization suggests matches between the worker's best-loved skills and some of the most challenging problems the organization faces. It helps workers to explore future career scenarios, to find the learning opportunities that match those opportunities, and to continually develop new skills. The software encourages constant curiosity and creativity. It captures information about what the worker learns, and the skills the worker develops, and reflects those gains in badges and other recognition metrics, data that instantly becomes available to others in the worknet ecosystem who may be seeking such talents. The software helps workers to manage both just-in-time/just-in-context learning experiences, as well as long-term learning, and to make learning a team sport with other workers as often as the worker prefers.

CASE STUDY

Involvement by Design

Ultranauts is an onshore software and data quality engineering firm based in New York that does website testing for large clients like Bloomberg, Berkshire Hathaway, BNY Mellon, Cigna, Comcast-NBCU, WarnerMedia and Slack. I met Ultranauts CEO Rajesh Anandan at a conference in 2018.

Founded in 2013, Ultranauts has team members in 29 states across America, 75 percent of whom are autistic. Since its inception, the company has been reimagining how an organization hires talent, manages teams, and enables career growth. Ultranauts uses data-driven recruiting to objectively assess talent, flexible business practices that allow it to build from each worker's unique strengths, and a "psychologically safe" culture that promotes continuous learning. Because it continues to deliver highly competitive value to its customers, the organization has been growing at over 50 percent annually.

"If you can create an environment where you can take a whole bunch of people who are very different, and create conditions where they can truly use their strengths, you end up being better," Rajesh said. "It's better for the team, it's better for the business, and it's better for clients."

Tools to Encourage Alignment across the Organization

The organization's vision and mission is explicit, and explicitly and frequently communicated and reinforced. The organization's authentic purpose is reflected in a set of goals and metrics, and benchmarked against other organizations. Today this is often known as ESG, tracking environmental, social, and governance issues. These are increasingly seen as critical statements about the organization's purpose, benefiting companies by everything from ESG-focused investors to worker recruiting and retention.

The organization has continuous and accurate knowledge and agreement about the core problems faced by its key stakeholders. That includes current and future customers, as well as your other stakeholders, such as workers, partners, suppliers, the communities in which you operate, and the planet. (Remember that your shareholders should be satisfied that if the needs of the other stakeholders are met, their needs will be met as well.)

The organization has a comprehensive view of the current skillset of its worknet and provides you the ability to do scenario planning for optimizing the organization's current skillset, as well as planning for future skills. It recommends career paths, identifies learning gaps, and suggests training opportunities.

I mentioned in Chapter 3 the balanced scorecard, a technique tool useful for encouraging alignment. The scorecard has been re-envisioned[6] for the multi-stakeholder era to encourage organizations to design the "positive sum ecosystem" of an organization and its interconnected partners, suppliers, and communities. A good tool to consider is its "ecosystem strategy map," to help those who lead to envision strategies that are aligned with the organization's key stakeholders. You can learn more at balancedscorecard.org.

What about *Digital* Transformation?

Digital transformation is the *strategy du jour* for many who see the successful practices of tech companies and want to pour the same secret sauce over their organizations. By encouraging workers to leverage technology that is infused throughout the organization, the thinking goes, they will emulate Silicon Valley, and therefore become successful.

A late 2020 survey[7] by McKinsey and Company of 800 executives across a range of industries found that 85 percent reported they had accelerated their digitization efforts in areas like employee collaboration and interaction, many due to the impact of the global pandemic. Though some believe that shifting from phones to video calls qualifies as "digital transformation," many organizations have reported significant acceleration of initiatives ranging from supply chain digitization to artificial intelligence software development.

There is no question that organizations with modern digital infrastructure are at an increasing advantage. A "digital-first" skillset supported by a flexible technology toolset means that an organization can react far more nimbly. Companies that had already invested in home broadband connections, powerful desktop computers, and team collaboration software were far better prepared to rapidly adapt in the face of the global pandemic.

Yet as I've mentioned, far too much of the focus of digital transformation has been on automating human tasks to reduce costs and increase efficiency. We need to completely change this mindset so that we develop a different toolset—technology that augments humans and gives them superpowers.

> We need to completely change our mindset so that we develop a different toolset—technology that augments humans and gives them superpowers.

This is perhaps the greatest possible investment that a Next Organization can make. By focusing on technologies that can help workers to understand their own skills, to learn more rapidly, to solve problems more effectively, to collaborate more rapidly and effectively—especially for distributed teams—and to augment human capabilities, organizations will gain a far more effective worknet.

Remember, though, that digital transformation has much less to do with a technology toolset, and everything to do with a Next Rules *mindset*. The technology side of the organization must indeed provide the kind of tools that are needed to enable the organization to continually embrace the Next Rules. But since digital transformation is far more a mindset shift than it is any particular set of technologies, those who lead organizations must approach digital initiatives first as a culture change, and second as a skills training requirement. The technology is necessary, but by itself not sufficient.

For a practical reference on steps that can be followed for digital transformation in the context of work, check out *Reinventing Jobs: A 4-step approach for applying automation to work*,[8] by Ravin Jesuthasan, senior partner and global leader for transformation services for the global consulting firm Mercer.

Next: What Tools Do Workers and Teams Need?

Understanding the opportunities for cross-functional tools that can enable effectiveness, growth, involvement, and alignment throughout the organization are important. But the true test of these techniques and technologies is how they enable each worker and team to solve problems and create value for the organization's stakeholders. In the next chapter, we'll examine a variety of approaches intended to fuel adoption of the Next Rules at the ground level.

08

The Next Toolset for Workers and Teams

Innovators are continually creating a range of breathtaking new technologies to power the Next Work of workers and teams. Though the specific tools and vendors will continually change, the workers' and teams' toolkits include:

- effectiveness, such as OKRs and reducing "work about work;"
- growth, such as self-knowledge and just-in-time/just-in-context learning;
- involvement, such as inclusive design thinking and inclusive hiring;
- alignment, such as rapid prototyping and distributed team alignment.

Empowering workers and teams with the toolset they need to solve problems and create value for the organization's stakeholders needs to be the most important priority of the organization.

When you finish this chapter, you'll have completed the tour of the Next Rules through mindset, skillset, and toolset. You'll then have the opportunity to connect all the dots by using the Strategic Arrow to map out the interconnections between all of these elements.

You and I Hop Back into the Time Machine

We set the dial again for 20 years from now. Our destination is São Paulo, Brazil.

You and I are standing in a park in the center of the city. We meet Gia, who is perhaps aged mid-twenties. We ask Gia to describe the work schedule for the previous day.

Gia says that yesterday, after a restful sleep enhanced by a smart pillow that was tuned to brainwaves, the first step in the morning had been to put on augmented reality contact lenses. An artificial intelligence coach came online and ran through Gia's schedule for the day, offering suggestions based on its understanding of Gia's interests, skills, and portfolio of work and learning. (Gia isn't a fan of the current fad of a neck-embedded computer chip for direct online access.)

Gia is fascinated by ancient Greece, and the AI coach had said that in one hour there was a flash gathering of Greek learners in a local park. The AI summoned an autonomous cab, and on the ride toward the meeting, a range of information was displayed on Gia's AI lenses about the history of buildings that the vehicle passed.

Gia joined a half dozen fellow learners, each of whom was also wearing AI-powered glasses or contact lenses. All of their lenses simultaneously switched to virtual reality mode, and suddenly it was as if they were walking down the virtual street of a Greek city, populated by the avatars of other people from around the world. Gia's group explored the ancient virtual city together, learning from each other about architecture, clothing, and commerce.

After an hour, Gia said goodbye to these new friends, and set up at a nearby co-working cafe to work on several projects. The cafe had spotty Internet connectivity, so Gia used a wireless gigabit connection through a satellite network.

Gia has been fascinated since youth by subjects as diverse as space, plants, artificial intelligence, and robots. The intersection of these is astrobotany, a topic that Gia had studied extensively, guided by the AI coach through a variety of just-in-time and just-in-context online and in-person learning projects.

Gia knows that one of the challenges of the future colony on Mars will be growing food designed to succeed in the harsh Martian environment, and so will probably have to be underground. It so happens that a brand new digital autonomous organization (DAO) had sent out a request for proposals through online work marketplaces for new designs for vertical farms on Mars. Based on a verified digital skills profile, Gia's AI was able to negotiate and successfully secure a paid project to design robotic systems to maintain plants on the Earth-orbiting space station, on the rocket to Mars, and on the planet itself.

At the cafe, Gia used a software tool to auto-generate robot designs, continually tweaking design criteria to increase the robot's combination of precision and gentleness with plants. Every now and then Gia sent off questions and responses to collaborators around the world, letting the AI coach translate into local languages.

Finally satisfied after several hours of design, Gia uploaded the new robot specifications, and logged off for the day. Having met the requirements for the project, Gia's bank account was automatically updated with a combination of direct payments and credits in the digital currency of the DAO.

We thank Gia for the great story. As we walk away, you and I smile at each other. What a breathtaking vision of the future.

Then we look at the dial on the time machine. It says the current year. We hadn't gone anywhen, again. (Maybe our time machine has a problem to be solved.)

In fact, all of the technologies I just mentioned exist at this writing:

- Smart pillows with embedded sleep tracking and soothing audio.

- Smart glasses with embedded AI, such as Amazon glasses with Alexa, as well as augmented reality contact lenses from several startups that provide heads-up visual displays are already available.

- A variety of university researchers have used embedded chips to allow paraplegic subjects to control robotic arms and hands through a combination of mental and motor impulses, and several researchers have demonstrated simple brain–computer information transfers.

- An immersive "virtual world" of ancient Greece is provided by game software company Ubisoft from its "Assassin's Creed" video game, allowing educators from around the world to create their own narrated tours.

- Fully autonomous taxis with no drivers are already operating in cities like San Francisco.
- Astrobotany is a thing.
- Digital autonomous organizations built on Ethereum software are also a thing.
- Elon Musk's Space Exploration Technologies Corp. (SpaceX) already has a "Mars & Beyond" program, with the tagline, "The road to making humanity multiplanetary."
- SpaceX's Starlink satellite network is already providing Internet access at over 100 megabits per second.
- Companies like Autodesk have software that performs "generative design" to create thousands of architectural model iterations based on human requirements.
- Emirates Airlines is building the world's largest vertical farm at Dubai Airport so its planes can provide fresh greens on its flights.
- A variety of online services already provide verified digital work experience credentials, real-time language translation, and digital conversion to currencies like bitcoin.

The future is indeed already here. But it isn't now, nor will it likely ever be, evenly distributed.

A Next Toolset for Individuals and Teams

As we saw in our brief tour of the future of work in the Introduction, the pace and scale of disruptive technologies continues to accelerate and expand. One important skillset that Next Organizations need to develop is the ability to continually find the right tools to solve specific problems for stakeholders. There is no bright line between techniques and technologies. If a technique is successful, some innovator will invariably step in with software to enable it.

The sampling of techniques and technologies listed below is not comprehensive by any means. They should help to catalyze your thinking and research to determine what additional tools would be helpful to you specifically in your organization to help fuel adoption of the Next Rules.

If there is one category of technology tools that offers the brightest future for the Next Rules, it's machine learning and artificial intelligence. At their best, next-generation tools to help offload mundane tasks, fuel learning, personal development, team collaboration, and goal-achievement will have a transformative impact on people and organizations. At their worst, though, technologies ranging from robotic process automation to flawed anti-bias software can disempower workers and reinforce the very behaviors they are trying to help improve. That's why it's so critical that you anchor your choices for the tools your organization uses in human-centric practices that actually deliver the empowerment you are looking for.

Tools to Empower *Effectiveness* for Workers and Teams

Objectives and Key Results (OKRs)

There is a simple reason that OKRs have eaten Silicon Valley: It's currently one of the most effective ways to ensure that (1) regular conversations occur between those who lead teams and team members, (2) there is aligned agreement on hoped-for goals, and (3) there is aligned agreement about the signposts for accomplishment of important steps along the way to those goals. Many organizations use OKRs to ensure that clear goals are in place, there is an understanding how to measure progress, and that there are frequent discussions about that progress. OKRs were initially managed as a set of techniques and practices, but there is a growing class of software tools that make it easier to structure the OKR planning and discussion process for teams and team guides.

OKRs are often yoked to key performance indicators, or KPIs. Workers need to know what agreed-upon metrics link their work to the problems solved and the value created for stakeholders, so they can track their own results. But I prefer to label these key *effectiveness* indicators, because many goals and indicators, such as meeting the needs of local communities, can not only be challenging to link to traditional performance metrics, they can force a profit-making lens on results that have no direct correlation, yet are still core to the organization's purpose.

A good reference for those who want to learn more is *Measure What Matters: How Google, Bono, and the Gates Foundation rock the world with OKRs*,[1] by the legendary venture capitalist John Doerr, whose position as early investor in some of Silicon Valley's most iconic companies lets him reference a range of familiar brands to show how structured work can help to build an effectiveness engine for an organization.

Reducing "Work about Work"

One of the challenges for workers and team guides is the sheer overhead of communication and coordination, which sees its worst examples in bureaucratic organizations. Companies like Asana and Atlassian provide tools to reduce the amount of work-about-work, making communication and coordination a natural part of a team's activities. Because it reduces the penalties of working remotely by channeling work through collaboration software, this approach not only increases the ability of a team to be distributed, it potentially increases involvement by distributed workers and alignment of the team's efforts.

Tools to Enable *Growth* for Workers and Teams

Self-Knowledge

Every organization should have a commitment to helping workers to continually gain new insights into their abilities, experiences, and interests. What are your best-loved skills—your superpowers? What subjects do you know the most about? What motivates you the most, in work and in learning? What are your values? We explored some of these issues with the Aristotle Canvas.

Self-inventory software can help you to gain insights into your know, flex, and self skills. For example, at eParachute.com we have posted a simple card-sorting exercise that helps young people do a basic skills inventory in just a few minutes, then suggests fields that might be of interest to check out for gathering more information. The popular *CliftonStrengths*, formerly known as *Strengthfinders*, walks through exercises to help inventory a variety of know, flex, and self skills (though it doesn't use those categories), then offers insights about strengths based on its proprietary skills model. Another tool that many find helpful is *Designing Your Life*,[2] a career-envisioning book created by instructors from Stanford d.school, the Hasso Plattner School of Design.

You'll find other exercises for several of the Aristotle Canvas topics included in "the Flower" from the book *What Color Is Your Parachute?* You'll remember that my father first wrote the book in 1970 and updated it dozens of times until he passed away in 2017. I co-founded eParachute, Inc., with him and our business partner Eric Barnett in 2014. The Flower walks you through a series of seven "aspects of you" that are also the main parts of a job. I've recorded an online course that walks people through the Flower exercises. You'll find the link to that course, and to my other online courses, at gbolles.com/toolset.

Hacking Your Own Behavior

The organization-wide mindset shift we discussed in Chapter 3 can be enabled not just by techniques for collaborative problem-solving, but by technology that can help encourage new behaviors. In Chapter 4, I talked about techniques from Cognitas Thinking Solutions and from the Stanford Behavior Design Lab's BJ Fogg. Another company offering support for self-driven behavior change is Cognician.com, which provides custom-designed learning experiences to help those who lead in organizations, as well as workers throughout the organization, to commit to and receive support for the adoption of a new mindset.

"Just-in-Time" and "Just-in-Context" Learning

These tools can help workers to learn what they need to know to solve the problem directly in front of them, and to learn as they are solving the problem. These technologies are best used when there is a clear problem to be solved. Many of the online learning services like LinkedIn Learning, Pluralsight, Edcast, and EdX offer "learning paths" that aggregate courses into learning experiences, providing short-form learning bursts with techniques that can immediately be put into action. To tailor these even more to specific recommendations, Pluralsight is powered by an underlying "skills ontology" that suggests learning opportunities for you based on its understanding of your skills. Some online learning services are beginning to offer "badges," which are credentials like micro-degrees that "certify" you've learned something. These will increasingly be "stackable," allowing you to layer them together to demonstrate that you have gained a set of skills that can be useful in your current or future work.

Tools to Ensure *Involvement* for Workers and Teams

Inclusive *Design Thinking*

Problem-solvers need techniques that empower them to better understand the problems they are working to solve, and to develop more effective solutions. Originally developed and championed by the consulting firm IDEO, design thinking offers an approach to problem-solving that walks a group through empathizing with the stakeholder's problem, defining the need, then ideating, prototyping, and testing potential solutions.

What is often missing from these practices is to make them inclusive, to involve the actual stakeholders, or people who have a deep knowledge of the lived experience of the stakeholders. Here's an example.

CASE STUDY

Empathy Instigator: Virginia Hamilton

Virginia Hamilton is a "public sector innovation catalyst." To some, that might sound like an oxymoron, since government isn't often considered a hotbed of innovation. But as the former US Department of Labor Regional Administrator for the eight Western states, Virginia knows how to use inclusive design thinking to help public servants and other workers to dramatically improve the ways they deliver value to citizens and customers.

Virginia described to me a time when she guided a design thinking session for a group of career services professionals in a public employment development office in Long Beach, California. The group wanted to improve the office's ability to meet the career needs of homeless youth. Their biggest concern was that homeless teens were often observed to come into the facility, but only stayed for a short time. Why weren't kids using the services that had been prepared for them? How could the office become more hospitable to them?

As they gathered for the session, one of the team suggested involving an unusual participant: a security guard. The thinking was that the guard saw the behavior of the teens all the time, so perhaps he would have a useful observation or two.

As the group began its design thinking exercise, the guard jumped immediately to the key source of the problem. They're homeless, he said. They have all of their worldly possessions with them when they walk in. They see that there's no safe place to put their belongings. Since they have so few things they own, they're deeply worried about losing anything. And because the world has not been kind to them, they are understandably worried that anything they value might be taken by someone. So they turn around and leave.

Based on the guard's input, the design team came up with a solution that would immediately repurpose a room near the reception desk, place a highly visible label on the room, and provide a secure place to lock up the teens' possessions. Result: a dramatic increase in the number of homeless teens using the services.

You can use this same inclusive mindset in your own design thinking exercises, such as when you co-create the definition of the organization's future desired mindset. Any workshop is far more likely to succeed with representatives of the stakeholder group in the room. And even in traditional problem-solving meetings, if you look around the room, and everyone looks like you, that's a fatal design flaw, since you're all likely to simply come up with the same solutions. Stop the meeting and find others who can help you expand the psychological diversity of the group, including people who have the actual lived experience of your stakeholders.

Technologies that can support inclusive design thinking by onsite groups include the ubiquitous whiteboards and sticky notes. Online technologies for distributed collaboration that attempt to emulate the same experience can be found at companies like Miro.com and Lucidspark.com.

Inclusive Hiring, Development, and Promotion

In Chapter 5, we explored an inclusive hiring process. An increasing number of innovators are creating software designed to identify potential biased requirements, language, and assumptions in job descriptions and corporate communications. It can be hard for any of us to admit or even be aware of the biases that we infuse into processes like hiring, promotion, and professional development. It can be even harder to root them out of bureaucratic processes that end up limiting access to work by those who are least advantaged.

First, let's agree that tacking on some software letting you slightly improve the diversity of your hiring pool, just so the organization can meet some advertised diversity targets, is a failure for everyone: the organization, society, and especially the candidates. You need to have authentic involvement processes baked into the DNA of your organization. It's essential to fix this first, in your strategic toolset, anchored in the organization's mission, values, and mindset.

Even after that, software tools alone won't solve the problem. Too many "anti-bias" tools have bias baked into them, because they use prior (biased) hiring practices as their datasets. Organizations need to commit to ongoing training to help stakeholders throughout the organization and beyond learn how to create and sustain inclusive practices that don't just try, but that *guarantee* diversity, equity, and inclusion.

Tools to Encourage *Alignment* for Workers and Teams

Rapid Prototyping

One of the most difficult challenges for teams is to be aligned around the solution to a problem. What many miss is that you can leverage design thinking to develop actionable insights in real time, by using rapid prototyping.

Just as the long-time practice of developing large-scale software products used to follow the "waterfall" model of months-long design and production processes, a lot of traditional non-technical product development can be just as ponderous. In an era of less disruptive change, the needs of potential customers might have remained static long enough that they could wait months or years for a new product to arrive. But the combination of nimble competition and rapidly changing customer demands requires an accelerated pace of innovation.

Effective real-time prototyping includes bringing a diverse set of thinkers into the exercise, each committed to rapid decision-making; having supportive resources available to them to solve specific problems, such as designers who can take a product vision and rapidly model a product or a user interface; and enforcing time constraints, to encourage quick insights and immediate implementation.

Real-time prototyping isn't just for products. It can be extremely useful for *processes* as well. In fact, I've used design thinking and real-time prototyping for processes like speeding the time to onboard consultants into an organization. You can use this approach to do "process camps" in your organization, taking existing processes that are widely acknowledged to take more time or resources than necessary, and revamp them with the actual stakeholders who implement the process.

CASE STUDY

Mr. Real-Time Prototyping: Tom Chi

Tom Chi was employee #6 at Google X, the company's "moonshot factory" that spawned new products such as the Waymo autonomous vehicle technology. When the new X team initially envisioned a computer display embedded in a pair of glasses, it could have followed a design process that could have taken weeks or months. But Tom jury-rigged a prototype in a few hours, allowing team members like Google co-founder Sergey Brin to test out their assumptions in real time. (We can of course argue that Google Glass as a product didn't end up meeting a critical market need at the time. But it's likely the product was ahead of its time, as a range of companies like Amazon are today delivering glasses infused with interactive technologies.)

Tom has since used that real-time prototyping mindset to help catalyze a range of innovations. Tom told me a story about a client that was designing the packaging for a high-end home product it intended to sell in big-box stores like Target. Though the company's design team had spent months on the project, progress was slow, and the team simply couldn't agree on the right approach.

Tom asked them where they might find their target customer. The answer: Whole Foods and Apple stores. So Tom had the company send several small interview teams at the same time in several different cities to stand with computer tablets outside these stores, testing designs with departing customers. What did the customer like about the product whose packaging design was being shown on the tablet? Would they buy this product?

The first rounds of responses were discouraging, as few of those interviewed understood what the product was or said they'd be interested in buying it. But as customers suggested changes, a design team at the company's home office were listening to this feedback in real time, worked those ideas into new designs in just a few minutes, and pushed them out to the test teams' tablets, who then asked for feedback from new rounds of customers mere moments later.

After several iterations over a few hours, the company not only had a successful design that many sample customers said they would buy, but had posted a website where the people could actually submit pre-orders to purchase the product—and several customers did.

So how does this approach work with *processes*?

Tom tells another story about an industrial equipment client that had agonized for over two years about the design of a succession planning process for executives who had been passed over for the job of division head. In a workshop, Tom had them take the idea that most executives thought would work, organized the leading team into small groups, and had each team prototype that process in a few minutes. Then each team "borrowed" a member of another design team, and ran a mock interview describing the program to that guinea pig.

In every single case, the guinea pig executive "quit" the company.

Okay, so that program wasn't going to retain executives. But at least the leading team figured it out in just an hour, after years of indecision. Tom then ran them through another exercise to prototype a set of new ideas, and within a few more hours the group had a new program designed, which was then rolled out to great success.

Both of these examples illustrate that the cycle time between idea and test can and should be measured in minutes, not years. With the proper preparation, and involving actual stakeholders in the prototyping process, tremendous results can be generated rapidly. And by giving workers experience with rapid prototyping, they can not only learn a new toolset usable in many situations, they can experience creative problem-solving techniques that can have a massive positive ripple effect throughout the organization.

The cycle time between idea and test should be measured in minutes, not years.

Team Alignment

In the same way that OKRs are the *strategy du jour* for individual and team effectiveness, agile project management practices have expanded from the world of software development into a range of team and project alignment processes throughout organizations.

Agile is essentially the strategic stepchild of design thinking and OKRs. It's a set of practices to determine a stakeholder's needs, define goals and project activities, collaboratively distribute team roles, continually iterate goals and design criteria based on stakeholder input, synchronize team activities on a daily basis, and drive toward a finished product as the primary deliverable. Agile has its own language, such as sprints, ceremonies, burn-down charts, scrum, scrum master, and scrum of scrums. Do an online search for *Agile Manifesto* to learn some of the basics.

Agile is as much mindset as it is toolset. As Adilson Borges, chief learning officer for Carrefour, the French multinational retailer with over 300,000 workers and 22,000 stores, told me, "We ask our leaders, what are you doing to become more agile? What are you doing to help your team become more agile?" He continued, "For us, it's making sure that we have the capacity to react to whatever comes up and being able to do that in an easy and fast way." Adilson also points to frequent use of "test and learn" processes like rapid prototyping, and is writing a book on the subject.

The same team techniques and software tools that increase effectiveness are often also valuable for ongoing alignment, with software companies ranging from IBM to small developers offering tools to enable agile project management practices. For an excellent overview of how agile practices can be used throughout the organization, read *The Age of Agile*[3] by Stephen Denning.

CASE STUDY

An Integrated Next Rules Toolset: Catalyte Cracks the Code

Empowering effectiveness, enabling growth, ensuring involvement, and encouraging alignment sounds like an impossibly broad set of functions to integrate into a toolset. But a US startup has done exactly that. Catalyte has literally cracked the code on an integrated toolset of technologies and techniques for the Next Rules. CEO Jacob Hsu and his team have designed software that combines effectiveness, growth, involvement, and alignment from the beginning of a candidate's interactions with the company.

Founded in 2000, Catalyte is a contract programming company based in Baltimore, Maryland. The organization offers an apprenticeship program that trains workers from around the US to become "full-stack" programmers. Successful trainees are then hired into the company's 600-person worknet, and their services are contracted to companies like Disney and Nike. It does this with:

- *Involvement:* To enable the constant hunt for new programmers, the company has created a series of software quizzes. Applicants are tested not just for their understanding of programming, but because the quiz series presents some seriously difficult challenges, a variety of flex skills like cognitive agility are also evaluated, as well as self skills like perseverance and determination. Jake says that an applicant can answer 80 percent of the quiz questions correctly, and still not pass if they don't exhibit enough tenacity. And they can answer 50 percent of the questions wrong, such as specific know skills about programming, yet still pass, because they pushed on through. That means that even applicants with minimal training can still successfully complete the tests and join the program. Catalyte is also committed to involving a diverse worknet, with training initiatives in cities like its hometown of Baltimore.

- *Growth:* Once accepted into the program, using evidence-based learning, Jake says his company can train a programmer in six months, learning at a level of proficiency equal to a traditional four-year computer science degree. One of the reasons for its success: Learners are apprentices from day one, given real-world problems to solve walking in the door. They learn just-in-time and just-in-context.

- *Effectiveness:* Throughout the training program, and after they are hired, workers receive ongoing and supportive feedback channeled by the software from their team lead and from fellow workers, not in a traditional creepy 360-degree review process, but as an authentic part of continuous skills development.

- *Alignment:* The same software serves as a set of project management services, helping teams to stay synchronized on goals and deliverables. And since Catalyte hires workers wherever they live, they learn from the beginning how to function as part of a distributed team.

The Top Priority for Next Organizations: Empowering the Worker and the Team

What should be abundantly clear from the insights and practices throughout this book is that the main deliverable for *every* organization is the empowerment of its workers and teams to continually solve problems and create value for stakeholders. And since the organization's workers and teams are *themselves* a core stakeholder group, it is the Next Organization's responsibility to provide the best techniques and technologies needed to ensure their success.

That sounds very recursive, I know. But there is a set of very simple questions to guide that work:

- Does every worker and team in the organization feel that they are more **effective** in their work than they were a year before? If not, fix that.

- Is every worker and team in the organization on a personal and group **growth** path? If not, fix that.

- Does every worker and team in the organization feel that they are **involved** in work that leverages their superpowers, the skills they love using and are best at? If not, fix that.

- And, finally, is every worker and team **aligned** with the organization's vision, mission, and strategy? Can they list their own personal and team objectives, and describe how those objectives are aligned with one or more of the organization's strategic goals? If not, fix that.

Now, let's tie everything that we've covered so far together into a useful framework.

TABLE 8.1   The Next Rules Landscape

The 3 Lenses for the Next Rules	The 4 Core Next Rules	The Next Skills for Individuals and Teams	The 6 Ws: Insights from the Aristotle Canvas
Mindset **Skillset** **Toolset**	• Empower **Effectiveness** • Enable **Growth** • Ensure **Involvement** • Encourage **Alignment**	**P**roblem-solvers *who are* **A**daptive *and* **C**reative *with* **E**mpathy	**W**hat **W**hy **W**ho **W**here **W**hen ho**W**

SOURCE © 2021 Charrette LLC. Used by permission.

Tying It All Together

Well, we've covered a lot of ground so far.

Throughout the book, we've explored many threads related to the Next Rules, through the lenses of mindset, skillset, and toolset. Now we'll connect all the dots to illustrate the work ecosystem of the organization.

Here's a way to envision all of those elements working together. I call this the Strategic Arrow. You'll see a lot of familiar elements that we've already discussed, such as the organization's purpose (its vision and mission), the organization's strategy, organization and team objectives, organization and team results, and projects. (Operations is the set of basic "blocking and tackling" work functions in the organization that aren't project-based, like maintaining facilities and keeping equipment functioning. It's still work, though, even for Next Organizations.)

Operations > Projects > Results > Objectives > Strategy > Mission > Vision

This is a "map" that those who lead in Next Organizations can continually use to encourage an aligned *mindset, skillset,* and *toolset* for the organization.

Think of the four core Next Rules as the cylinders powering the organization's human engine:

- Effectiveness is enabled by the combination of results and objectives, and the projects to deliver them.

- Alignment comes through the connection of the objectives to the organization's strategy for solving problems and delivering value to stakeholders (mission).

- Involvement is a key aspect of the value created for the organization's workers—who are, of course, one of the key stakeholder sets. Another important element of involvement is the encouragement of "talent flows" into and throughout the organization, through practices ranging from apprenticeships to project-based work.

- Growth is fueled by the continuous development of the mindset and skillset needed to solve problems and create value.

The six Ws of the Aristotle Canvas provide ideas that can be infused throughout the Arrow, providing depth and nuance to many of these elements:

- *Why* lives mainly in the realm of the organization's vision and mission, and the needs of its core stakeholders.

- *Who* lives in the organization's mission, by the characteristics of the worker stakeholders.

- *How* is mainly in the realm of strategy.

- *When* is typically defined in the strategy, objectives, and results of the organization, and in the objectives and results of teams.
- *What* is the set of problems and skills needed to deliver results.
- *Where* lives in the set of projects to be delivered.

If you see these differently, you can map them according to your own perspective.

Here are some general insights from the Strategic Arrow:

- The more strategic a function, like the organization's mission and vision, the more a consistent mindset is usually involved. *Communicating* that vision is a skillset. But working to encourage an entire organization to align around the vision and mission is a *mindset.*
- The more tactical a function, such as executing projects and performing base operations, the more a skillset is involved.
- The more repetitive an activity is, such as in the operations bin, the more likely it is in the realm of the robots, and either a machine or software will perform an increasing amount of those functions. Or, it will be outsourced, since it's not core to the stakeholder value the organization delivers.

Figure 8.1 shows the organizational work ecosystem in all its marvelous richness.

You will find a blank PDF copy of the Strategic Arrow at gbolles.com/strategy. I urge you to download and print it, and fill in the various elements that are relevant to your organization and your team. You can also use it with others in your organization to help them pull the various elements of their own work onto a single sheet.

I'll reiterate here the way we started the book. Learning and living the Next Rules is a journey. In a world of disruptive change and uncertainty, it will always be a work in progress just like we are as humans.

Pick the corner of the work ecosystem where you have the most agency, whether it's your own work, or the work of one or more teams. Build from that activity. Enlist a "coalition of the willing" to join you.

Remember: no human left behind.

FIGURE 8.1 The Strategic Arrow and Next Rules Landscape

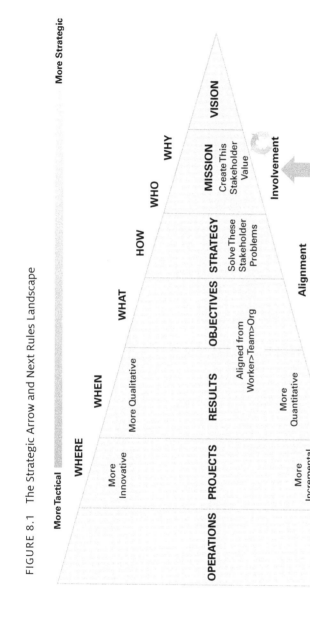

This Is the Start of the Future We All Want

Doing this in your own work, and the work of the organization, is actually a key step toward building a more inclusive future of work.

Now, how can we 10× that?

Read on.

Conclusion

The Future We All Want

There are four domains for creating an inclusive future of work: individuals, organizations, communities, and countries. Every organization and every worker functions in one or more communities, and in one or more regions or countries. We can only co-create the future we all want through deep coordination and collaboration within and across each of these domains.

At the intersection of societies and economies sits a set of decisions about the priorities of *work economies*, defining the balance of power between organizations and workers. Leaders must co-create adaptive and inclusive practices in the countries where they operate, so that workers will have the ability to find or create meaningful, well-paid work, and that organizations will have the talented workers they need, today and tomorrow.

You have tremendous power to use your mindset and skillset to help co-create that future. Here's how.

Magic Wand Time, Again

I wave a magic wand, and suddenly it is the time before you first set foot on the planet.

I tell you that you will be born into a family whose income is in one of five levels spanning the economic pyramid, from the poorest one-fifth of people with the lowest incomes, through the three levels in the middle, to the wealthiest one-fifth at the apex of the pyramid.

You won't get to choose which of these "quintiles" (as economists are fond of calling them) into which you will be born. But you *can* decide on just one rule that will make it a more fair and just society, for you and for others. What is your one wish for a rule to determine how this society can be fair?

You think deeply for some time. Then, suddenly, an idea occurs to you. Here is what you say to me.

"No matter which of the five levels of the economy I am born into," you suggest, "I should have an equal chance of moving up one rung on the economic ladder, in my lifetime, as anyone else. If I'm born at the base of the pyramid, I could have an equal chance of at least increasing my income to the second level. And if I'm born in the second level, I'd have an equal chance of moving up to the third. And so on."

I nod. "Tell me more."

You continue. "I should have access to meaningful, well-paid work. If I work hard, I grow my skills, I'm effective in my work, and I'm aligned with the goals of the organizations with which I work, I should be able to make and save more money, and eventually make more than my parents did. And my kids would have the same opportunity after me."

I applaud. "Brilliant," I respond. "If everyone could be guaranteed those outcomes, it would indeed be a much more fair and just society. *That's* the world we all want."

The Four Domains of an Inclusive Future of Work

Of course, that's not the work economy that most people in the world live in.

Why not? Well, it's a wicked problem.[1]

Wicked problems are a class of challenges that are complex, have ecosystems that span multiple arenas, resist easy solutions, and often continue to exist because some people make a lot of money from the way things work today. That's true of wicked problems like the high cost of healthcare in the US, the rising cost of a college education, and human impact on climate change.

And it's the same with work economies. There are dozens of issues that are intertwined like snarled yarn, often so complex that the history and the data can be twisted to any perspective.

We need to get our arms around the core issues so we can make some sense of how we can solve for tomorrow. That's why I've distilled all of the dozens and dozens of issues related to the future of work into four domains: *individuals*, *organizations*, *communities*, and *countries*.

Think of the four domains as a new lens. Even if the problem you want to impact is helping a single person in your community to make good career decisions in a world of disruptive change, you will give far better assistance if you have a well-informed image of the landscape where that person lives. And if you are trying to encourage your organization to follow its authentic purpose, in the context of work, you can craft far more persuasive arguments if you have a comprehensive view of the ecosystem of work and learning.

Each of the four domains has a core problem to solve:

- **For individuals:** Throughout the years, as I've talked with people ranging from refugee youth in Amman, Jordan, to formerly incarcerated adults in San Francisco, I'd state their articulated needs in a single request: **How can I find or create meaningful, well-paid, stable work, today and tomorrow?** There are many other things we need in our lives to thrive. But if everybody on the planet had this kind of opportunity, from a work perspective, we'd be in pretty good shape.

- **For organizations:** As I've consulted with and lectured to those who lead organizations, from startups to massive multinational corporations, and from project managers to CEOs and boards of directors, I'd synthesize their perspectives into one problem statement: **How can we have the talented workers we need to solve problems and create value for our stakeholders, today and tomorrow?** There are many other things that those who lead organizations want. But if every organization had the people with an aligned mindset and skillset, those organizations could deal with *any* problem and create *any* value for their stakeholders.

- **For communities:** When I sit down with people in rural and urban communities around the world, from small towns in the US to large cities in developing economies, I find that those who are trying to co-create solutions for their communities are effectively asking: **How can we function as ecosystems in which all of our constituents can thrive?**

- **For countries:** When I've spoken with everyone from ministers of labor and education, to policymakers trying to craft effective legislation, to changemakers trying to catalyze scaled change, they consistently want to know: **How can we have an inclusive economy?**

We've already focused extensively throughout this book on individuals and organizations. But now we have a new lens: How can we create a more inclusive future of work and learning for all, and do this as an integral part of our work and our organizations?

You may find this surprising, but I have found that virtually every problem you can name related to work markets has already been solved somewhere. It's just that the solution isn't well known, easily transferable, or highly scaled—yet.

Some of these strategies are listed below, by their domain. Given the complexities of work ecosystems, these are meant to be inspirational but not comprehensive. We continue to update broader lists of

FIGURE 9.1   The Four Domains of the Future of Work

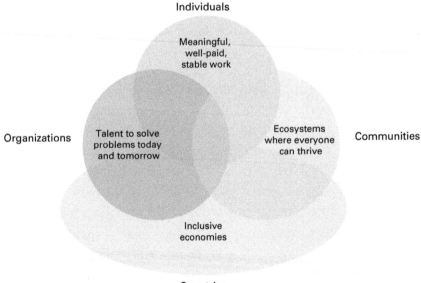

SOURCE © 2021 Charrette LLC. Used by permission.

insights, and encourage your insights and suggestions, at gbolles. com/domains.

These are complicated issues: I urge you not to look away. I've included a number of statistics below: I encourage you to see the patterns they illuminate. And though I suggest some solutions, I invite you to make them better, and to create your own.

> Virtually every one of our biggest challenges in the worlds of work and learning has already been solved somewhere. It's just that the solution isn't well known, easily transferable, or highly scaled—yet.

Individuals: Balance the Table

I'm often asked: Do we need to empower individuals so they can continually be successful today and tomorrow, or should we change a system that isn't yet fair and just for all?

The answer, of course, is yes. We must do both. One or the other is not sufficient. Change will not slow down, nor will existing systems suddenly become fair and just. But we need to acknowledge that the lack of balance between the needs of individuals and the functions of work markets is a power dynamic.

In the Age of the Smart Machine[2] author Shoshana Zuboff appropriately subtitled her 1988 book, "The Future of Work and Power." Work systems have *always* been fundamentally about power dynamics.

Picture the dynamic between workers and the organization as a table. The structure and assets of an organization—its physical resources and its legal status—exist independent of its workers, and any worker can be independent of an organization. But organizations need people to solve problems and create value for stakeholders (including for those same workers), and workers often need organizations to help them channel their collective energies.

Some people reject this framing as overly transactional. Organizations are in part people, so it's a false dichotomy to picture workers on one side and "the organization" on the other. But the more exalted an executive position in an organization, the more vested a worker becomes in that organization's power dynamic. Just like the "fuzzy" nature of work, executives over time gain *a higher degree of membership* in that power structure. That's pretty clear in gig platform companies, which always have three players: demand (the customer), the platform, and supply (messy, expensive humans). Two out of three always win: the customer and the platform. The gig worker is the commodity.

And people *do* work, and organizations pay them for that work. It *is* transactional. That's not bad, or wrong. It's just that often it's a game, and one player not only has more cards, that player also gets to influence a lot of the rules of the game.

Organizations and workers can and should have a symbiotic relationship. Their interdependence is defined by each of their goals. Workers want meaningful, well-paid, reliable work with good working conditions. And organizations need talented workers to solve the problems of today and tomorrow, at a cost aligned with the organization's business model. If workers are continually learning to solve new problems, they have incentives to ask for increasingly better rewards. But in a competitive world, with shareholders breathing down the necks of those who lead, organizations have incentives to continually reduce those costs. That means paying people less, or shifting them to easily severed relationships like gig work.

That's a power dynamic.

I've worked in Silicon Valley since the early 1980s. I've seen just how much the world has become infected by the entrepreneurial fervor of hi-tech. I bought the rhetoric that anybody can be an entrepreneur, and that anyone just needs to work hard, work smart, and get a little bit of luck, and they would be successful. And I thought that there would be so much new economic growth, everyone would benefit equitably.

I was wrong. I was *very* wrong. And it turns out that the country that has been the most affected by that disconnect is America, where the table went from reasonably balanced in the 1950s to such a steep angle that it's not even the same table it used to be. And technology and globalization are exaggerating the tilt by giving the table a big shove.

In the gig economy, all-powerful algorithms determine who makes money and who doesn't, and the ways tech companies run their black-box processes means there is often little recourse for people caught up in their AI gears. An app-based driver can suddenly receive an unjustified income-killing rating, or find their access to work crash, and the data driving those "decisions" are buried deep in powerful code. And when that code can span country boundaries, the code becomes even more powerful, because it can find ever-cheaper workers.

It turns out there are consequences for the Valley mantra of "move fast and break things." Like, well, parts of society.

Look at how much less workers overall are making in the modern economy. Economists measure the size of an economy (like GDP), compare that total to the amount of money that people earn from their work, and call that "labor's share of income," the percentage of money in the pockets of workers. It turns out that from 1945 to the 1990s, labor's share of income in the US was basically even. But from 1998 to 2016, the US economy doubled[3]—and labor's share of income *dropped* about 10 percent in real dollars.[4]

That's a *very* unbalanced table.

What changed? The power dynamic.

The Organization for Economic Co-operation and Development (OECD) is a consortium of 37 Western countries that tracks and follows a variety of metrics for healthy economies. On average in OECD countries today more than 50 percent of all salaried workers are covered by some kind of collective work agreement, often through unions. According to the Pew Research Center, in 1954 over a third of US workers were covered by labor agreements. But by 2019 it was only about one in ten.[5] And in the private sector alone, it was only about 6 percent of salaried workers.

The precipitous drop in worker collectivism wasn't because the average person hated unions (though union behavior can sometimes be hard to defend). An August 2019 Gallup poll rated public approval of unions in the US at 64 percent. So why the disconnect? Why would nearly two-thirds of all adults approve of unions, yet only 1 in 15 private sector workers be covered?

Power dynamics. Again.

So how do we balance the table? We need "AI governance" that makes algorithms visible, and data owned by humans, so that increasingly platform-driven work is transparent. We need to reinvent the ways in which humans collaborate together to increase their individual power, such as freelancer unions and cooperative organizations. And those who lead organizations need to *invite* collective voice, collective representation, and collective action, because workers who feel more engaged with the organization's mission, and who are better compensated through group-negotiated pay and micro-benefits, will be far more effective at solving problems and creating value for the organization, customers, and other stakeholders.

That's just good business.

GOOD WORK, NOT GHOST WORK, IS GOOD BUSINESS

According to Mary L. Gray, a senior principal researcher at Microsoft Research and faculty associate at Harvard University, around a quarter of Americans work full-time, but make less than a living wage. In her book, *Ghost Work*,[6] she shows that while the tech-fueled trend toward contract and gig work increases the flexibility of work hours for some, to many it means unreliable work. In 2020, Mary was named a MacArthur Fellow for her research at the intersection of technology and society. When I asked Mary what workers need most, she said, "Give people the capacity to control their time, what they work on, and with whom they work." And, of course, pay them a fair wage, with commensurate benefits.

There are very good business reasons to do just that. In *The Good Jobs Strategy: How the smartest companies invest in employees to lower costs and boost profits*,[7] Harvard University's Zeynep Ton offers a rationale why organizations should treat workers as stakeholders. Zeynep points to examples like the low-price retail and gas station chain Quiktrip, with more than 800 stores and \$11 billion in annual sales, which pays workers well and offers excellent benefits. Yet its sales per square foot beat the industry average by 50 percent, and its profit per store was more than *double* the industry average. How? Quiktrip treats its workers as stakeholders, as professionals dedicated to making happy customers. That's an example of baking purpose into the organization's business model: Workers give great customer service because they're paid well, which in turn drives tremendous profitability. That's very good business.

Organizations: Purpose-Driven in their DNA

We have spent a significant amount of the book diving into practices intended to help your organization to increase effectiveness, growth, involvement, and alignment to its authentic purpose. Like augmented reality glasses, the Next Rules offers a set of filters to understand and align mindset, skillset, and toolset throughout the organization.

Now I want to offer a new lens. You will be far more likely to be successful at achieving your organization's purpose if *your business model itself* delivers on that purpose.

It's a uniquely human characteristic to appreciate irony. But if an organization uses its profits from selling cigarettes to fund cancer research, is the world a net better place? An organization's attempts to define an authentic purpose that will benefit people or planet is far more guaranteed to be successful when its core business model is directly connected to the value it's creating. Doing less bad isn't doing good. Doing good to mitigate an inevitable bad isn't doing good, either. When a business model is dependent on, say, manipulating our attention, it's very difficult to maintain a net positive impact on society.

You might forgive someone who leads an organization that is still anchored in the Old Rules for asking, *Aren't we overloading the responsibilities of organizations and the work to be done by those who lead them?* Diversity and inclusion. Focusing on the environment. Responsible for workers' full lives. The list seems to go on and on.

But the opposite is actually true. Organizations can do so much more. Since the Next Organization is a platform for channeling human energy to create value for customers and other stakeholders, there is far more that can be done to make the organization a living ecosystem that continually delivers integrated value to an expanded list of stakeholders, ensuring that its mission remains authentically executed. But it forces those who lead Old Rules Organizations to look at some pretty fundamental issues about how, where, and why they make money.

You could simply have your organization's purpose sit in PowerPoint presentations and on the walls of company micro-kitchens. Or you can choose to send deep roots into the ground, ensuring that commitment will remain sustainably strong. What do those practices look like?

- **Next Organizations are driven by purpose in their DNA.** A rapidly growing list of people and organizations are committing to an expanded set of stakeholders, from the 2019 policy statement from the Business Roundtable,[8] to the "Profit & Purpose" letter[9] written in the same year by Larry Fink, the CEO of BlackRock, one of the largest hedge funds in the world. At Singularity University, a common framing suggested for those who lead organizations is to identify a massive transformative purpose, or MTP, a purpose so big that it helps to move the world.

- **Next Organizations make contractual commitments to their mission.** One of the movements that has grown since the mid-2000s is the "benefit corporation." Those who want to align their long-term organization mission with the interests of other stakeholders can either start or change their legal structure to explicitly define the value to be created for people or planet. As outlined at benefitcorp.net, it's a legal structure supported in 21 states and the District of Columbia in the US, and a similar approach is used in a number of European countries. Well-known examples of benefit corporations include Patagonia, Unilever's Ben & Jerry's and Seventh Generation divisions, Procter & Gamble's New Chapter division, Allbirds, and Danone North America.

- **Next Organizations guide themselves by metrics.** That targeted impact is explicit and tracked. For example, the $55 billion Latin American bank Bancolombia uses the B Corp B Impact Management Tools to benchmark its purpose and impact, not just for its environmental, social, and governance metrics, but across its business ecosystem. There are over 600 ESG metrics used around the world, and though that arena could use much more consistency, there is no lack of opportunity for Next Organizations to guide their decisions and actions through metrics sanctioned by investors, markets, and governments.

- **Next Organizations treat workers as key stakeholders.** And that means treating them as whole people, intent on enabling their well-being. By ensuring that part of the organization's purpose is to ensure meaningful, well paid work, the organization treats workers as *critical* to its mission.

- **Next Organizations reject "negative externalities" and take responsibility for their footprint in the world.** They are committed to collaborating with communities and other stakeholders to understand the consequences of their actions. A purpose-driven technology company doesn't simply write some artificial intelligence software and release it on an unsuspecting world. Instead, it co-creates products inclusively with stakeholders, tests relentlessly, analyzes its impact, admits when it makes errors, and corrects them immediately.

- **Next Organizations ideally make money *because* of their mission.** The most effective way to guarantee purpose long term is to ensure that the company delivers purpose as it makes money. If your organization's business model is dependent on gathering massive amounts of information about potential customers, using social networks to bombard them with persuasive messages to buy products they don't necessarily want, and squeezing every last dime of margin out of its supply chain, how authentic would it be to claim a mission to improve lives? But if each time someone buys and uses your product you know that they have greater well-being, delivering your purpose is unavoidable.

- **Next Organizations bake the purpose into their products and production.** In some cases, that authentic purpose is in a "buy one/give one" model, such as TOMS, Warby-Parker, and Allbirds. In other cases, it is fused into the company's supply chain, such as Unilever's commitment to build production markets in the developing economies where they sell their products.

As we march inexorably toward more inclusive capitalism, investors will increasingly urge those who lead companies to significantly increase their commitment to purpose, especially related to social impact, environmental stewardship, and internal governance. For example, in late 2020 the Nasdaq stock exchange announced a rule proposal that would require at least one woman and one diverse board director at each of its 2,500 listed companies. And in early 2021, BlackRock's Fink told CEOs they must start factoring the business costs and opportunities of climate change into their business models and reporting. These are incremental steps: They need to be 10×'d.

Communities: Ecosystems Where Everyone Can Thrive

Your organization and its workers operate in one or more communities. How can your organization authentically help those communities to thrive?

Imagine a breakthrough model of community empowerment, one based on the assumption that families and communities with economic challenges actually know what they need to improve their lives and can be trusted to do just that.

Sounds pretty radical. And it works, phenomenally well.

Mauricio Lim Miller grew up poor in the San Francisco Bay Area, the son of an immigrant mother with a third-grade education. He saw how many poverty programs simply reinforced the same economic dynamics that encouraged the conditions for poverty in the first place. After getting the attention of then-mayor of Oakland, California, Jerry Brown, Mauricio launched the Family Independence Initiative (FII).

FII's "alternative" is inspiringly simple. Ask people what they need and give them the money to do that. You want your kid to be first in the family to go to college? Great. Put together a plan. Publish your plan on the FII community website. Receive a no-questions-asked grant to support your plan, such as after-school coaching. Report your family's progress to your goal on the community website. Get the advice of other families who have achieved similar goals. Offer your own support to other families in the community. And contribute some volunteer time to support the operations of FII, so the organization will need few staff.

No government oversight. No well-meaning people from non-profits. No hoops to jump through. No shame.

Mauricio and his team have expanded the FII peer-support model into the Community Independence Initiative, a global cooperation platform driven completely by the peer-driven decisions of each community's members. Communities from Liberia to the Philippines have launched projects leveraging the mutuality model to address challenges ranging from pandemic response to creating new businesses. And for his work, Mauricio received a MacArthur Foundation "genius grant."

If you want to put on a completely new pair of virtual reality glasses to see the world in a different light, read Mauricio's book, *The Alternative: Most of what you believe about poverty is wrong.*[10]

This kind of *mutuality* is nothing new. Communities have decided for centuries what matters to them and marshalled resources to address their most challenging problems. What is different about Mauricio's approach to mutuality is that it begins with the assumption that families and communities know what they need, and never wavers from that belief. Foundations and organizations support the work because the results speak for themselves.

What is often missing is the commitment to mutuality by those who lead organizations.

Your organization operates in one or more communities. It employs workers, leverages supply chains, works with partners, and solves problems and creates value for customers, each of whom also lives and works in one or more communities. You may believe that simply providing employment to some people in those communities is enough of a contribution. But there are negative externalities even from such basic relationships. Even though tech companies are by far the largest industry employer in the San Francisco Bay Area, some of the greatest backlash against Silicon Valley companies comes from rapid gentrification, the extensive use of ghost work, and the profound lack of diversity in hiring and development. These were not inevitable outcomes, but they happened due to a stunning lack of co-creation with communities.

Mutuality offers a way forward to address these challenges. By partnering with community members, organizations can better understand the negative externalities to which they contribute, and co-create authentic solutions anchored in unshakeable commitments that won't be simply forgotten by the next team of executives.

For two great examples of organizations that are helping communities to co-collaborate on a better future, check out the Innovation Collective and the Center on Rural Innovation. And for some great stories about how communities have worked to knit together their own work ecosystems, read *Our Towns: A 100,000-mile journey into the heart of America*[11] by Deborah Fallows and James Fallows.

Countries: Same Storm, Different Boats

You may be intensely focused on the future of your organization, your team, and your own work. You may feel that if you simply help to build an organization that makes happy customers, that you are contributing to the economy, and therefore to society, and that's plenty. And in the Old Rules, that may indeed have been enough.

But you, your team, and your organization each function in the ecosystems we call a society and an economy. Your society has certain norms, laws, and regulations. Your economy has a set of design heuristics that determine who benefits, and how much.

In the West, we call our peculiar form of an economy "capitalism," and our peculiar form of societal decision-making "democracy." Certainly, no democracy is ideal. As Winston Churchill is quoted as saying in 1947, "No one pretends that democracy is perfect or all-wise. Indeed it has been said that democracy is the worst form of Government except for all those other forms that have been tried from time to time...."[12]

We can say the same is true of capitalism. It has historically by far been the worst system for distributing economic benefit—except, of course, for all the other systems. Many people have benefited tremendously from the potential for opportunity that capitalism offers. But that doesn't mean that capitalism doesn't need a serious overhaul. Or that we can't hack capitalism for good.

Capitalism's flaws are systemic *and* systematic. They are not accidents. They're not bugs. They're features. The system has been built and rebuilt throughout the years as an unbalanced table. And the very complexity of the system makes it hard to agree on the sources of the imbalance, or even if imbalance is somehow not a problem, or doesn't even exist, much less on solutions.

The good news is that rules of societies and economies are not laws of nature. They are decisions by humans. And we can make different decisions.

> The rules of societies and economies are not laws of nature. They are decisions by humans. And we can make different decisions.

The Fair and Just System We All Want

Remember the thought exercise at the beginning of the chapter? It's actually a theory put forth by the influential economist John Rawls in his book *A Theory of Justice*.[13] Rawls called it "the Veil of Ignorance." You don't get to know what quintile you'd arrive in. You just know that if you worked hard, things would get better throughout your lifetime, for you and for your children.

But wait a minute. There's a lot of money sloshing around the world. How could we all possibly believe the same about the way it should be distributed? Surprisingly, it turns out that we all pretty much agree.

The proof is in research by behavioral economist Dan Ariely, who, as I mentioned in Chapter 4, is the world's expert on why we do things against our own interests. In 2012, Dan conducted one of his most important studies, with researcher Mike Norton. They asked two simple questions of over 5,000 people. The first was: How equal do you think that wealth in the US economy is? (That's money in the bank and other assets, not income.) Their responses were remarkably similar. The respondents thought that the people in the top fifth of the economy had 59 percent of the wealth, and the bottom fifth had 9 percent.

The second question was: What *should* it be?

Wealthy or poor, Republican or Democrat, the responses were again surprisingly consistent. The top fifth in the country should have a total of 32 percent of all wealth, and those at the base of the pyramid 11 percent. (Incidentally, the same survey was conducted in Australia, for the listeners of National Public Radio in the US, and for the affluent readers of *Forbes Magazine*, all with the same results.)

However, no country in the world today comes even *close* to those percentages. Especially not the US. At the time of the study, the wealthiest fifth in the US actually had two and a half times as much as the ideal, about 84 percent of the wealth. And the poorest had *one-thirty-sixth* as much as the ideal, about 0.3 percent of the wealth in the country. And in 2020, the wealthiest one-fifth had 96 percent of the wealth. (Eighty-four percent of all stock value in the country was held by just 10 of the wealthiest families.[14])

We already have abundance. It's just not very evenly distributed.

Two years after Dan's study, with *Capital in the 21st Century*,[15] economist Thomas Piketty set off a firestorm with his research pointing to what he called systemic inequality in the latter half of the second millennium. But it really wasn't new information. The OECD's Gini Index, named for Italian statistician Corrado Gini, measures the distribution of income or wealth across an economy. The US rate in

FIGURE 9.2   US Wealth Distribution

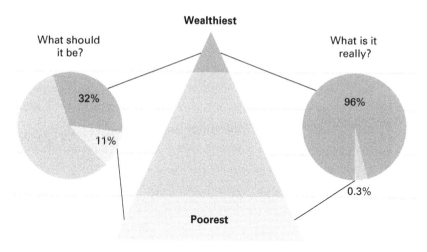

SOURCE © 2021 Charrette LLC. Used by permission.
DATA SOURCE © Dan Ariely. Used by permission.

2020 was 0.48, about the same as Turkey. (The Netherlands was 0.90, which is about as equitable as it gets.) What many find controversial isn't that the table is so unbalanced; it's that fixes to the system take the combination of mass agreement that it's a problem and mass will to change it. The enemies of the future have but one strategy: delay. So we continue to argue whether the table actually is unbalanced, when we should be focusing on how everyone can win with more inclusive capitalism.

We already have abundance. It's just not very evenly distributed.

The domains of individuals, organizations, and communities are all intertwined with the work economies in which they operate. Any country's economic system establishes the ground rules for which constituents benefit, and how much they benefit, in any work economy.

Take, for example, the employment impact from the initial response to the global pandemic. In just three months, official US unemployment *tripled*, spiking from 5 percent in January 2020 to nearly 15 percent in April. But at the same time in Germany, unemployment in comparison barely budged, going from 5 percent to 6.4 percent.

Why? Same storm, different boats.

In 2003, national decision-makers in Germany launched the Hartz labor reforms to strengthen the country's employment policies, creating a series of incentives to keep people employed, discourage mass layoffs, and train people when layoffs are unavoidable. There are costs, of course, including making it more difficult to terminate employment even of those who might be relentlessly unaligned with their work roles. But the German system clearly proved itself far more resilient in the face of a global pandemic, which seems like a pretty good test case. (Germany also has *four times* the ratio of robots to humans that the US does, but has experienced far *less* impact on employment than in America.[16])

And as America's economy slowly righted itself, the power dynamic I had pointed out in April 2020 in "The Great Reset" article[17] became crystal clear. Many of those who were already disadvantaged became even more so in the recovery.

So, even if you try to change the mindset of an organization to have a greater purpose, less can truly be accomplished if the Old Rules of your work economy fight against your efforts. Suppose your organization invested heavily in technologies that enable it to avoid polluting the ocean, but there is no cost for your competitors to continue fouling the planet. Your products and services are likely to be more expensive than theirs, limiting your ability to compete, and therefore limiting your ability to keep your workers employed.

You'll find similar challenges in many economies when it comes to finding trained workers. If you want to hire a broad range of people in your organization who have the Next Mindset and Skillset you need, and you want them all to have diverse backgrounds, you may encounter substantial challenges, depending on the way an economy functions. These are often labeled "pipeline problems," as if certain populations simply didn't have enough interest in the most in-demand jobs. But education and economic systems in many societies place numerous barriers for diverse populations to gain the mindset, skill-set, and worknet they need for success.

These are all solvable problems. But they take ecosystem thinking and action.

CASE STUDY

Hacking Capitalism for Good

In the late 1990s, I met Kevin Jones, a staff writer for *Inter@ctive Week*, a magazine where I had previously been the editorial director. Kevin and I became good friends, and I watched as he and his wife Rosa Lee Harden started a newsletter about the budding arena of online marketplaces. That newsletter grew into a fast-growing conferences business, and Kevin and Rosa Lee were able to sell that business just before the year 2000 market meltdown.

Kevin and I spent a lot of time in the early 2000s talking about the fundamental flaws of an American economic system that was clearly benefiting fewer people. We joined forces with Mark Beam, a former investment banker I'd met in a birthing class when both our wives were pregnant. Kevin, Mark, and I started a small non-profit consulting organization called Collective Intelligence. Our founding question: *How can we help accelerate the flow of capital to good?*

Historically in the US, a little over 2 percent of the economy[18] is philanthropy, and nonprofits are a little less than 6 percent.[19] Government is about 36 percent.[20] That leaves over half the economic activity in the US in the for-profit realm. We could have tried to make the impact arena better, but that was in total less than a seventh of the entire business arena. If we could help to catalyze more positive behaviors by organizations and investors, even a small percentage increase in their societal and environmental good could have huge benefits to society.

Our efforts didn't exactly take off.

As the US economy rebuilt itself in the early 2000s, most corporate executives we spoke with rejected our thesis that business could both do well and do good for society. Investment advisory firms laughed at our suggestion that they would one day have high-net-worth clients clamoring for investments with positive societal impact. Chief investment officers for philanthropies told us they would never put the bulk of the foundation's money at risk by investing in companies that fit their theory of change.

But after a few years, we found enough people were interested in the topic that we thought we could at least get a few together for a small conference. So in 2008, Kevin, Mark, and I, along with my wife and business partner Heidi Kleinmaus, Rosa Lee, and social capital guru Tim Freundlich, announced that we would be starting *SoCap: Social Capital Markets*, a conference that bridged across traditional silos to bring together investors, entrepreneurs, foundations, consultants, government, and researchers to talk about "the intersection of money and meaning."

And then, three weeks before our little event, Lehman Brothers cratered, and the financial world crumbled. Hundreds of executives fled the economic carnage in New York to join us at Fort Mason in San Francisco.

SoCap grew as an annual event. After several years, Heidi and I handed the reins to our co-founders, and years later they did the same to an acquiring company. The SoCap community continued to grow rapidly, and in 2019 the event drew over 4,000 attendees. By 2020, the global impact investing market had grown to $715 billion. "Mission investing" of a foundation's core financial assets had become the hottest trend in philanthropy. The benefit corporation movement continued to gain tremendous momentum. Going forward, Deloitte has estimated[21] that the stocks of companies with strong environmental, social, and governance commitments may comprise as much as half of all managed assets by 2025, totaling $35 trillion.

I personally take credit for none of the successes in the inclusive capitalism movement. But I tell the SoCap story for two reasons.

First, though my co-founders of SoCap were all world-class change-makers, we were all just ordinary people. We simply saw that there might be a better future, and we channeled our energies to gathering a "coalition of the willing." By bridging across the silos of business, finance, philanthropy, nonprofits and NGOs, entrepreneurs, and government, we were able to find other like-minded people committed to co-creating the future we all wanted. We were lucky enough to do it during a disruptive period where many people were ready for systemic change. If you are an investor, and "zero is the new up," you are much more open to new possibilities.

The second reason for the story is that we have undeniable proof that markets *can* be hacked for good. Those who lead in organizations *can* think and act differently. People with money *can* think and act differently. Governments *can* encourage organizations and investors to think and act differently. Inclusive capitalism isn't a dry theory in an economics textbook. It's a living, breathing, positive future that we are all co-creating together.

If the change you want to see is compelling enough, there are others in your organization, in your community, in your country, and around the world who also see that potential future and will join a coalition of the willing to co-create it. Just pick the domain where you believe you can have an impact, from helping to empower a single person to change their life, to catalyzing your organization's commitment to purpose, and to hacking work markets for good.

THE FIFTH DOMAIN: REGIONAL AND GLOBAL COLLABORATION

For those interested in "10x-ing" their perspective, as I'm sure you have already intuited, there is a fifth domain. Multiple countries, industries, and institutions can collaborate across country boundaries, at scale. Regions can build integrated strategies. Economic and societal ecosystems and communities of purpose can build tighter connections across geopolitical and physical boundaries.

Think of this as "radically inclusive globalization." We know that traditional globalization created a broad range of benefits, especially in developing markets. But it also has negative ripple effects on communities and industries that have not been able to move nimbly enough to take advantage of new market opportunities.

Rather than traditional globalization on steroids, disruptive collaboration in the fifth domain uses the same kind of ecosystem thinking that fuels local cooperation in communities, expanding exponentially to involve a growing set of stakeholders in the redesign and incentives baked into new economic systems. Think of the Sustainable Development Goals as one example of a fifth domain engine.

You may choose to focus your energies on simply creating a better future of work for you and your family. Or you may choose to launch yourself into problems in the fifth domain. Or something in between.

Work markets *can* be hacked for good. For a good example of ecosystem thinking at the national level, check out the Centre for Public Impact's (CPI) overview of the German Hartz reforms.[22] By rating the initiative on issues such as stakeholder commitment, alignment, and evidence/objectives/measurement (do these all sound like Next Rules?), CPI provides an excellent case study illustrating how something as complex as a work market can be moved. The reforms were not broadly popular when they were instituted. But they served as a defibrillator to restart the German economy after its post-unification doldrums.

> You *can* hack work markets for good.

And capitalism *can* be hacked for good. We are at a unique time in modern economic history when the drumbeat for inclusive capitalism is growing ever louder. Our economic systems can and must be deeply anchored in the needs of the broad set of stakeholders in society, not just shareholders.

For an excellent exploration of these strategies, I urge you to dive into *Reimagining Capitalism in a World on Fire*.[23] Author Rebecca Henderson, the John and Natty McArthur University Professor at Harvard Business School, offers specific examples for the ways that those who lead organizations can effectively and profitably expand their stakeholder sets to include communities and the planet, deeply anchored in moral and ethical frameworks. Rebecca suggests a variety of approaches for "building cooperation at scale," pointing to hundreds of self-regulatory efforts around the world that link ecosystems of stakeholders working together for mutual benefit.

Next

The irony of calling this chapter "Conclusion" is that I intend it to be the opposite: a start for a new way of thinking and taking action. I hope that this chapter has helped to provide a vision of the ways that individuals, organizations, communities, and countries can all be seen as interconnected ecosystems. And I hope you have a sense of where it is that you can use your mindset and skillset to contribute to the co-creation process to help impact the wicked problems of work markets. As Tim Brown, chairman of the iconic design firm IDEO, told me, "The moments of greatest disruption are where the greatest examples of collective solutions are created." He calls this new opportunity to collaborate at scale "design collectivism."

The global pandemic has given us a new start date. By taking whatever action you can to help create a more inclusive future of work, you can help to build the next economy.

> According to IDEO's Tim Brown, "The moments of greatest disruption are where the greatest examples of collective solutions are created."

Most of all, I hope that you will hope. What we have accomplished together as humans is amazing. We have eradicated diseases. We have encouraged conditions under which billions could rise from poverty. The world's information is at our fingertips. We have digitally connected half the people on the planet, and we are using satellites to begin connecting the other half. Smart software increasingly solves more of the complex and challenging problems that have bedeviled humans for millennia. The autonomous and flying cars of our science fiction dreams will soon be at our doors. We are at the cusp of breakthrough insights into our human cognition that will completely reshape how humans work and learn. And in our lifetimes we are likely to visit another planet in our solar system.

Through all of these disruptive shifts, the Old Rules will continue to erode. Traditional skillsets will no longer be rewarded by work markets. New skills will continually be needed. We will all need to continually understand and leverage the Next Rules that will enable us to solve the problems of today and tomorrow.

I hope that many of the insights and techniques suggested throughout this book will be helpful to you, your team, and your organization. I want to reiterate that this is a journey. In the same way that an organization's vision of the world it wants to create can never be fully attained, we will never fully embody the Next Rules—because, of course, many of the rules will continually change, as we co-create new ones.

What will *never* change is the need to anchor the rules of work and organizations in human-centric values.

I want you to join me in co-creating an inclusive world of work. I believe that we can do well, and do good. Individuals, organizations, communities, and countries can all build that future, together. We can all make a simple but powerful commitment, for today and tomorrow.

No human left behind.

APPENDIX

Strategic HR: Build a New Table

If you scan back through the book, you'll see that I haven't mentioned much about HR. I haven't offered any clever new name for the department. I haven't suggested any response to the frequent question I hear from those who lead in HR: "How can I have a seat at the table with the C Suite?"

There are several reasons for this.

The first is that every person within the organization needs to understand, adopt, and help teach the Next Rules of Work. That process shouldn't be outsourced to HR. It needs to be infused throughout the organization. HR is the flashpoint, but that's because it's the traditional nexus point in the organization for people processes. It doesn't mean that HR is necessarily prepared to take on the mantle of the Next Rules.

The second reason is that we have been to this rodeo before, and we're doing it wrong.

In the early 1990s, I was the editor-in-chief of *Network Computing Magazine*, a monthly print publication focused on computer networks in large organizations. I spoke frequently with a variety of chief information officers (CIOs), who often lamented that they felt like second-class leaders in their companies. They wanted to be seen as strategic contributors, viewed by their CEOs as having "a seat at the table" with the other divisional leaders of the organization. (This was long before the label "CxO" came into vogue.)

I told them there were several barriers to that kind of goal.

The first challenge was that it was going to be very difficult for them to have the cognitive bandwidth to truly contribute to organizational strategy. At the time, computing and communications were extremely complicated. Many large organizations had mainframes, minicomputers, workstations, PCs, and a spaghetti-plate of wired networks to connect all of that technology. Yet few large organizations at the time outsourced much of their IT infrastructure. There seemed to be some mythical limit around 15 percent, and beyond that CIOs decided that it was a core competency to maintain all that technology themselves. Yet with the commitment to "99.99 percent uptime," it wasn't likely that these CIOs were ever going to unshackle themselves from the fire-drill life the technology demanded. They believed that holding tightly onto these functions was a competitive advantage for them, despite the fact that so many CIOs in other organizations were clearly doing *exactly* the same things, with little actual differentiation.

The other major challenge for CIOs at the time was that few had business backgrounds. They often began their careers as engineers or technicians, and lacked experience in other parts of the business. So their CEOs rarely looked to them for strategic advice. To the C Suite, they were bit-pushers. Their lingo was tech-speak, not the language of business.

Fast forward to today, and many IT executives have worked in other parts of the business outside IT. Many have handed off their computing infrastructure to cloud providers. CIOs have done the calculus about "what is core and what is context," as Geoffrey Moore, author of the venerable *Crossing the Chasm*,[1] was fond of saying, offloading many of the "context" operational distractions that don't truly differentiate the "core" of their businesses.

This has coincided with the rise of the need for technology to become a critical core competency of virtually every organization. The CIO no longer has to ask for a seat at the table, since many organizations would be at a competitive disadvantage if the CIO wasn't already there. And since many CIOs have experience from various facets of the organization, they know the challenges and opportunities well.

Today's chief human resources officer (CHRO) has a hauntingly familiar complaint, asking for a seat at the table. But CHROs need to stop asking for a seat at the table. Instead, they need to build a new table.

We've already seen what that is: turning the organization into *a platform for channeling human energy to create value for customers and other stakeholders.*

Yet many CHROs have far too many operational responsibilities that are as repetitive and undifferentiated as CIOs had with those early computing networks. And since many who lead in HR grew up in HR, too often they are seen in the C Suite as paper-pushers.

The first priority of those who lead people has to be co-creating a vision of the organization's human worknet, painting a clear picture of the ways to become a Next Organization that can perpetually increase human potential to continually create value for customers and other stakeholders. The vision of that new table has to be so compelling that others who lead in the organization will crawl through broken glass to help make that vision real.

The second priority is to expand the worker and experience pool. Begin recruiting heavily from other parts of the organization. Take assignments yourself that will embed you into business units. Learn first-hand about the lived experiences of the humans in those parts of the organization.

The next priority has to be to automate or offload processes, so that the mind-numbing bureaucracy of administering things like benefits and processing vacation requests can be handled with far less process and cognitive load. It isn't that these activities are unimportant to workers: far from it. They need to be performed with great effectiveness and reliability. But the process of delivering them doesn't differentiate your organization in the slightest.

Automating those tasks is, of course, a circular challenge. You're automating work that humans are doing, but "people" people can't simply robotize a raft of jobs out of existence. That would be a deeply ironic failure.

Yet this is a unique time when those who lead in HR can completely reshape the dialog. They can lead the organization to understand the seismic opportunity for dramatically increasing the capacity of the organization by promoting deeply human-centric practices. As Kelley Steven-Waiss, the former CHRO of HERE Technologies and co-author of *The Inside Gig*,[2] told me, if you are the CHRO, "[y]ou need to lead the entire company's agenda for transformation."

It's not that someone with a traditional HR background can't do that. It's just a lot harder. Start hiring from non-traditional backgrounds, now, to build your team's psychological diversity bench as rapidly as you can. Empower them as risk-takers and give them the psychological safety to move rapidly and make new mistakes. Embed them in business units whenever possible.

You have a historic opportunity. We are at an inflection point in the history of the organization where we are redefining what it is for humans to collaborate and create value. Many of the major strategies we have used to organize our activities—corporate hierarchies, fiefdom managers, jealously guarded assets, placing people in predetermined slots—are fading away as Old Rules. You can, and must, be the champion and the co-creator of the Next Rules for your organization.

Channeling Existing HR Functions into the Next Rules

Since our human energy engine doesn't exist (yet), we are dependent today on a seemingly endless catalog of people- and work-related techniques and technologies. Here's how those traditional offerings fit into the four core Next Rules:

- **Growth.** Online learning systems. Learning management systems. Virtual reality- and augmented reality-based training. Career planning and career management tools. "Reskilling, upskilling, cross-skilling, outskilling." Future skills training. Self-inventory. Testing. Assessment. Employee engagement monitoring. Management training. Leadership development. Health, wellness, and well-being. Whole-person development.

- **Effectiveness.** Productivity tools. Agile process techniques and tools. Performance management systems. Competency management. Compensation and rewards negotiation and management. Benefits management. Recognition systems. Succession management. Relocation apps. Innovation process tools. Internal innovation marketplaces. Workplace environment design. Co-working facilities.

- **Alignment.** Synchronous and asynchronous communication and coordination tools. Collaboration tools. Project management. Culture surveys. Organizational alignment software. Distributed work technologies. Environmental impact awareness. Sustainability practice monitoring.

- **Involvement.** Recruiting. Resume management. Digital interviewing. Onboarding. Employee experience. Diversity/equity/inclusion. Hiring bias detection and avoidance. Harassment training, monitoring, and reporting. Digital work marketplaces. Collective worker voice, representation, and action. Surveying. Analytics. Worker security management.

And that's not even a complete list.

I'm only offering this to help show just how messy the landscape of people-related tools has become. Here we're really just shoehorning many Old Rules practices into Next Rules categories. Sure, your organization needs many of these technologies for basic blocking and tackling issues related to human work. But in the same way that IT organizations have jettisoned many of the operational functions that once consumed their attention, Next Organizations must be committed to a constant process of focusing on the most strategic needs of the human worknet. And that means prioritizing the technology toolset to focus on the ones that will enable the Next Organization, and streamlining and handing off processes where they don't differentiate you.

But the most critical work to be done is to crack the code on human skills. Here's how.

Cracking the Code on Human Skills: We Need a Work Genome

Imagine that you could have perfect information about all the human potential in your organization, and perfect knowledge of the problems to be solved, today and tomorrow. With the right technology, you could help people to more rapidly understand their own abilities, develop new skills, and continually solve the problems of the organization's stakeholders. Because the software could model what kinds of career paths could be interesting to the worker, people would have great information on which to base their career goals. Everybody wins. Every human gets great information about themselves and their future opportunities, the organization gets to optimize its worknet, educators better understand the skills future workers will need, and governments get a self-optimizing workforce. The entire world of credentials would shift over time from large, multi-year experiences called degrees, to more granular and stackable credentials based on experience and learning. People would own their own skills data, carrying it flexibly from schools to employers to government programs.

I first had this vision in 1995 as chief operating officer for a human resources information system startup that was eventually called Evolve Software. However, the technology of the time wasn't up to the task, so it remained just a vision.

There has been one big persistent problem with this vision. Most of us can't agree on what a skill is, much less what different skill labels mean. We don't often agree on what a particular level of proficiency might be, or how to measure it. And that lack of consistency is true not just between employers, educational institutions, communities, and governments, but actually *inside* many of these organizations and institutions.

What is needed is a flexible, open, and global *ontology* that serves as a living, data-driven information space, coalescing around labels for skills based on rigorous usage analysis. By looking at the skills and other attributes of workers present and past, and by looking at the work roles of today and tomorrow, an organization could far more effectively help its workers to dynamically align with the most appropriate problems.

I call this the Work Genome. Think of our human skills and other attributes as having very similar characteristics to our DNA. The basic building blocks of DNA are recombinant, allowing for near-infinite variation and mutations. The same is true of our human capabilities.

Of course, there needs to be some mechanism that allows different organizations, education institutions, governments, and languages to each have their own adapted set of that skills information space. So, we need what I call "The Rosetta Stone for Skills," an open, virtual information exchange that would allow innovation to continue to occur wherever possible. There are already numerous startups, consortia, and initiatives focused on some aspect of the Work Genome and the Rosetta Stone for Skills. I believe that in the future we will look back to this as the time when, just as we have cracked the code of human DNA, we will say that we cracked the code on human skills.

If this vision is compelling to you, you can learn more at gbolles. com/genome.

Today, those who lead in HR have the ability—the responsibility—to redefine how humans create value together by channeling their human energies. And so does every single person who leads in the organization.

ENDNOTES

Introduction

1 Kurzweil, R (2005) *The Singularity is Near: When humans transcend biology*, The Viking Press, New York

2 Seba, T and Arbib, J (2020) *Rethinking Humanity: Five foundational sector disruptions, the lifecycle of civilizations, and the coming age of freedom*, Tony Seba

3 Desjardins, J (2018) The rising speed of technological adoption, *Visual Capitalist*, February 14, https://bit.ly/2MLocbl (archived at https://perma.cc/NT5T-AX9T)

4 Toffler, A and Farrell, A (1970) *Future Shock*, Random House, New York

5 Aristotle (350 BCE) *Politics*, translated by Jowett, B, https://bit.ly/3reAcBp (archived at https://perma.cc/M6WZ-TJ6S)

6 Keynes, JM (1930) *Economic Possibilities for our Grandchildren*, https://bit.ly/3opWdeD (archived at https://perma.cc/RHE3-T6UG)

7 Keynes, JM (1930) *Economic Possibilities for our Grandchildren*, https://bit.ly/3opWdeD (archived at https://perma.cc/72U3-987G)

8 Keynes, JM (1930) *Economic Possibilities for our Grandchildren*, https://bit.ly/3opWdeD (archived at https://perma.cc/YP4G-NE85)

9 Wiener, N (1961) *Cybernetics: Or control and communication in the animal and the machine*, MIT Press, Cambridge, MA

10 Pauling, L et al (1964) *The Triple Revolution*, https://bit.ly/36uhJbS (archived at https://perma.cc/6TKH-36AR)

11 King, Jr., ML (1964) Prospects for '64 in the civil rights struggle: The leaders speak, *Negro Digest*, January, https://bit.ly/3pDKCKr (archived at https://perma.cc/34M7-9KD4)

12 Fullerton, H (1999) *Labor Force Participation: 75 years of change, 1950–90 and 1998–2025*, US Bureau of Labor Statistics, Monthly Labor Review, https://bit.ly/3j4fD7K (archived at https://perma.cc/X7P4-9JZE)

13 Ford, H (no date) *Henry Ford 150 Quotes*, Ford Motor Co., https://ford.to/3suoROO (archived at https://perma.cc/G3MH-BSW3)

14 Steincke, KK (1948) https://bit.ly/3ulWNhQ (archived at https://perma.cc/D25B-2HVU)

15 Wilde, O (1891) *The Soul of Man under Socialism*, https://bit.ly/3slpeeM (archived at https://perma.cc/FN2Y-ZWKJ)

16 Ford, M (2015) *Rise of the Robots: Technology and the threat of a jobless future*, Basic Books, New York

17 Gates, B (2014) Bill Gates: People don't realize how many jobs will soon be replaced by software bots, *Business Insider*, https://bit.ly/2Xs8Ivi (archived at https://perma.cc/6QZW-JJ38)

18 Hawking, S (2016) This is the most dangerous time for our planet, *The Guardian*, 1 December, https://bit.ly/35tROAy (archived at https://perma.cc/SRP8-JXFZ)

19 Wiles, J (2021) *Gartner Top 3 Priorities for HR Leaders in 2021*, Gartner, Inc., https://gtnr.it/2LX8DNV (archived at https://perma.cc/HF4D-B2XP)

20 Vardi, M (2016) AI and robots threaten to unleash mass unemployment, scientists warn, *Financial Times*, 14 February, https://on.ft.com/3q0BdMw (archived at https://perma.cc/SGJ3-PM5V)

21 Quote verified and permission granted.

22 Musk, E (2019) Elon Musk and Jack Ma debate AI at China summit, *Bloomberg News*, https://bloom.bg/2LBnhtA (archived at https://perma.cc/UY9W-A74M)

23 Frey, CB and Osborne, M (2013) *The Future of Unemployment*, Oxford Martin School, https://bit.ly/3oALoHu (archived at https://perma.cc/8UQ6-7DWR)

24 Markoff, J (2015) *Machines of Loving Grace: The quest for common ground between humans and robots*, Ecco Press, New York

25 Knight, D (1950) *To Serve Man*, Galaxy Science Fiction, https://en.wikipedia.org/wiki/To_Serve_Man (archived at https://perma.cc/QQ3V-5F6S)

26 Andreessen, M (2014) This is probably a good time to say that I don't believe robots will eat all the jobs…, *The Robot Tweetstorm by @PMARCA*, https://bit.ly/2L87T8p (archived at https://perma.cc/8XHN-WSAC)

27 Pollak, J et al (2018) *The Future of Work*, ZipRecruiter, https://bit.ly/3oJ5DmB (archived at https://perma.cc/P78T-UEAQ)

28 Reese, B (2019) AI will create millions more jobs than it will destroy. Here's how, *Singularity Hub*, https://bit.ly/38qdpfh (archived at https://perma.cc/3L3S-X8AF)

29 *Employment Projections 2019–2029 – Occupations with the Most Growth*, US Bureau of Labor Statistics, https://bit.ly/3il4hf7 (archived at https://perma.cc/5JKB-MQ2M)

30 Zuboff, S (1988) *In the Age of the Smart Machine: The future of work and power*, Basic Books, New York

31 *Future of Work Talent Crunch*, Korn Ferry, https://bit.ly/3iU2FsY (archived at https://perma.cc/KJ7Y-UASQ)

32 World Economic Forum (2016) *The Future of Jobs*, World Economic Forum, 18 January, https://bit.ly/2KSiCDy (archived at https://perma.cc/F23M-PML3)

33 Forrester Research (2017) *The Top Emerging Technologies to Watch: 2017 to 2021*, Forrester Research, https://bit.ly/3j3C6lz (archived at https://perma.cc/9LT5-3JQW)

34 Susskind, D (2020) *A World Without Work: Technology, automation, and how we should respond*, Metropolitan Books, New York

35 Schumpeter, J (1950) *Capitalism, Socialism, and Democracy*, Harper & Brothers, New York

36 ILO (2021) *ILO Monitor: COVID-19 and the world of work*, 7th edition, https://bit.ly/2M73DXb (archived at https://perma.cc/DN6T-HR27)

37 Oxfam (2021) *The Inequality Virus: Bringing together a world torn apart by coronavirus through a fair, just and sustainable economy*, https://bit.ly/3iYXt7n (archived at https://perma.cc/9ZAF-V77M)

38 NAHB (2020) *Labor Shortages Remain Top Concern for Builders*, National Association of Home Builders, https://bit.ly/3ptzZty (archived at https://perma.cc/L97W-MQ9N)

39 Ludwig Institute for Shared Economic Prosperity, lisep.org (archived at https://perma.cc/44TJ-3YGK)

40 Manyika, J, Lund, S, Chui, M et al (2017) *Jobs Lost, Jobs Gained: What the future of work will mean for jobs, skills, and wages*, McKinsey Global Institute, https://mck.co/3q3BwX6 (archived at https://perma.cc/F8L7-SPQ2)

Chapter 1

1 Tilgher, A (1977) *Work: What it has meant to men through the ages*, Ayer Co., New York

2 Smith, V (2013) *Sociology of Work: An encyclopedia*, Sage Publications, Thousand Oaks, CA

3 Hill, R (1992) *Historical Context of the Work Ethic*, https://bit.ly/39p4KtQ (archived at https://perma.cc/B3NP-4FQR)

4 Acemoglu, D and Robinson, J (2012) *Why Nations Fail: The origins of power, prosperity, and poverty*, p 182, Random House, New York

5 https://www.britannica.com/biography/Jethro-Tull (archived at https://perma.cc/G3X8-T9WV)

6 https://www.historycrunch.com/enclosure-movement.html/ (archived at https://perma.cc/PHK7-T9KW)

7 Clark, G (2018) Average earnings and retail prices, UK, 1209–1217, *MeasuringWorth.com*, https://bit.ly/2JXaH7t (archived at https://perma.cc/DSB8-BW96)

8 Taylor, FW (2010) *The Principles of Scientific Management*, Cosimo Classics, New York

9 Drucker, P (1946) *Concept of the Corporation*, John Day, New York

10 Suzman, J (2021) *Work: A deep history, from the stone age to the age of robots*, Penguin Press, London

11 Wojcicki, E and Izumi, L (2015) *Moonshots in Education: Launching blended learning in the classroom*, Pacific Research Institute, San Francisco, CA

12 Bolles, RN (1970) *What Color Is Your Parachute?*, Ten Speed Press, Berkeley, CA

13 Gratton, L and Scott, A (2016) *The 100 Year Life: Living and working in an age of longevity*, Bloomsbury Information, London

14 Bolles, R (1976) *The Three Boxes of Life, and How to Get Out of Them*, Ten Speed Press, Berkeley, CA

15 Denning, S (2010) *The Leader's Guide to Radical Management: Reinventing the workplace for the 21st century*, Jossey-Bass, San Francisco, CA

16 Schlosser, J (2006) Trapped in cubicles, *Money.cnn.com*, https://cnn.it/30ZFaqB (archived at https://perma.cc/PNR8-KWEE)

17 US Census Bureau (2021) Search results, United States Census Bureau, https://bit.ly/2MmZbDE (archived at https://perma.cc/6EBD-Q7UW)

18 Orwell, G (1945) *Animal Farm*, Secker and Warburg, London

19 Mishel, L and Wolfe, J (2019) CEO compensation has grown 940 percent since 1978, *Economic Policy Institute*, 14 August, https://bit.ly/3nQ17B7 (archived at https://perma.cc/PR57-X8C8)

Chapter 2

1 Gibson, W, as attributed by Quote Investigator, https://bit.ly/39skEnj (archived at https://perma.cc/Z5WA-65UK)

2 Li, C (2019) *The Disruption Mindset: Why some organizations transform while others fail*, IdeaPress Publishing, Washington, DC

3 Bridges, W (1994) The end of the job: As a way of organizing work, it is a social artifact that has outlived its usefulness. Its demise confronts everyone with unfamiliar risks—and rich opportunities, *Fortune*, 19 September, https://bit.ly/3nFFzaA (archived at https://perma.cc/8PS7-Q483)

4 Bridges, W (1994) *Jobshift: How to prosper in a workplace without jobs*, Addison-Wesley Publishing Co., Boston

5 Levinson, JC (1979) *Earning Money Without a Job*, Holt, Rinehart & Winston, New York

6 Johnston, D (1978) Scientists become managers: The 'T'-shaped man, *IEEE Engineering Management Review*, 3, pp 67–68, https://bit.ly/3pzWf5b (archived at https://perma.cc/ZUJ2-AMLB)

7 Moghaddam, Y, Demirkan, H and Spohrer, J (2018) *T-Shaped Professionals*, Business Expert Press, New York, https://bit.ly/3t2VbbM (archived at https://perma.cc/4JDE-D56R)

8 Wojcicki, E and Izumi, L (2015) *Moonshots in Education: Launching blended learning in the classroom*, Pacific Research Institute, San Francisco, CA

9 Jones Lang LaSalle (2020) *The Impact of COVID-19 on Flexible Space: What the future holds in a fast-paced world affected by the pandemic*, https://bit.ly/2LtKAFW (archived at https://perma.cc/J2ZS-PWNJ)

10 Kahneman, D (2011) *Thinking, Fast and Slow*, Farrar, Straus and Giroux, New York

11 Ries, E (2011) *The Lean Startup: How today's entrepreneurs use continuous innovation to create radically successful businesses*, Currency, New York

12 Sinek, S (2011) *Start with Why: How great leaders inspire everyone to take action*, Penguin, New York

13 Seidman, D (2011) *How: Why how we do anything means everything*, Wiley, Hoboken, NJ

Chapter 3

1 Dweck, C (2006) *Mindset: The new psychology of success*, Random House, New York

2 Harter, J (2020) Historic drop in employee engagement follows record rise, *Gallup*, 2 July, https://bit.ly/3cxkxsv (archived at https://perma.cc/7T5K-X7Q7)

3 Li, C (2019) *The Disruption Mindset: Why some organizations transform while others fail*, IdeaPress Publishing, Washington, DC

4 Grant, A (2021) *Think Again: The power of knowing what you don't know*, WH Allen, London

5 Solomon, LK (2016) *Design a Better Business: New tools, skills and mindset for strategy and innovation*, Wiley Publishing, Hoboken, NJ

6 Taleb, N (2010) *The Black Swan: The impact of the highly improbable*, 2nd edn, Random House, New York

7 Bolles, G (2020) Welcome to The Great Reset, *Techonomy.com*, 8 April, http://bit.ly/2OQKzgY (archived at https://perma.cc/SRY9-EWY6)

8 Schwab, K and Malleret, T (2020) *COVID-19: The Great Reset*, Agentur Schweiz, Zurich

9 Institute for Corporate Productivity (2019) *Culture Renovation: A Blueprint for Action*, Institute for Corporate Performance, (behind membership paywall) https://bit.ly/3p83hxG (archived at https://perma.cc/994G-PYFY)

10 Oakes, K (2021) *Culture Renovation: 18 leadership actions to build an unshakeable company*, McGraw-Hill Education, New York

11 Li, C (2019) *The Disruption Mindset: Why some organizations transform while others fail*, IdeaPress Publishing, Washington, DC

12 Synergy Research Group (2019) *Amazon, Microsoft, Google and Alibaba Strengthen their Grip on the Public Cloud Market*, Synergy Research Group, https://bit.ly/3iR3AL1 (archived at https://perma.cc/EH6N-ENNB)

13 Nadella, S (2017) *Hit Refresh: The quest to rediscover Microsoft's soul and imagine a better future for everyone*, Harper Business, New York

14 Synergy Research Group (2020) *Cloud Market Growth Rate Nudges Up as Amazon and Microsoft Solidify Leadership*, Synergy Research Group, https://bit.ly/3qYJ9hS (archived at https://perma.cc/AE5G-4FDD)

15 Hagel, J (2021) *The Journey Beyond Fear: Leverage the three pillars of positivity to build your success*, McGraw-Hill, New York

16 Ogburn, C (1957) Merrill's marauders: The truth about an incredible adventure, *Harper's Magazine*, January. Often mis-attributed to the Roman courtier Petronius, but verified as Ogburn's by Quote Investigator, https://bit.ly/3sVvtWK (archived at https://perma.cc/ZZF6-JB98)

17 Kaplan, RS and Norton, DP (2001) *The Strategy-Focused Organization: How balanced scorecard companies thrive in the new business environment*, Harvard Business School Press, Boston

Chapter 4

1 Ursell, L, Metcalf, J, Parfrey, L and Knight, R (2012) Defining the human microbiome, *Nutrition Reviews*, 70, pp S38–S44

2 Howell, E (2018) How many stars are in the Milky Way?, *Space.com*, 30 March, https://bit.ly/36pJ8vv (archived at https://perma.cc/6F9Q-CNY7)

3 Hamer, A (2019) How many megapixels is the human eye?, *Discovery.com*, 1 August, https://bit.ly/3j23LDg (archived at https://perma.cc/BB2M-EHHM)

4 Ariely, D (2009) *Predictably Irrational: The hidden forces that shape our decisions*, Harper, New York

5 Re:Work (no date) *Guide: Understand team effectiveness*, Project Aristotle, Google, https://bit.ly/3iF1Vbj (archived at https://perma.cc/JAJ9-BX76)

6 Business Insider (2021) Workplace Evolution: Execs from Netflix, P&G, Dell, tackle the future, *Business Insider*, https://bit.ly/2MAyc7o (archived at https://perma.cc/2KM7-8BAH) (Preissner's session, "The new workplace landscape," begins at 1:12.)

7 Buettner, D (2008) *Blue Zones: Lessons for living longer from the people who've lived the longest*, National Geographic, Washington, DC

8 Diamandis, P and Kotler, S (2012) *Abundance: The future is better than you think*, Free Press, New York

9 Ismail, S, Malone, MS and Van Geest, Y (2014) *Exponential Organizations: Why new organizations are ten times better, faster, and cheaper than yours (and what to do about it)*, Diversion Books, New York

Chapter 5

1 Gallup (no date) *State of the American Manager: Analytics and advice for leaders*, Gallup, https://bit.ly/3teujpI (archived at https://perma.cc/225A-UJV2) (requires free registration)

2 Isaacson, W (2011) *Steve Jobs: The exclusive biography*, Simon & Schuster, New York

3 Eggers, W, Hagel, J and Sanderson, O (2012) Mind the (skills) gap, *Harvard Business Review*, 21 September, https://bit.ly/3oP99fb (archived at https://perma.cc/9MTA-W4ZG)

4 Weiner, J (2018) *LinkedIn's Jeff Weiner: How compassion builds better companies*, Wharton School, 17 May, https://whr.tn/2NCeqcd (archived at https://perma.cc/2YYC-5SQH)

5 Goldberg, E and Steven-Waiss, K (2020) *The Inside Gig: How sharing untapped talent across boundaries unleashes organizational capacity*, LifeTree Media/Wonderwell, Los Angeles, CA

6 Mottola, M and Coatney, M (2021) *The Human Cloud: How today's changemakers use artificial intelligence and the freelance economy to transform work*, HarperCollins Leadership, New York

7 Lencioni, P (2008) *The Five Temptations of a CEO: A leadership fable*, Jossey-Bass, San Francisco, CA

Chapter 6

1 World Economic Forum (2020) *The Future of Jobs Report 2020*, World Economic Forum, https://bit.ly/2LYo88g (archived at https://perma.cc/SQ4W-GC6V)

2 McGown, H and Shipley, C (2020) *The Adaptation Advantage: Let go, learn fast, and thrive in the future of work*, John Wiley & Sons, Hoboken, NJ

3 Ibid.

4 Dzombek, R (2018) *The Future of Collaboration in the Future of Work*, Blum Center for Developing Economies, Berkeley, CA

5 Woolf, M (2021) Is remote work here to stay?, *LiveCareer.com*, https://bit.ly/39twkpT (archived at https://perma.cc/95CQ-CPA4)

6 O'Duinn, J (2018) *Distributed Teams: The art and practice of working together while physically apart*, Release Mechanix

7 Grant, A (2018) A world without bosses, *TED.com*, https://bit.ly/2YrPeqQ (archived at https://perma.cc/48AE-5YYD)

8 Fried, J and Hansson, DH (2013) *Remote: Office not required*, Currency, London

9 Ismail, S, Malone, MS and Van Geest, Y (2014) *Exponential Organizations: Why new organizations are ten times better, faster, and cheaper than yours (and what to do about it)*, Diversion Books, New York

Chapter 7

1 Secondary source: Kaplan, A (1962) quoted in *Journal of Medical Education*, as cited in Quote Navigator, https://bit.ly/395jZbb (archived at https://perma.cc/XH7R-ZCTT)

2 Maslow, A (1966) *The Psychology of Science*, Van Nostrand Publishing, New York, p 15

3 Ballerini, M et al (2008) Interaction ruling animal collective behavior depends on topological rather than metric distance: Evidence from a field study, *Proceedings of the National Academy of Sciences of the United States of America*, https://bit.ly/3ck99jR (archived at https://perma.cc/TQ65-HVH5)

4 Ismail, S, Malone, MS and Van Geest, Y (2014) *Exponential Organizations: Why new organizations are ten times better, faster, and cheaper than yours (and what to do about it)*, Diversion Books, New York

5 Ismail, S (2018) *Exponential Transformation: The ExO sprint playbook to evolve your organization to navigate industry disruption and change the world for the better*, Diversion Books, New York

6 Kaplan, R and McMillan, D (2021) Reimagining the balanced scorecard for the ESG era, *Harvard Business Review*, 3 February, https://bit.ly/3aRbLTX (archived at https://perma.cc/LS9X-WXJ7)

7 McKinsey Global Institute (2020) *What 800 executives envision for the post-pandemic workforce*, McKinsey Global Institute, https://mck.co/ 3hYEvgE (archived at https://perma.cc/MN54-UCNL)

8 Jesuthasan, R (2018) *Reinventing Jobs: A 4-step approach for applying automation to work*, Harvard Business Review Press, Boston

Chapter 8

1 Doerr, J (2018) *Measure What Matters: How Google, Bono, and the Gates Foundation rock the world with OKRs*, Portfolio, New York

2 Burnett, B and Evans, D (2017) *Designing Your Life: Build the perfect career, step by step*, Vintage, New York

3 Denning, S (2018) *The Age of Agile: How smart companies are transforming the way work gets done*, AMACOM, New York

Conclusion

1 Rittel, H and Webber, M (1973) *Dilemmas in a General Theory of Planning*, Elsevier Scientific Publishing Company, Amsterdam

2 Ibid.

3 World Bank data, visualized on Google Public Data, https://bit.ly/ 2YAnFf9 (archived at https://perma.cc/257X-UGTD)

4 McKinsey Global Institute data, visualized by VisualCapitalist.com, https://bit.ly/3aERVvd (archived at https://perma.cc/F8QS-SUPG)

5 Bureau of Labor Statistics, https://bit.ly/2N9wuKo (archived at https:// perma.cc/8J5R-2KNL)

6 Ibid.

7 Ton, Z (2014) *The Good Jobs Strategy: How the smartest companies invest in employees to lower costs and boost profits*, New Harvest, New York

8 *One Year Later: Purpose of a corporation*, Business Roundtable, https://purpose.businessroundtable.org (archived at https://perma.cc/ 5EYW-6TD9)

9 Fink, L (2019) *Profit & Purpose*, BlackRock, https://bit.ly/3bSCp0Y (archived at https://perma.cc/CRC9-U44R)

10 Miller, M (2017) *The Alternative: Most of what you believe about poverty is wrong*, Lulu Publishing Services, Morrisville, NC

11 Fallows, J and Fallows, D (2018) *Our Towns: A 100,000-mile journey into the heart of America*, Vintage Press, New York

12 Churchill, W (1947) quoted by International Churchill Society, https://bit.ly/3lzYyng (archived at https://perma.cc/W795-SXQT)

13 Rawls, J (1999) *A Theory of Justice*, Belknap Press of Harvard University Press, Cambridge, MA

14 Wolff, E (2017) *Household Wealth Trends in the United States, 1962 to 2016: Has middle class wealth recovered?*, National Bureau of Economic Research, https://www.nber.org/papers/w24085 (archived at https://perma.cc/E5K9-KKPN)

15 Piketty, T (2014) *Capital in the 21st Century*, Belknap Press, Cambridge, MA

16 Dauth, W, Findeisen, S, Sudekum, J and Woessner, N (2017) *German Robots—The impact of industrial robots on workers*, Centre for Economic Policy Research, https://bit.ly/38Vmmxw (archived at https://perma.cc/F2H6-HPPE)

17 Bolles, G (2020) Welcome to The Great Reset, *Techonomy.com*, 8 April, http://bit.ly/2OQKzgY (archived at https://perma.cc/682A-7VBB)

18 Charity Navigator, 2017 statistics, searched January 2021, https://bit.ly/3nAFpRP (archived at https://perma.cc/SY9D-DACT)

19 Urban Institute, 2016 statistics, searched January 2021, https://urbn.is/3oK4jja (archived at https://perma.cc/6QYF-VADH)

20 Statista, 209 statistic, searched January 2021, https://bit.ly/3qipVnk (archived at https://perma.cc/A9M2-EU3N)

21 Collins, S and Sullivan, K (2020) Advancing environmental, social, and governance investing: A holistic approach for investment management firms, *Deloitte Insights*, 20 February, https://bit.ly/38C8DeC (archived at https://perma.cc/49NW-22NS)

22 Jopp, J (2019) *The Hartz Employment Reforms in Germany*, Centre for Public Impact, https://bit.ly/2NfOYJm (archived at https://perma.cc/W2LT-L36Z)

23 Henderson, R (2020) *Reimagining Capitalism in a World on Fire*, PublicAffairs, New York

Appendix

1 Moore, G (1991) *Crossing the Chasm: Marketing and selling high-tech products to mainstream customers*, Harper Business, New York
2 Goldberg, E and Steven-Waiss, K (2020) *The Inside Gig: How sharing untapped talent across boundaries unleashes organizational capacity*, LifeTree Media

INDEX

CPSIA information can be obtained
at www.ICGtesting.com
Printed in the USA
JSHW010259010821
17422JS00003B/7